latin

DeMYSTiFieD

Richard E. Prior

McGraw Hill

New York Chicago San Francisco Lisbon London Madrid Mexico City
Milan New Delhi San Juan Seoul Singapore Sydney Toronto

5 6 7 8 9 10 11 12 13 14 15 16 17   DOC/DOC   1 9 8 7 6 5 4 3 2 1 0

ISBN 978-0-07-147727-7
MHID   0-07-147727-6
Library of Congress Control Number: 2007048727

CONTENTS

Contents

Contents

Contents

INTRODUCTION

Latin is a dead language,
That is plain to see.
First it killed the Romans,
And now it's killing me!

This schoolkid rhyme is almost as old as Latin itself. What's all the fuss? More to the point, what's the *mystery*?

Clearly, Latin is not impossible to learn. Two thousand years ago, the ancient Romans used it daily to do everything from running an empire to picking up a loaf of bread on the way home from work. People in Italy still speak it at the bakery, but after two millennia of growth and change, Latin is now called Italian. In France, they call it French; in Spain, it's Spanish; in Portugal, Portuguese. The list of Latin's daughter languages is very long. Romance languages get the "Rom-" in their names from "Rome." You might even consider the English language a stepdaughter, since over 60 percent of English comes directly or indirectly from Latin roots.

The source of frustration in the ditty above—and what needs demystification—is the intricate architecture of the Latin language itself. In fact, Latin grammar is so different from that of English that the first chapter of this book is devoted to an overview of the entire language. There is a Japanese saying that one eats first with one's eyes. Chapter 1 is a buffet. Following this chapter are 15 more, each focusing on a specific linguistic feature of Latin, and each builds on what you have learned before.

Latin Demystified is designed to establish a firm foundation in the fundamentals of the Latin language. Each chapter has plenty of exercises for you to practice what you have learned; this is the best way for you to monitor your progress. Some exercises include a short list of vocabulary words needed specifically for them. At the end of each chapter, there is a Key Vocabulary section. The words here are extremely common in Latin, and you should take care to memorize them thor-

oughly. You will find an Answer Key at the back of the book, along with a Latin-English Glossary.

At the end of each chapter, there is also a short quiz to test what you have learned. For the most part, it is a spot check on your mastery of forms. There are many endings for you to learn, and your progress will rely on your command of them. Therefore, it is advised that you score at least 80 percent before moving on to the next chapter.

Latin Demystified is divided into three parts. Part One establishes fundamentals, Part Two builds on those fundamentals, and Part Three presents more advanced grammatical concepts. Unfortunately, not all the finer points of Latin grammar can be included here. At the end of each part there is a test, and at the end of the book there is a final exam, which reviews all that you have learned throughout the book. Scoring at least 75 percent on the part tests and final exam is a marginal benchmark of sufficient mastery to continue on, but 100 percent should be your goal. Remember, these quizzes, tests, and exam are chances for you to see what you know, not what you can look up—so put away your notes and refrain from flipping around in the book. The ghost of Caesar will be watching you!

Take your time in this pursuit. Vergil has waited this long for you to hear his poetry, so there's no hurry. I hope you enjoy this mental exercise as much as I have and continue to.

Fēlīciter et tibi! *I hope that things are going as well/happily/luckily for you as they have been going for me!*

Acknowledgments

Major thanks go to all my students, especially those from last year. They broke my eye to things Latin that I hadn't seen before.

My boys Tarquinius, Numa, and Sherman were always there for me, especially T. Can't not love a border collie!

My deliciously obnoxious neighbors Sam and Fred also deserve thanks. They have propped me up and delivered "enhanced enthusiasm" at every moment.

Most of all, my gratitude goes to Scott, my life partner and soulmate of 21 years and counting, who has with me more patience than Job, and knows how to use commas, semicolons, *et cetera*.

PART ONE

FUNDAMENTALS OF THE LATIN LANGUAGE

CHAPTER 1

Overview of the Latin Language

In this chapter, you will learn about:

Parts of Speech

Pronunciation

Inflection Versus Analysis

Latin Nouns

Latin Verbs

This chapter is an overview of the entire Latin language. When you have finished the whole book, you'll be able to look back at this chapter and grin knowingly. In the meantime, as you persevere through chapter after chapter, bear in mind that as a speaker of an analytical language such as English, but a student of an inflected language such as Latin, you may slip into an analytical mindset and curse Latin for not being more like Modern English. Word endings rule here, not word position. Learn the word endings and their uses—and, of course, their meanings—and then relax and try to read Latin like the Romans did.

As the Romans used to say, **Incipiant lūdī!** (*Let the games begin!*)

Parts of Speech

Like all fields of study, Latin has its fair share of specialized terminology. Some of the terms that you will encounter, such as **_noun_**, will be familiar; others, such as **_rhotacism_**, will probably be new to you. Whichever is the case, most of these terms have to do with grammar.

All of us learned parts of speech in elementary school. But since it may have been a long time since you've thought about them, let's do a quick review.

A **_noun_** is a person, place, or thing, e.g., *men, Rome, bagpipe.* (The abbreviation **e.g.** stands for the Latin phrase **exemplī grātiā**, which means *for the sake of example.*)

A **_pronoun_** stands in for a noun, e.g., *those, she, who.*

A **_verb_** shows action or existence, e.g., *drink, was, happen.*

An **_adjective_** describes a noun, e.g., *green, tall, seventeenth.*

An **_adverb_** modifies a verb, e.g., *yesterday, quickly, often.* It may also modify an adjective, e.g., *highly, considerably,* or another adverb, e.g., *very, quite.*

A **_conjunction_** connects words, phrases, or clauses, e.g., *yes **or** no, over the river **and** through the woods, I'll be here **when** they come.*

A **_preposition_** shows a relationship between words, e.g., *the fool **on** the hill.*

An **_interjection_** is an exclamation word, e.g., *yeah!, uh-oh.*

Pronunciation

Modern foreign language study involves four skills: Two are active (speaking and writing), and two are passive (listening and reading). Because Latin is no longer spoken (it's an ancient language), we will concern ourselves only with reading.

These days, the only Latin you might hear is Ecclesiastical (Church) Latin, which is spoken using the pronunciation rules of modern Italian. For example, the Latin word **ecce** (*look!*) in Church Latin is pronounced *ay-chay,* but in Classical Latin—which is what we're studying in this book—it is pronounced *ay-kay.*

Even though the English alphabet is called the Roman alphabet, there are some important differences in pronouncing the same letter in English and Latin. In Latin, each letter represents only one sound. The same is not true in English. For example, the nonexistent word *ghoti,* given the seemingly random rules of pronunciation in Modern English, could be pronounced as *fish* (*gh* as in *laugh, o* as in *women, ti* as in *nation*).

Latin is much more strict: one letter, one sound. The following table shows how Caesar (a famous Roman general and dictator) pronounced the letters of the Roman alphabet.

Letter	Sounds like English ...	Latin Example	Phonetically ...
a	ah!	arma	AHR-mah
b	bottle	bibō	BEE-boh
c	cake	cornū	KOHR-noo
d	dog	dux	DOOKS
e	angel	docēre	doh-KAY-ray
f	fun	fugiō	FOO-gee-oh
g	get	gerō	GAY-roh
h	house	hodiē	HOH-dee-ay
i	machine	Cicerō	KEE-kay-roh
k	keep	kalendae	kah-LAYN-deye
l	lime	pila	PEE-lah
m	more	multus	MOOL-toos
n	not	nihil	NEE-heel
o	tango	tangō	TAHN-goh
p	pear	pirum	PEE-room
q	quiet	quiēs	KWEE-ays
r	rut	ruō	ROO-oh
s	second	secundus	say-KOON-doos
t	table	tabula	TAH-boo-lah
u	ruse	figura	FEE-goo-rah
v	wine	vīnum	WEE-noom
x	exit	exit	AYKS-eet
y	—	zythum	—
z	fits	zōna	TSOH-nah

PRONUNCIATION NOTES

C and **g** are always pronounced hard, as in English *cable* and *get*—never soft, as in *mice* and *general.*

I may be used as a consonant as well as a vowel; as a consonant, it is pronounced like *y* in English *yes.* Several hundred years ago, writers started putting a little tick beneath this consonantal **i** to distinguish it from the vowel, creating a new letter: **j.** You can often see the effect of this new letter in English derivatives of Latin words, such as *justice,* which comes from Latin **iustitia.**

K is very rare in Latin. The letter **c** is usually used instead.

Q in Latin is always followed by **u.** The two letters are pronounced /kw/, and the **u** is not counted as a vowel in this pairing.

V is pronounced like English *w.* The letters *u* and *v* have an interesting history. They evolved from a single letter that the Romans wrote as **u** in lowercase and as **V** in uppercase. Have you ever wondered why inscriptions often have *V* where there ought to be *U* (e.g., COVNTY COVRTHOVSE) or why the name for the letter *W* is "double-*u*"? That's why!

X is actually a double consonant and stands for **c** + **s** and **g** + **s.**

Y appears only in loan words from other languages, usually Greek, and represents a sound that we don't have in English. It sounds like the vowel *u* in French. To make the sound, purse your lips as if you are going to say *oo,* but—keeping your lips pursed—say *ee* instead.

Z is another letter that isn't native to Latin, and it appears only in words borrowed from other languages.

VOWELS

The five Latin vowels have the same pronunciation value they have in Italian and Spanish. Say the sentence *Ma made these old boots* out loud and you will hear the Latin vowels **a, e, i, o, u** in order.

Latin vowels can be long or short. If a vowel is long, it will have a long mark called a macron above it. The Romans did not use macrons. For us, they are important only when scanning poetry, so don't feel that you have to memorize them. The difference in pronunciation between long and short vowels is very slight. Basically, long vowels take twice as long to say as short ones. (Think of half and quarter notes in music.) Here are some English equivalents of long and short Latin vowels.

ā	father	a	ago
ē	prey	e	set
ī	machine	i	pin

ō	over	o	on
ū	tube	u	put

DIPHTHONGS

A diphthong is a pair of vowels spoken like one vowel. You wouldn't pronounce the word *aisle* as ay-EES-ul, would you? In fact, that word is a good example for the table of diphthong pronunciations that follows.

Diphthong	Sounds like English ...	Latin Example	Phonetically ...
ae	aisle	**ae**quus	EYE-kwoos
au	owl	**au**t	OWT
ei	freight	d**ei**nde	DAYN-day
eu	feud	**eh**eu	ay-HOO
oe	boy	**foe**dus	FOY-doos
ui	we	h**ui**c	HWEEK

CONSONANT COMBINATIONS

There are a few other letter combinations in Latin that deserve attention.

Combination	Sounds like English ...	Latin Example	Phonetically ...
bs	lapse	ur**bs**	OORPS
gu/cu	goo/coo	**cu**ius	KOO-yoos
qu	quick	**qu**is	KWEES
ch	baker	pul**ch**er	POOL-kayr
ph	uphill	**ph**iloso**ph**ia	^{h}ee-loh-soh-^{h}EE-ah
th	outhouse	**th**eatrum	tay-AH-t^{h}room

ACCENT

The rules for placement of stress in Latin words are very simple. The last three syllables of a word have special names: The last one is called the ***ultima***, the syllable before it is the ***penult***, and the syllable third from the end is the ***antepenult***. Put the stress on the penult if the penult is long; otherwise, put it on the antepenult. For example, you say **hó-mi-nēs** because the **mi** is short, but **a-mā́-tus** because the **mā** is long.

Inflection Versus Analysis

(**Versus** is Latin for *turned against* or *opposing*.)

To learn Latin, you must understand the difference between inflected and analytical languages. Latin is inflected, and English is analytical. For this reason, you cannot read Latin as if it were English.

The key difference between these two types of languages lies in their approach to *syntax*. Syntax is the way words show their relationships to each other in a sentence (i.e., how each word functions grammatically. Incidentally, **i.e.** is an abbreviation for Latin **id est**, which means *that is*). Analytical languages rely on word order to show these relationships. For example, in the sentence *Caesar conquered the Gauls,* you know *Caesar* is the subject because it comes *before* the verb. If we change the word order to *The Gauls conquered Caesar,* then the outcome of the battle would be the opposite! If we tinker with this sentence a little more and say *Conquered Caesar Gauls the,* it becomes gibberish. So, to repeat: The syntax of analytical languages is based on word order. An English sentence makes sense—or, to be more accurate, we make sense of an English sentence—because of how the words are arranged.

Inflected languages like Latin use word *endings,* not *order,* to make sentences comprehensible. Look closely at the following Latin sentences.

Caesar Gallōs vīcit.	*Caesar conquered the Gauls.*
Caesar vīcit Gallōs.	*Caesar conquered the Gauls.*
Gallōs Caesar vīcit.	*Caesar conquered the Gauls.*
Gallōs vīcit Caesar.	*Caesar conquered the Gauls.*
Vīcit Caesar Gallōs.	*Caesar conquered the Gauls.*
Vīcit Gallōs Caesar.	*Caesar conquered the Gauls.*

They all mean the same thing! Now watch how we can turn the tables on the famous general.

Gallī Caesarem vīcērunt.	*The Gauls conquered Caesar.*
Gallī vīcērunt Caesarem.	*The Gauls conquered Caesar.*
Caesarem Gallī vīcērunt.	*The Gauls conquered Caesar.*
Caesarem vīcērunt Gallī.	*The Gauls conquered Caesar.*
Vīcērunt Gallī Caesarem.	*The Gauls conquered Caesar.*
Vīcērunt Caesarem Gallī.	*The Gauls conquered Caesar.*

Actually, while they all translate the same way, there is a slight difference among them. Usual Latin word order is Subject-Object-Verb. When that order is disturbed, it's usually for emphasis. For instance, **Caesar Gallōs vīcit** answers the question *Who conquered the Gauls?,* while **Gallōs Caesar vīcit** answers the question *Whom did Caesar conquer?*

Take another look at the examples above. See how the endings changed from the first set to the next? Clearly, word endings are crucial in Latin. The upshot of this is, of course, that you will have to memorize a fair number of word endings. Don't feel intimidated. Keep a notebook or begin an index card file for easy future reference. We will be taking things bit by bit, building on what you have learned previously, and paying close attention to patterns as they emerge.

As an Indo-European language, English was also highly inflected at one point in its history. Even though word order sets the rules now, a few inflections still exist in Modern English. We still add *-ed* to most verbs to show past tense, and add *'s* to show possession. The plural of *hoop* is *hoops,* but—less predictably—the plural of *foot* is *feet,* not *foots.* We use *he* for the subject of a sentence, *him* for the direct object, and *his* to show possession. If you are a native speaker of English, thank your lucky stars!

The Latin language is highly inflected, especially its nouns and verbs. The following sections will acquaint you with some basic concepts regarding these two parts of speech. Again, the goal here is to familiarize you with the landscape you're about to enter, not to give you a bunch of material that must be memorized immediately. We'll be covering all this information methodically over the course of the book. You may want to dog-ear this chapter and return to it for future reference as needed.

The heart of a Latin sentence is the verb. The job of all the other words and word groups in the sentence is to modify the verb in some way. As you saw in the previous section, English shows the relationship of all those words and word groups to the verb by means of word order, while Latin uses special endings to modify the verb in various ways. We use special terms to refer to these different ways.

Latin Nouns

DECLENSIONS

Latin nouns are divided into five groups called *declensions,* which have the utterly uninspired names of "first declension," "second declension," etc. (**Etc.** is short for **et cētera,** meaning *and the other things,* which usually refers to the rest of a finite number of items, often called a "closed set.") The classification of nouns into the five declensions is based on common patterns of endings. Something similar can be done with English nouns. Imagine if we assigned all English nouns to groups based on the way they form their plural. All nouns that add *-s* (e.g., one *dog*, but two *dogs*) go in the "first declension," ones that add *-es* (e.g., one *ditch*, but two *ditches*) we can put in the "second declension," and so on.

CASES

For speakers of Proto-Indo-European (PIE), Latin's mother language, nouns could interact with verbs in eight ways. Each way was designated by what we call *case*. Here are the original cases in PIE and the basic ideas behind them.

Case	Basic Function	Example
Nominative	Subject of action	*He walked the dog.*
Genitive	Links nouns	*His idea was ridiculous.*
Dative	Personal interest	*It was an interesting day **for him**.*
Accusative	Where action stops	*I smacked **him**.*
Ablative	Where action starts	*This bookcase was built **by him**.*
Instrumental	Goes alongside action	*We went to Rome **with him**.*
Locative	Where action takes place	*A bug was crawling **on him**.*
Vocative	Person addressed	***Dude**!*

Language is a living entity. Over time, living entities change. Today, how many English speakers know what "FUBAR" (slang from World War Two) means? Or "heading down the pike" (a phrase from the 1860s)? Or more to the point, can you—or anyone you know—explain the difference between *who* and *whom*? English continues to change.

In Modern English, all those PIE grammatical cases have collapsed into three: the nominative, genitive, and accusative. And you'll notice that English uses prepositions to make up for the loss of these endings.

The start of the PIE case collapse some 2,000 years ago also affected Classical Latin. In short, the ablative case absorbed the instrumental and locative cases. This resulted in an ablative case that appears to have 1,001 household uses, which have historically tended to give students of the language fits! Fret not. We'll examine this case use by use as the book unfolds.

NUMBER AND GENDER

The grammatical term **number** refers to *singular* or *plural*.

In addition to number, a Latin noun has grammatical **gender**: *masculine, feminine,* or *neuter*. Don't let the term **gender** throw you off. The Romans didn't designate **nāvis** (*ship*) feminine because there was anything physically womanly about it. Admittedly, *she* is the appropriate English pronoun to refer to *ship,* but it is the only word for an inanimate object left in Modern English that retains grammatical gender! English has gravitated toward *natural* gender, as opposed to *grammatical* gender. *Natural* gender classifies nouns by physical characteristics, which means that words such as *woman* and *girlfriend* are deemed feminine. Likewise, *masculine* gender is assigned to words like *man* and *boyfriend.* All other nouns are considered neuter.

Latin and her daughter modern languages, such as Italian, French, Spanish, Portuguese, et al., operate with both natural and grammatical gender. (**Et al.** is the abbreviation for **et alia**, meaning *and (an unknown number of) other things,* which is often referred to as an "open set.")

Grammatical gender is assigned to objects based on the class of endings they take. For example, the word **mensa** (*table*) is considered grammatically feminine because it follows the same pattern of endings as **puella** (*girl*), which is naturally feminine. The neuter gender gets its name from Latin **neuter**, which means *neither.* The patterns of endings for neuter nouns have neither masculine nor feminine models to follow, although their forms are essentially the same as those of masculine nouns, with a few variations.

HOW TO READ DICTIONARY ENTRIES FOR NOUNS

There are four items presented in dictionary entries for Latin nouns. Let's take the following noun as an example.

pēs, pedis *m.* foot

Pēs is the nominative singular form. (Nominative is the case form used for the subject of a sentence.) It is the main part of the dictionary entry. The second word, **pedis**, is the genitive singular form. (Genitive is the case used to show possession, like *'s* in English.) This second word provides two crucial bits of information. The first is the stem change for the word if there is one. What do we mean by stem change? It sometimes happens that a word changes a little when any of the other nine possible endings is attached to it. To know which part stays the same (the stem), you simply drop the genitive ending. For **pēs**, the stem to which you would

attach any of the other nine possible endings is **ped-**. The **-is** part, which is the genitive ending, alerts you to the declension this word belongs to. A noun is sorted into one of the five declensions *based on its genitive case ending,* so if you know the genitive, you know which declension it belongs to; this is the second crucial bit of information. In this example, the **-is** tells us that **pēs** is a third-declension noun.

The following table lists the genitive endings of all five declensions.

Declension	Genitive Ending
First	-ae
Second	-ī
Third	-is
Fourth	-ūs
Fifth	-ēī

The *m.* in the dictionary entry refers to the gender of the Latin word; the entry above indicates that **pēs** is considered grammatically masculine. The abbreviations *f.* and *n.* indicate feminine and neuter, respectively.

When studying Latin vocabulary, you need to learn all four elements in the listing for a noun, not just the meaning of the word!

Latin Verbs

The verb is the heart of a Latin sentence and carries an amazing amount of information. Latin is a very economical language, so a single verb can easily translate into an entire sentence in English. A Latin verb can do this by virtue of—yes, you guessed it—the many forms it can take. While a noun can appear in any of ten forms, a verb can show up in over 250 forms! Here are a few factors that make that daunting figure possible (and manageable).

An English verb has at most five forms. There are two present tense forms (e.g., *drink* and *drinks*), one past tense form (*drank*), and usually two participles (*drinking* and *drunk*). (In simplest terms, participles are verbs that function as adjectives.) All other senses of the main verb have to be communicated via auxiliary, or "helping," verbs, such as *I hope that she **will have** drunk,* as opposed to Latin's **bibat** (which means the same thing). Seven English words are needed to express what Latin can convey in a single five-letter word. Endings can do amazing things!

Verbs have five basic characteristics: person, number, tense, mood, and voice. Let's consider each of these one at a time.

The term *person* refers to the speaker's point of view. *First person* is the speaker: *I* if alone, *we* in a group. *Second person* is whomever is being spoken to: *you* if one person, *you, y'all, y'uns, yous guys,* et al. if more than one, depending on your dialect. *Third person* is anyone else: *he, she, it, they.*

Number refers to whether the verb is singular or plural.

Tense is more complicated than you might expect. It doesn't just involve time, as in past, present, and future. It also involves the linguistic concept of *aspect*, which refers to the way the speaker views an action, as either in progress or a single completed act. Consider the difference between *I was going* and *I went* and you'll understand aspect perfectly. There are six verb tenses in Latin: three for the "continuous" aspect, and three for the "completed" aspect (one each for the present, past, and future). These tenses are *present tense* (*I am going*), *imperfect tense* (*I was going*), *future tense* (*I will go*), *perfect tense* (*I went*), *pluperfect tense* (*I had gone*), and *future perfect tense* (*I will have gone*).

Mood refers to the way the speaker treats an action. In the *indicative mood*, the speaker treats the action as a fact: *He is here.* In the *imperative mood*, the speaker treats the action as a command: *Be here!* The *subjunctive mood* treats the action as an idea or a wish: *If he were here....* Finally, there is the *infinitive mood*, which refers to an action in general without assigning any person to it: *to be.*

Voice has to do with the grammatical subject's relationship to the verb. When the subject is performing the action, the verb is in the *active voice*: *He loves me.* If the subject receives the action, the verb is in the *passive voice*: *I am loved.* There is a third voice you will encounter on occasion, called the *middle voice*; here, the subject performs the action on himself or for his own benefit: *I love myself.*

Verbs also have other forms, including *gerunds* (verb forms that function as nouns—*Buying a house can be a lengthy process*) and *supines* (special verb forms that indicate purpose—*Betty went to the store **to buy** tapioca*). A Latin verb may have four *participles*: the *present active participle* (*buying*) and the *perfect passive participle* (*bought*) like English has, plus two future participles that English does not, the *future active participle* and *future passive participle*. While present participles refer to something happening *at the same time* as the main verb, and perfect participles refer to something that happened *before* the action of the main verb, future participles refer to something that will take place *after* the action of the main verb. There is no English equivalent, so future participles can present a challenge in their translation. One has to be creative and say something like *about to buy* or *about to be bought.* Furthermore, because participles are verbal adjectives, they must agree with (i.e., have the same gender, case, and number as) the words they modify. Latin illustrates agreement by endings, which is why a participle can appear in any of 30 forms!

THE CONJUGATIONS

Just as nouns are organized into declensions, verbs are arranged into four groups called *conjugations*, based on the ending of the present infinitive, which is a form that appears as the second principal part.

Conjugation	Infinitive Ending
First	-āre
Second	-ēre
Third	-ere
Fourth	-īre

A few Latin verbs are irregular and don't belong to any conjugation.

PRINCIPAL PARTS OF VERBS

When you look up a Latin verb in the dictionary, you will see a list of four, or sometimes only three or even two, words. These are its *principal parts*. English verbs also have principal parts that serve pretty much the same function. Take, for example, *drink, drank, drunk*; *go, went, gone*; *lie, lay, lain*. The first form for English verbs is the present tense, next is the simple past tense, and the third form is the past participle. Armed with knowledge of these parts, you can create any possible form for a verb.

Principal parts for Latin verbs give you all the information you need to make any of the more than 250 possible forms for a verb. Obviously, memorizing all four principal parts of a verb when studying vocabulary is crucial! Let's take a sample dictionary entry for a garden-variety Latin verb and discuss each of its parts.

moneō, monēre, monuī, monitum to warn

Do you remember the concept of verbal aspect you read about earlier? The *continuous aspect* shows action in the midst of happening. This aspect is traditionally called the *present system,* a misleading name since it encompasses tenses other than the present. The first two principal parts of a Latin verb give you all the information you need to make all the forms for this aspect: the present, imperfect, and future tenses, the present active and future passive participles, and present infinitives. The *completed aspect*, often called the *perfect system*, refers to an action that has been or will have been completed ("perfected") in past, present, or future time. The last two principal parts (or the last one if the verb has only three parts) tell you what you need to know to make these forms: the perfect, pluperfect, and future perfect tenses, the supine, the future active and passive infinitives, the perfect active and passive infinitives, and the perfect passive and future active and passive participles.

So, back to our verb **moneō** …

The first principal part, **moneō**, is first-person singular, present tense: *I am warning.* This is the main entry in dictionary listings. This part also tells you whether or not this is an **-iō** verb. Verbs that have a first principal part ending in **-iō** have a few peculiarities, as you will learn in Chapter 4.

The second principal part, **monēre**, is the present infinitive: *to warn.* Its main job is to let you know to which conjugation a verb belongs. This is important, because each conjugation has its own way of adding endings to the verb stem (verbs, like nouns, have stems). In the conjugation chart above, you'll see that **moneō** belongs to the second conjugation. You might also take note of the macron (i.e., the long mark) over the first **e** of the infinitive ending. The macron marks the difference between second (**-ēre**) and third (**-ere**) conjugations, and, as you will learn, the difference is vast. There are only a few macrons that are crucial. This is one of them.

The third principal part, **monuī**, is first-person singular, perfect tense: *I warned.* If you drop the final **-ī,** you'll have the stem needed to make all the perfect system forms, but for the active voice only. For perfect system passive voice forms, we move on to the last principal part.

The fourth principal part, **monitum**, has an interesting history. One tradition is to list the supine (ending in **-um**) for it in dictionary entries. The other tradition uses the perfect passive participle (ending in **-us**). This book follows the former tradition, but either is valid. Whether an **-um** or **-us** is dropped, we are left with the same stem: **monit-**.

Another consideration is that some verbs do not have a supine or perfect passive participle. Some of these verbs, however, do have a future active participle; if this is the case, the future active participle is given as the fourth principal part. Future active participles are easily recognized by their ending, **-ūrus**. (The **-ur-** in the English word *future* is not a coincidence!) If the verb does not have a future active participle, then it has only three principal parts.

QUIZ

Although the aim of this chapter has been to give you an overview of the Latin language and introduce you to new grammatical terms, it might be fun to see how much you have retained.

Choose the most appropriate answer to complete each statement.

1. Latin nouns are divided into groups called _____.
   (a) declensions
   (b) conjugations
   (c) suits
   (d) inflections

2. Latin verbs are divided into groups called _____.
   (a) declensions
   (b) conjugations
   (c) suits
   (d) inflections

3. The grammatical term for an exclamation word is _____.
   (a) nominative
   (b) interjection
   (c) expletive
   (d) conjunction

4. The Latin abbreviation that means *that is* is _____.
   (a) et al.
   (b) viz
   (c) i.e.
   (d) e.g.

5. The Latin abbreviation that means *and the others* is _____.
   (a) et al.
   (b) viz
   (c) i.e.
   (d) e.g.

6. The term _____ refers to a change in the form of a word to show grammatical function.

   (a) declension

   (b) conjugation

   (c) style

   (d) inflection

7. Passive is an example of grammatical _____.

   (a) mood

   (b) gender

   (c) voice

   (d) case

8. Indicative is an example of grammatical _____.

   (a) mood

   (b) gender

   (c) voice

   (d) case

9. Accusative is an example of grammatical _____.

   (a) mood

   (b) gender

   (c) voice

   (d) case

10. Neuter is an example of grammatical _____.

   (a) mood

   (b) gender

   (c) voice

   (d) case

CHAPTER 2

The Perfect and Imperfect Tenses

In this chapter, you will learn about:

Verbal Aspect

Perfect Tense

Perfect Stem Recognition

The Conjugations

Imperfect Tense

Key Vocabulary

Verbal Aspect

In Chapter 1, you learned about verbal aspect and principal parts. The grammatical term *aspect* refers to the way a speaker views an action, either as something in progress (like watching a movie) or something completed (like looking at a photograph). The former aspect is called the **continuous aspect,** or present system. The latter aspect is called the **completed aspect,** or perfect system. Each aspect has three tenses, one for each time frame, as the following chart illustrates.

Time Frame	Continuous Aspect (Present System)	Completed Aspect (Perfect System)
Now	Present tense	Perfect tense
	he is going / he goes	*he has gone / he went*
Earlier	Imperfect tense	Pluperfect tense
	he was going	*he had gone*
Later	Future tense	Future perfect tense
	he will go	*he will have gone*

Of the four (or sometimes only three) principal parts of a verb, the first two provide all the information you need in order to form all the present system tenses. The third and fourth (if there is one) principal parts provide the information necessary for creating the perfect system tenses.

The tenses that describe actions in the past are the imperfect, perfect, and pluperfect. It may seem counterintuitive that the perfect is considered a past tense, since it sits on the present timeline in the chart above. The reason for this is that although it refers to an action that occurred in the past, the emphasis is on the fact that, as of right now (i.e., in the present), that action has been *completed.*

Perfect Tense

Of the three tenses used to refer to past events, the perfect is the most common. In fact, the perfect is used more than any other tense in the entire language. This should come as no surprise. When we speak or write, it is most often about things that have already happened.

The perfect tense is used to show a single, completed event. The word *perfect* comes from the Latin prefix **per-** (*thoroughly*) and **-fectum** (*done*). Let's talk about how to form the perfect tense before moving on to its usage.

PERFECT TENSE FORMATION

The first thing you will need is a verb stem, which, by the way, you will be able to use for all the perfect system tenses in active voice. The third principal part minus the final **-ī** provides the stem. To this stem, we attach a personal ending.

> **bibō, bibere, *bibī*, bibitum** to drink
> **bib-** + personal ending

In Latin, verbs have special endings that allow subject pronouns to be built into the verb itself. The endings correspond to the person and number of the subject. In English, on the other hand, a subject pronoun must be expressed. For example, *drank* doesn't tell you who was drinking; you have to supply a subject pronoun like *you*. The personal endings on Latin verbs can identify the subject, so the word **bibistī** all by itself means *you drank*. It's the ending **-istī** that supplies the *you*. Of course, there *does* exist a pronoun for *you* in Latin. The point for now is that you don't need it for the Latin verb to work. We'll talk about the role of personal pronouns very soon.

All Latin verb tenses use the same set of personal endings except one—the perfect. The personal endings you are about to learn belong to the perfect tense only. The following chart shows these special perfect personal endings and the person and number each represents.

Singular

First person	-ī	*I*
Second person	-istī	*you*
Third person	-it	*he/she/it*

Plural

First person	-imus	*we*
Second person	-istis	*you*
Third person	-ērunt	*they*

Now that you know how to determine the verb stem for perfect tense and know the special perfect personal endings, it's time to put theory into practice. For our model, let's use the verb **currō, currere, cucurrī, cursum** (*to run*). (Note that this is a full dictionary entry for this verb with all its principal parts. Consult Chapter 1 for a refresher on principal parts if you're not sure what they are.)

Step 1: Go to the third principal part: **cucurrī**.

Step 2: Drop the final **-ī**: **cucurr-**.

Step 3: Add personal endings.

Singular

First person	cucurr**ī**	*I ran*
Second person	cucurr**istī**	*you ran*
Third person	cucurr**it**	*he/she/it ran*

Plural

First person	cucurr**imus**	*we ran*
Second person	cucurr**istis**	*you ran*
Third person	cucurr**ērunt**	*they ran*

The perfect tense does not have to be translated into English as a simple past. English has a couple of other ways to express the perfect tense. For example, in addition to *they ran* for **cucurrērunt**, you could also translate it as *they did run* or *they have run*.

Written Practice 2-1

Conjugate (i.e., put into all their forms) the following verbs in perfect tense and translate each in at least one way.

	Latin	**English**

1. **petō, petere, petīvī, petītum** to look for

   Singular

   First person _____ _____

   Second person _____ _____

   Third person _____ _____

   Plural

   First person _____ _____

   Second person _____ _____

   Third person _____ _____

2. **cadō, cadere, cecidī, cāsum** to fall

   Singular

   First person _____ _____

   Second person _____ _____

   Third person _____ _____

Plural

First person   _____   _____

Second person   _____   _____

Third person   _____   _____

3. **videō, vidēre, vīdī, vīsum** to see

Singular

First person   _____   _____

Second person   _____   _____

Third person   _____   _____

Plural

First person   _____   _____

Second person   _____   _____

Third person   _____   _____

4. **sum, esse, fuī, futūrus** to be

Singular

First person   _____   _____

Second person   _____   _____

Third person   _____   _____

Plural

First person   _____   _____

Second person   _____   _____

Third person   _____   _____

5. **dīcō, dīcere, dixī, dictum** to say

Singular

First person   _____   _____

Second person   _____   _____

Third person   _____   _____

Plural

First person   _____   _____

Second person   _____   _____

Third person   _____   _____

Written Practice 2-2

Using the Key Vocabulary at the end of this chapter, translate the following verb phrases into Latin.

1. you (*pl.*) made   _____
2. they did have   _____
3. I heard   _____
4. we have looked for   _____
5. they gave   _____
6. you (*sg.*) fell   _____
7. I led   _____
8. they have heard   _____
9. he did say   _____
10. she came   _____

Written Practice 2-3

Using the Key Vocabulary at the end of this chapter, translate the following verb forms into English.

1. dixit   _____
2. fēcistis   _____
3. vīdī   _____
4. habuimus   _____
5. dedit   _____
6. vēnit   _____
7. audīvī   _____
8. petīvērunt   _____
9. duxistis   _____
10. cecidistī   _____

Perfect Stem Recognition

Look closely at the principal parts of the verbs in the Key Vocabulary at the end of this chapter. The first two principal parts are where you go to get the stem for the present system tenses, and the last two are the parts you use for the perfect system tenses. You'll notice that there are four ways that perfect stems differentiate themselves from present stems. Knowledge of these four ways will come in quite handy, so here are explanations of what to watch for in order to recognize a perfect verb stem.

SYLLABIC AUGMENT

One way you can recognize a perfect stem is to look for a *syllabic augment*. The English word *augment* comes from the Latin verb **augeō** (*to increase*). In short, some verbs form their perfect stems by—you guessed it—adding a syllable to the end of the present stem, usually **-āv-**, **-īv-**, or **-u-**. Examine the following examples.

*am*ō, amāre, *amāv*ī, amātum to love

*cupi*ō, cupere, *cupīv*ī, cupītum to desire

*mone*ō, monēre, *monu*ī, monitum to warn

TEMPORAL AUGMENT

Another way to recognize a perfect stem is to look for a *temporal augment*. The English word *temporal* comes from Latin **tempus** (*time*). Some verbs form their perfect stems by increasing the length of the present stem's vowel. (As you may recall from the pronunciation section in Chapter 1, the difference between a long and short vowel in Latin is the amount of time it takes to say it.) Identifying perfect stems in this way can be tricky at times, because there is often a slight vowel change as well.

*move*ō, movēre, *mōv*ī, mōtum to move

*em*ō, emere, *ēm*ī, emptum to buy

*capi*ō, capere, *cēp*ī, captum to take

AORIST

A third way to recognize the perfect stem is to look for an *aorist* marker. The term *aorist* refers to an Indo-European verbal aspect that ancient Greek retained but Latin did not. Its key sign was the attachment of **-s-** to the present stem. In the following examples, don't forget that the letter **x** is a double consonant composed of either **c** + **s** or **g** + **s**. There are also some other odd consonant issues for certain linguistic, phonic reasons, but we won't get into those right now.

> *maneō*, manēre, *mansī*, mansum to stay
>
> *claudō*, claudere, *clausī*, clausum to close
>
> *intellegō*, intellegere, *intellexī*, intellectum to understand
>
> *mittō*, mittere, *mīsī*, missum to send

It is amusing how the verb **mittō** seems paranoid enough to use both aorist and temporal augment to assert its perfect system distinction!

REDUPLICATION

The fourth way some Latin verbs form their perfect stem from the present stem is *reduplication*. By this method, the first two letters of the present stem are repeated and added to its beginning rather than end, although at times the vowel in the present stem changes slightly. Once again, this is for linguistic, phonic reasons.

> *currō*, currere, *cucurrī*, cursum to run
>
> *pellō*, pellere, *pepulī*, pulsum to drive

There is one trick about the reduplication method that you need to be aware of. When a reduplicating verb has a prefix, the prefix takes the place of the reduplicated syllable.

> *currō*, currere, *cucurrī*, cursum to run
>
> *pellō*, pellere, *pepulī*, pulsum to drive

but

> *recurrō*, recurrere, *recurrī*, recursum to run back
>
> *expellō*, expellere, *expulī*, expulsum to drive out

Recognizing these patterns in Latin will be very helpful in internalizing the language. By "internalizing," I mean reaching a point in your study where you don't have to think about things so much; they become "gut." When you hear *swam* as opposed to *swim,* or *this* as opposed to *these,* or *children* as opposed to *child,* you don't need to sit back and ponder what those form changes mean. Whatever peculiarities or irregularities there are, you take them in stride as part of your linguistic landscape. It's only by being in Latin's environment for a while that things won't seem so odd anymore.

The Conjugations

As you remember from Chapter 1, Latin verbs are divided into pattern groups called ***conjugations***. Each of the four conjugations constructs the present system tenses (i.e., the present, imperfect, and future) in its own special way. You'll recognize a verb's conjugation from its infinitive, which is its second principal part. The following chart shows the markers to look for to distinguish the conjugations.

First conjugation	amō, am**ā**re, amāvī, amātum *to love*
Second conjugation	teneō, ten**ē**re, tenuī, tentum *to hold*
Third conjugation	mittō, mitt**e**re, mīsī, missum *to send*
Third conjugation **-io**	cap**iō**, cap**e**re, cēpī, captum *to take*
Fourth conjugation	dormiō, dorm**ī**re, dormīvī, dormītum *to sleep*

A few remarks on each of the conjugations would be worthwhile.

First-conjugation verbs have **ā** for their theme vowel. The principal part pattern (**-ō, -āre, -āvī, -ātum**) is the same for nearly all first-conjugation verbs.

Second-conjugation verbs have **ē** for their characteristic vowel. The macron here is very important, since third-conjugation verbs have short **e** and the two conjugations can have quite different endings. About half of all second-conjugation verbs have the principal part pattern shown here (**-eō, -ēre, -uī, -itum**).

Third-conjugation verbs, perhaps the most common, have short **e** for their theme vowel, but this is very unstable phonetically. There is no predominant pattern in its principal parts.

Third-conjugation -iō verbs are considered third-conjugation verbs because of their infinitive. You can recognize them by their first principal part, which ends in **-iō**. They conjugate like regular third-conjugation verbs except that, in the present system tenses, **-i-** is added between the stem and the ending if the ending doesn't already begin with **-i**.

Fourth-conjugation verbs have ī for their theme vowel. Nearly all of their endings in the present system tenses look the same as those of third-conjugation **-iō** verbs. The principal parts pattern shown above (**-iō, -īre, -īvī, -ītum**) is extremely common.

Imperfect Tense

The imperfect tense works as the present system's counterpart to the perfect tense. As you may recall, the word *perfect* means "thoroughly done." The word ***im**perfect* means "**not** thoroughly done." It shows an action that was in progress in the past and may or may not still be going on in the present. It doesn't matter if it is *still* happening, because the emphasis is that it was *in the midst of happening* at some earlier time. The imperfect contains a range of ideas that can be translated in quite a few different ways. For example, you could translate **audiēbam** in the following ways.

I was hearing
I used to hear
I kept hearing
I began hearing
I started hearing
I heard

This last option, however, only works if there is another word or phrase in the sentence, such as *every day,* that makes it clear that the action was ongoing or repeated, and not a single, completed one, e.g., *I wrote to him every day.*

IMPERFECT TENSE FORMATION

Formation of the imperfect tense is a little more complicated than formation of the perfect tense. The perfect system tenses are made the same way for all verbs, regardless of which conjugation they belong to. This is not the case for present system tenses such as the imperfect.

The basic steps for formation are simple.

Step 1: Go to the infinitive (the second principal part).

Step 2: Drop the infinitive ending (**-āre, -ēre, -ere, -īre**) and add **-ā-** for first conjugation, **-ē-** for second and third, and **-iē-** for third **-iō** and fourth conjugations.

Step 2 provides the stem.

Step 3: Add the tense indicator **-ba-**.

This syllable is added to the present stem of verbs of all conjugations and is an easy-to-spot marker for imperfect tense.

Step 4: Add personal endings.

Don't forget that the personal endings for the perfect tense that you learned earlier in this chapter are unique to the perfect tense. The imperfect uses a set of endings common to all the present tenses. These endings are shown in the following chart.

Singular

First person	-ō/-m	*I*
Second person	-s	*you*
Third person	-t	*he/she/it*

Plural

First person	-mus	*we*
Second person	-tis	*you*
Third person	-nt	*they*

N.B. (**notā bene** (*note well*)): For the first-person singular, there is a pair of alternate endings, **-ō** and **-m**. They are not interchangeable. Some tenses use one, other tenses use the other. The imperfect uses **-m**.

The following chart gives sample conjugations of the imperfect tense in each of the conjugations.

First Conjugation amō, amāre, amāvī, amātum to love

Singular

First person	amābam	*I was loving*
Second person	amābās	*you were loving*
Third person	amābat	*he/she/it was loving*

Plural

First person	amābāmus	*we were loving*
Second person	amābātis	*you were loving*
Third person	amābant	*they were loving*

Second Conjugation teneō, tenēre, tenuī, tentum to hold

Singular

First person	tenēbam	*I was holding*
Second person	tenēbās	*you were holding*
Third person	tenēbat	*he/she/it was holding*

Plural

First person	tenēbāmus	*we were holding*
Second person	tenēbātis	*you were holding*
Third person	tenēbant	*they were holding*

Third Conjugation mittō, mittere, mīsī, missum to send

Singular

First person	mittēbam	*I was sending*
Second person	mittēbās	*you were sending*
Third person	mittēbat	*he/she/it was sending*

Plural

First person	mittēbāmus	*we were sending*
Second person	mittēbātis	*you were sending*
Third person	mittēbant	*they were sending*

Third Conjugation -iō capiō, capere, cēpī, captum to take

Singular

First person	capiēbam	*I was taking*
Second person	capiēbās	*you were taking*
Third person	capiēbat	*he/she/it was taking*

Plural

First person	capiēbāmus	*we were taking*
Second person	capiēbātis	*you were taking*
Third person	capiēbant	*they were taking*

Fourth Conjugation **dormiō, dormīre, dormīvī, dormītum** to sleep

Singular

First person	dormiēbam	*I was sleeping*
Second person	dormiēbās	*you were sleeping*
Third person	dormiēbat	*he/she/it was sleeping*

Plural

First person	dormiēbāmus	*we were sleeping*
Second person	dormiēbātis	*you were sleeping*
Third person	dormiēbant	*they were sleeping*

Written Practice 2-4

Conjugate the following verbs in imperfect tense and translate each in at least one way.

Latin   **English**

1. **portō, portāre, portāvī, portātum** to carry

   Singular

   First person   _____   _____
   Second person _____   _____
   Third person   _____   _____

   Plural

   First person   _____   _____
   Second person _____   _____
   Third person   _____   _____

2. **cadō, cadere, cecidī, cāsum** to fall

   Singular

   First person   _____   _____
   Second person _____   _____
   Third person   _____   _____

   Plural

   First person   _____   _____
   Second person _____   _____
   Third person   _____   _____

3. **moveō, movēre, mōvī, mōtum** to move
   Singular
   First person   _____   _____
   Second person   _____   _____
   Third person   _____   _____
   Plural
   First person   _____   _____
   Second person   _____   _____
   Third person   _____   _____

4. **sentiō, sentīre, sensī, sensum** to feel
   Singular
   First person   _____   _____
   Second person   _____   _____
   Third person   _____   _____
   Plural
   First person   _____   _____
   Second person   _____   _____
   Third person   _____   _____

Written Practice 2-5

Using the Key Vocabulary at the end of this chapter, translate the following verb phrases into Latin.

1. you (*pl.*) used to have   _____
2. they kept hearing   _____
3. I was coming   _____
4. we began to think   _____
5. they were giving   _____
6. you (*sg.*) started to see   _____
7. I fell   _____
8. they were leading   _____

9. he used to say _____

10. she kept looking for _____

Written Practice 2-6

Using the Key Vocabulary at the end of this chapter, translate the following verb forms into English in at least one way.

1. faciēbat _____

2. habēbāmus _____

3. vidēbam _____

4. veniēbāmus _____

5. petēbant _____

6. veniēbātis _____

7. cadēbās _____

8. dūcēbant _____

9. dabat _____

10. faciēbās _____

Key Vocabulary

Here are some of the most important verbs in Latin. Be sure to memorize them before moving on to the Chapter Quiz! In square brackets at the end of most entries, you'll find an English derivative or a related word that may help you learn it. Be careful with them, though—they're aids, not meanings!

Verbs

audiō, audīre, audīvī, audītum to hear [audio]

cadō, cadere, cecidī, cāsum to fall [cadence]

dīcō, dīcere, dixī, dictum to say, tell [dictation]

dō, dare, dedī, datum to give [data]

dormiō, dormīre, dormīvī, dormītum to sleep [dormitory]

dūcō, dūcere, duxī, ductum to take (someone/something somewhere), lead [duct]

faciō, facere, fēcī, factum to make, do [factory]

habeō, habēre, habuī, habitum to have, hold; consider, regard [habit]
moveō, movēre, mōvī, mōtum to move [movable]
petō, petere, petīvī, petītum to look for, ask; head for a place; attack [petition]
portō, portāre, portāvī, portātum to carry [portable]
putō, putāre, putāvī, putātum to think [compute]
sentiō, sentīre, sensī, sensum to feel [sensitive]
veniō, venīre, vēnī, ventum to come [convention]
videō, vidēre, vīdī, vīsum to see [video, vision]

QUIZ

Choose the best Latin translation for each English verb phrase.

1. they used to hear
   (a) audiēbant
   (b) audīvērunt
   (c) audiunt
   (d) audīverint

2. you (*pl.*) kept falling
   (a) cadēbās
   (b) cecidistī
   (c) cadō
   (d) cadēbātis

3. we said
   (a) diximus
   (b) dixērunt
   (c) dīcimus
   (d) dīcerēmus

4. we were giving
   (a) dabant
   (b) dedērunt
   (c) dedimus
   (d) dabāmus

5. they have led
   (a) dixērunt
   (b) duxērunt
   (c) dūcunt
   (d) dīcēbant

6. he has done
   (a) facit
   (b) fēcit
   (c) faciēbat
   (d) fēcistī

7. they used to have
   (a) habēbant
   (b) habuērunt
   (c) habērent
   (d) habuerant

8. you (*sg.*) used to ask
   (a) petis
   (b) petēbās
   (c) petīvistī
   (d) petīvistis

9. I came
   (a) veniō
   (b) vēnī
   (c) veniēbam
   (d) vēnistī

10. I saw
    (a) videō
    (b) vīdī
    (c) vidērem
    (d) vīderim

CHAPTER 3

The Basics of a Latin Sentence

In this chapter, you will learn about:

How Latin Nouns Work
Transitive Versus Intransitive Verbs
Accusative Case
Direct Objects
Nominative Case
Personal Pronouns
Key Vocabulary

How Latin Nouns Work

In Chapter 1, you learned that the Latin noun system is not nearly as complicated as its verb system. The noun system does, however, have some very important concepts that bear reviewing. These are declension, gender, case, and number, as well as how to read a dictionary entry.

THE DECLENSIONS

Just as a deck of playing cards can be divided into four suits, all Latin nouns are sorted into five groups called *declensions*, based on their endings. We could do the same thing with English nouns, based on the endings they take to form plurals: *dog/dogs, man/men, mouse/mice, foot/feet, child/children, church/churches.* English nouns take other endings as well. They also have genitive case endings. (A grammatical "case" is the form a word takes to show its relationship to other words in a sentence.) Here is a sample declension of an English noun.

Case	Singular	Plural
Nominative (shows subject)	*dog*	*dogs*
Genitive (shows possession)	*dog's*	*dogs'*
Accusative (shows direct object)	*dog*	*dogs*

For English nouns, the nominative and accusative forms are identical. The difference is more obvious with certain pronouns; consider *they* and *them.*

In our English noun classification system, we use the nominative plural ending to determine which group (declension) a noun belongs to. Latin uses a noun's genitive singular ending to determine its declension.

NOUNS IN THE DICTIONARY

When you study Latin vocabulary, you will find that noun listings have four parts. Let's analyze a couple of examples.

> **āla, ālae** *f.* wing
>
> **homō, hominis** *m.* person, human being

The first word in the dictionary listing is nominative case, the form used when the word is the subject of a sentence. In first declension, it always ends in **-a.** In third declension, however, the nominative singular is a wild card and totally unpredictable. There is no standard nominative singular ending; each third-declension noun has its own, and this simply has to be memorized.

The second word in the dictionary entry of a Latin noun is genitive case. We'll talk about genitive case later, but for the moment you should know that this form provides two crucial pieces of information. One is the stem change, if there is one, because it is to this modified stem that all other endings are attached. The first example above, **āla**, has no stem change from nominative to genitive. The second example has an extreme change. The nominative **homō** is unique. Once you drop the **-is** from the genitive **hominis**, you have the stem **homin-**, to which all the remaining case endings attach.

The following chart shows the genitive case ending for each of the five Latin declensions.

First declension	-ae
Second declension	-ī
Third declension	-is
Fourth declension	-ūs
Fifth declension	-ēī

After the genitive singular form comes a letter signifying gender: *f.* for feminine, *m.* for masculine, and *n.* for neuter. There are two kinds of gender in grammar, *natural* and *grammatical.* This is confusing for English speakers, since the English language has retained only natural gender. The Latin language, however, has grammatical gender as well as natural gender. Appropriate gender is assigned to naturally masculine and feminine beings, so the word **puella** (*girl*) is considered feminine. The word **āla** is considered grammatically feminine merely because it behaves like the naturally feminine word **puella**. Neuter gender is assigned to words that behave a different way, with neither naturally masculine or feminine words to follow as models.

N.B. Occasionally in a dictionary entry, you will find the letter *c.* This stands for ***common gender***. Common gender is sometimes assigned to a natural gender noun that could refer to either a male or female person, for example, **cīvis** (*citizen*), which might refer to a man or a woman.

The final item in the dictionary entry for a noun is its meaning. This is actually a bit tricky. No language is a code for any other language. Translation isn't just a matter of replacing words. Language is a reflection of culture, and since cultures differ from one another—sometimes greatly—they often have concepts, ideas, and objects that others don't. They also often have a very different view of the world. There are words in Latin that have no equivalent in English, and **vice versā** (which is Latin for *with the opposites having been turned around*). For example, there are no Latin words for *yes* and *no*. Instead, the Romans said things like **vērō**, which literally means *really,* and **minimē**, which means *in the least*! Latin also lacks the article adjectives *a, an,* and *the.* Apparently, the Romans didn't think the concepts behind these words were important.

Latin also has words for which there are no equivalents in English. This is easy to see in words for colors. In antiquity, all colors were natural—there was no yellow dye No. 5, for instance. Take the color **caeruleus**. Dictionaries usually list meanings such as *blue, green,* or *gray*. It's actually none of those colors. No, the Romans weren't color-blind. **Caeruleus** is the color where the sky meets the sea, or just the sea itself; it's too blue to be green, too green to be gray, too gray to be blue. The upshot of this is that no matter how you translate **caeruleus**, you're wrong. Apart from creative names on paint chips at the hardware store or on crayons, we have no native English word for what it refers to.

This is true for virtually all Latin words. **Ergō** (Latin for *therefore*), translations can only be near misses from the original language, which is why we study foreign languages to begin with! In order to encounter the ancient Romans and their literature, we have to hear and read them in their own words. So when you study vocabulary, try to imagine a word's true meaning as something of an approximate intersection of all the possibilities presented.

Written Practice 3-1

To which declension does each of the following nouns belong?

1. _____ **servus, servī** *m.* slave
2. _____ **rēs, rēī** *f.* thing
3. _____ **rex, rēgis** *m.* king
4. _____ **māter, mātris** *f.* mother
5. _____ **crāpula, crāpulae** *f.* hangover
6. _____ **ēventus, ēventūs** *m.* outcome
7. _____ **aetās, aetātis** *f.* age
8. _____ **ager, agrī** *m.* field
9. _____ **nāvis, nāvis** *f.* ship
10. _____ **culpa, culpae** *f.* guilt

Transitive Versus Intransitive Verbs

Verbs don't always show action **per se** (Latin for *by themselves*). Sometimes they describe inaction.

There are two kinds of verbs, transitive and intransitive. The term *transitive* is from Latin **trans** (*across*) and **it** (*go*). Transitive verbs describe an action that "goes across" from a subject to an object. For example, in the sentence *We picked elderberries, picked* is a transitive verb. *Someone* has to pick *something*! The act of picking requires a pick*er* (subject) and a pick*ee* (direct object). One agent has a direct impact on something else; thus, transitive verbs require a direct object in order to make a complete thought.

The prefix *in-* of the term *intransitive* suggests that these verbs don't "go across." Intransitive verbs describe states of being, such as in *He is sleeping.* He isn't doing anything to anyone; that's just the state of his being. A sleep*er* doesn't need a sleep*ee* to make sense, so it should be easy to see how intransitive verbs don't, and in fact can't, have direct objects. Verbs of motion also fall into this category. For example, in the sentence *I was going to the store,* I wasn't doing anything to the store; my state of being was just in motion in that direction.

It is important to be able to distinguish between transitive and intransitive verbs for the rest of this chapter to make sense. Let's take a moment to review verbs that we encountered in Chapter 2.

Written Practice 3-2

Indicate whether each of these verbs is transitive or intransitive.

1. dīcō   _____
2. faciō   _____
3. videō   _____
4. habeō   _____
5. dō   _____
6. veniō   _____
7. audiō   _____
8. petō   _____
9. dūcō   _____
10. cadō   _____

Accusative Case

The heart of a clause or sentence is its verb. All the other words around it either serve in some way to modify the verb, or they modify the words that are modifying it. Ultimately, it all comes back to the verb.

Since intransitive verbs cannot take direct objects—and since a Latin verb's subject can be known from its personal ending—a Latin sentence can easily be expressed in one word, i.e., the verb. Other words are piled on to describe the scene more fully. Here is a very simple sentence that we can beef up with other words to illustrate this concept.

Dormiēbam.	*I kept sleeping.*
Altē dormiēbam.	*I kept sleeping soundly.*
In lectō altē dormiēbam.	*I kept sleeping soundly in bed.*
In lectō amīcī altē dormiēbam.	*I kept sleeping soundly in the bed of a friend.*
In lectō amīci meī altē dormiēbam.	*I kept sleeping soundly in the bed of my friend.*
In lectō amīcī meī tōtam noctem altē dormiēbam.	*I kept sleeping soundly for the whole night in the bed of my friend.*
In lectō amīcī meī, quī repente Rōmā heri pervēnerat, tōtam noctem altē dormiēbam.	*I kept sleeping soundly for the whole night in the bed of my friend, who had unexpectedly arrived from Rome yesterday.*
Commissātiōne strepente, in lectō amīcī meī, quī repente Rōmā heri pervēnerat, tōtam noctem altē dormiēbam.	*Even though a drinking party was making a terrible racket, I kept sleeping soundly for the whole night in the bed of my friend, who had unexpectedly arrived from Rome yesterday.*

Each item added to the preceding sentence adds details to the circumstances under which the verb was taking place. (You might have also noticed that what Latin could say in 15 words was spun out into 31 words in English. Latin is a very tight, economical language!)

Intransitive verbs can't take a direct object, so one-word sentences like the first example above are possible. Transitive verbs, however, require a direct object. A sentence with a transitive verb must have at least two words.

The main—but not only—job of the accusative case in nouns is to mark direct objects required by transitive verbs. In Latin, an accusative case ending marks the word where an action stops or is at its limit. If you answer the phone, the phone is what stops the answering. If a chef makes chicken and rice, the finished chicken and rice is where the cooking stops and the stove is turned off. These are direct objects. The accusative is used in the same spirit with respect to verbs of motion and destination. If I'm going to Rome, getting to Rome is where the going stops.

The ending for the accusative case is attached to a Latin noun to show this point of termination. The endings themselves are very easy to learn and recognize. For singular nouns, look for **-m**, and for nouns in the plural, look for **-s**.

The following chart presents full declensions (i.e., all the forms) for nouns of first, second, and third declensions. These three declensions are the most common. Fourth and fifth declensions will be saved for another chapter. Only the accusative case forms are important for you to focus on and learn at the moment. We will work with the nominative case later in this chapter. All the forms are presented here to satisfy any curiosity you may have. It is not a bad idea for you to memorize each chart in its entirety, even if you don't know what to do with all the other cases or forms yet.

Case	Singular	Plural
First Declension		
Nominative	-a	-ae
Genitive	-ae	-ārum
Dative	-ae	-īs
Accusative	**-am**	**-ās**
Ablative	-ā	-īs
Second Declension		
Nominative	-us/-er	-ī/-rī
Genitive	-ī	-ōrum
Dative	-ō	-īs
Accusative	**-um**	**-ōs**
Ablative	-ō	-īs
Third Declension		
Nominative	*Wild card!*	-ēs
Genitive	-is	-um
Dative	-ī	-ibus
Accusative	**-em**	**-ēs**
Ablative	-e	-ibus

Written Practice 3-3

Write the singular and plural accusative case forms for each of the following nouns.

	Singular	Plural
1. **Germānus, Germānī** *m.* a German	_____	_____
2. **comes, comitis** *c.* buddy, companion	_____	_____
3. **mens, mentis** *f.* mind	_____	_____
4. **forma, formae** *f.* shape, image	_____	_____
5. **ventus, ventī** *m.* wind	_____	_____
6. **ager, agrī** *m.* field	_____	_____
7. **arbor, arboris** *f.* tree	_____	_____
8. **fāma, fāmae** *f.* reputation	_____	_____
9. **mīles, mīlitis** *c.* soldier	_____	_____
10. **lingua, linguae** *f.* tongue; language	_____	_____

Written Practice 3-4

The following nouns are all in accusative case, either singular or plural. Indicate their declension and the nominative singular form as you would find it in the dictionary. For third-declension nouns, the nominative singular ending is not standard; mark an *X* in these blanks. The purpose of this exercise is to practice recognition and back-formation, so it doesn't matter if you don't know what the words mean.

	Declension	Nominative Singular
1. deam	_____	_____
2. principem	_____	_____
3. hortum	_____	_____
4. mensam	_____	_____
5. magnitūdinēs	_____	_____
6. morbōs	_____	_____
7. agricolās	_____	_____
8. gregem	_____	_____

	Declension	Nominative Singular
9. lupum	_____	_____
10. canēs	_____	_____
11. geminōs	_____	_____
12. insulās	_____	_____
13. ensēs	_____	_____
14. avum	_____	_____
15. ūtilitātem	_____	_____

Direct Objects

The most important, even crucial, point of this chapter is that you remember, now and for always, that a clause or sentence with an intransitive verb needs nothing but the verb itself—everything else simply adds detail. However interesting a detail may be, it is unnecessary from a grammatical standpoint. A clause or sentence containing a transitive verb, however, *will* have a direct object. Watch for it! That stray noun in the accusative is an essential part of the sentence. All things considered, it is an essential part of a transitive verb. You should consider the verb and direct object as a single unit.

Verb Type	Basic Sentence Components	Example Latin Sentence	English Translation
Intransitive	Verb alone	Periit.	*He died.*
Transitive	Verb with direct object	Canem revocāvī.	*I called the dog back.*

He didn't "died" anything. Dying was the state his being was in. I certainly "called the dog back," though, and just in time before he bit the postman. I couldn't just "call." I had to call back someone or something.

This is a vital concept. In time, you will discover that sentences in Latin can become incredibly long, which, to a student of the language, can be very intimidating. There is no reason to be overwhelmed if you bear in mind that a sentence only requires one or two words, depending on which type of verb it is, and that all the rest is extra information.

This book strives to introduce you to the most basic and frequently encountered concepts and constructions right from the start. In this way, you will have a strong foundation to build on, and if for whatever reason you are not able to finish the course, you will at least be able to get a gist of something written in Latin when you encounter it.

With that said, it's time to put into practice what you have read in this chapter and the last one. In Chapter 2, you learned about the perfect and imperfect tenses: how to recognize and form them, how they differ in aspect, and how there are many ways those aspects can be expressed in English.

As a refresher, here are a couple of examples borrowed from the most basic type of sentence.

Canēs revocāvī.	*I called the dogs back.*
	I did call the dogs back.
	I have called the dogs back.
Canēs revocābam.	*I was calling the dogs back.*
	I used to call the dogs back.
	I kept calling the dogs back.
	I began to call the dogs back.
	I started calling the dogs back.
	I called the dogs back.

How do you know which translation is right? Grammatically speaking, they all are. To a Roman, the first example, which uses perfect tense, means simply that the calling is over. The second example, which uses imperfect tense, indicates that the calling occurred repeatedly or was in the midst of occurring. The point of the imperfect tense is to stress that it wasn't a one-time, over-and-done deal.

Written Practice 3-5

Translate each of the following sentences in at least two different ways. They're tiny sentences and will probably sound goofy, but when you started learning to read English, you didn't start with Shakespeare.

1. Cadēbant.

    _____

    _____

2. Hominēs accipiēbāmus.

    _____

    _____

3. Patrēs vīdērunt.

   _____

   _____

4. Mātrem amābat.

   _____

   _____

5. Vōcēs audiēbam.

   _____

   _____

6. Equōs ēgit.

   _____

   _____

7. Librum lēgistī.

   _____

   _____

8. Librōs lēgistis.

   _____

   _____

9. Mīlitem tenēbāmus.

   _____

   _____

10. Stetit.

   _____

   _____

11. Fugiēbās.

   _____

   _____

12. Hostēs cēpērunt.

   _____

   _____

13. Librum scrīpsī.

_____

_____

14. Puerōs petīvimus.

_____

_____

15. Virum dūcēbant.

_____

_____

Nominative Case

Now that you have learned about the basic structure of a Latin sentence, it's time to start learning about the information you can add!

After the accusative, the next most important case is the *nominative*. The primary function of the nominative case is to identify the subject of the verb. Thanks to personal endings, the verb itself already tells you quite clearly who the subject is for the first and second persons. For the third person, however, things are not so clear.

Canēs dūcēba**m**.	*I was leading the dogs.* I am I. No confusion.
Canēs dūcēba**nt**.	*They were leading the dogs.* Who are these "they" people?
Puerī canēs dūcēba**nt**.	*The boys were leading the dogs.* Ah! That's who "they" are!

There's a very important thing for you to notice in this last sentence. Even though the nominative plural **puerī** indicates the subject, the personal ending of the verb, **-nt**, still has to be there. This is called subject-verb agreement. From a linguistic standpoint, you might think this is redundant. It is, but we have subject-verb agreement in English too. For example, you say "I have," not "I has." Also, remember that the function of everything in a clause or sentence other than the verb serves to modify that verb. In the sentence above, the word **puerī** is in nominative case in order to clarify to whom the **-nt** refers.

For the most part, the nominative case only has gossip value, i.e., it communicates details. It's time to formally add more case forms to your inventory.

Case	Singular	Plural
First Declension		
Nominative	**-a**	**-ae**
Genitive	-ae	-ārum
Dative	-ae	-īs
Accusative	**-am**	**-ās**
Ablative	-ā	-īs
Second Declension		
Nominative	**-us/-er**	**-ī/-rī**
Genitive	-ī	-ōrum
Dative	-ō	-īs
Accusative	**-um**	**-ōs**
Ablative	-ō	-īs
Third Declension		
Nominative	*Wild card!*	**-ēs**
Genitive	-is	-um
Dative	-ī	-ibus
Accusative	**-em**	**-ēs**
Ablative	-e	-ibus

If you look closely at the nominative and accusative plural forms in third declension, you will notice a potential problem—they both end in **-ēs**.

> Hostēs mīlitēs cēpērunt.   *The enemy captured the soldiers.*
> OR *The soldiers captured the enemy.*

Since word order doesn't matter in Latin, and subjects and direct objects are very different entities, how can you know which version is intended? There are two things to bear in mind in this situation. First, although word order in Latin doesn't matter technically, the usual order is subject-object-verb. In this example, odds are that the first translation is the correct one.

Second, it is extremely rare that anything we say or write doesn't occur in some context. We live in a sea of language and take most of it for granted. Stop for a moment today and jot down a single, simple sentence that you see or hear outside of this book. Then come back to it later and think about how truly dependent it is on the sentences that went before and after it.

Personal Pronouns

In Latin, there are personal pronouns corresponding to *I, you* (sg.), *we,* and *you* (pl.). The nominative case for them is unnecessary, of course, given that personal endings already provide that information. Those forms are used to show emphasis.

Puerōs custōdiēba**m**.	*I was taking care of the boys.*
Ego puerōs custōdiēba**m**.	*I (not anyone else) was taking care of the boys.*

Here is a chart of the personal pronouns for first and second person.

Case	Singular	Plural
First Person		
Nominative	ego	nōs
Genitive	meī	nostrī/nostrum
Dative	mihi	nōbīs
Accusative	mē	nōs
Ablative	mē	nōbīs
Second Person		
Nominative	tū	vōs
Genitive	tuī	vestrī/vestrum
Dative	tibi	vōbīs
Accusative	tē	vōs
Ablative	tē	vōbīs

There are also pronouns for *he, she, it,* and *they.* In fact, there are four pronouns for each! To satisfy your curiosity: There's a *he* for "this here guy" (**hic**), "that there guy" (**ille**), a guy I don't like (**iste**), and "the guy I was just talking about" (**is**). Clearly, the topic is complicated enough to merit its own chapter, which will come later.

Written Practice 3-6

All of the following nouns are in the accusative case, either singular or plural. Write the nominative form of each, keeping singular for singular and plural for plural. Whether you know the meaning or not doesn't matter; the important thing is form recognition. For a third-declension noun, you can't know for sure what the nominative singular form is, but take a guess. There are some patterns in third declension, and over time you'll become acquainted with them enough to hone your prediction skills. In the second column, guess the meaning of the word. You'll be surprised at how much you already know!

	Nominative Form	Meaning (Guess!)
1. dolōrem	_____	_____
2. flammam	_____	_____
3. sermōnem	_____	_____
4. litterās	_____	_____
5. cīvēs	_____	_____
6. campōs	_____	_____
7. invidiam	_____	_____
8. pudōrem	_____	_____
9. lapidēs	_____	_____
10. rāmum	_____	_____

Written Practice 3-7

Translate the following sentences into English in at least two different ways.

1. Puer canem petēbat.

   _____

   _____

2. Māter puerum tenēbat.

   _____

   _____

3. Hostēs nōs cēpērunt.

   _____

   _____

4. Tū vōcem audīvistī.

   _____

   _____

5. Ego flōrēs collēgī.

    _____

    _____

6. Virī equōs agēbant.

    _____

    _____

7. Vōs dominum habēbātis.

    _____

    _____

8. Librum tū lēgistī.

    _____

    _____

9. Mātrem amābant puerī.

    _____

    _____

10. Canēs mīlitēs duxērunt.

    _____

    _____

Key Vocabulary

Don't forget that the words in square brackets at the ends of entries are only derivatives (i.e., English words that are derived from the Latin words) or closely related words, *not* meanings. They are provided because they can be useful in helping you remember what the Latin words mean.

Nouns

dominus, dominī *m.* master [dominate]
equus, equī *m.* horse [equine]
flōs, flōris *m.* flower [floral]
homō, hominis *m.* person, man (*as opposed to* animal) [homicide, *homo sapiens*]
hostis, hostis *c.* enemy [hostile] (*In the plural,* **hostēs** *means* the *enemy.*)

liber, librī *m.* book [library]

māter, mātris *f.* mother [maternity]

mīlēs, mīlitis *c.* soldier [military]

pater, patris *m.* father [paternity]

puer, puerī *m.* boy [puerile] (*In the plural*, **puerī** *can refer to children in general.*)

vir, virī *m.* man (*as opposed to* **fēmina** woman) [virile]

vox, vōcis *f.* voice [vocal]

Verbs

accipiō, accipere, accēpī, acceptum to welcome, receive; take [accept]

agō, agere, ēgī, actum to do, drive; lead; be busy [act]

amō, amāre, amāvī, amātum to like, love [amorous]

capiō, capere, cēpī, captum to take, catch [capture]

colligō, colligere, collēgī, collectum to gather, collect [collectible]

fugiō, fugere, fūgī to run away, flee, escape [fugitive]

legō, legere, lēgī, lectum to choose, pick, gather; read [legible]

scrībō, scrībere, scripsī, scriptum to write, scratch, carve [scribe]

stō, stāre, stetī, statum to stand, stay [stand]

teneō, tenēre, tenuī, tentum to hold, have [tentacle]

QUIZ

Indicate whether each of these verbs is transitive or intransitive.

1. dīcō   _____

2. fugiō   _____

3. stō   _____

4. dūcō   _____

5. petō   _____

6. scrībō   _____

7. capiō   _____

8. dō   _____

9. cadō   _____

10. legō   _____

CHAPTER 4

The Present Tense

In this chapter, you will learn about:

Present Tense

In Chapter 2, you learned about the perfect tense. You learned that in the perfect system, the tenses are formed in the same way for all conjugations, irregular verbs included.

We are not so lucky with the present system tenses, i.e., the present, imperfect, and future, so it is vital to know which conjugation a verb belongs to. Of the present system tenses, the imperfect has the most consistent forms across the conjugations. In this tense, all conjugations have the same tense indicator: **-ba-**. What differs among them is the verb stem to which the **-ba-** is attached. It is **-ā-** for first-conjugation verbs, **-ē-** for second- and third-conjugation verbs, and **-iē-** for third-conjugation **-iō** and fourth-conjugation verbs.

In the present system, the Latin present tense is the "now time" tense. The ideas it contains are expressed in three different ways in English. One way is as an action in progress right now, which is totally in the spirit of the continuous aspect. It can also represent an action that happens in general, not only in the present as we speak. English also sometimes uses the helping verb *to do* to put emphasis on the generality of an action.

Since Latin doesn't use helping verbs, it has only one way to express present tense. But as we noted above, English has more than one. Following is an example illustrating the different ways you can translate the Latin present tense into English; the best way depends on the context.

Vīnum bibis.	*You are drinking wine.* (in progress) I'm watching you as you do it.
	You drink wine. (in general) You do from time to time, just not at the moment.
	You do drink wine. (in general, emphatically) Don't deny it!

The present is the only tense in Latin that has a unique pattern of endings in each conjugation. It is also the only tense where nearly all irregular verbs show irregularity. The most common, not to mention the most important, of these irregular verbs, is **sum** (*to be*), whose present tense conjugation you will learn later in this chapter.

Since present tense varies from conjugation to conjugation, let's consider the conjugations one at a time.

First Conjugation

As you know, Latin verbs are sorted into their conjugation groups based on the ending of their infinitive (the second principal part). The infinitive ending that signals a first-conjugation verb is **-āre**. The pattern seen in the principal parts of almost all first-conjugation verbs is **-ō, -āre, -āvī, -ātum**, so verbs of this conjugation are easy to learn. If you are looking in a dictionary and you see an entry such as "**portō** (1)," you can assume that the principal parts for that verb follow this pattern.

The key characteristic, or signature vowel, of first-conjugation verbs is **ā**. This theme vowel appears as the stem vowel for every form in all the present system tenses—with one exception, as you will see.

In order to form present tense in first conjugation, follow these simple rules.

Step 1: Go to the second principal part (the infinitive).

Step 2: Drop the **-re**.

Step 3: Add personal endings.

Person	Singular	Plural
First	-ō	-mus
Second	-s	-tis
Third	-t	-nt

N.B. For the first-person singular, the personal ending is either **-m** or **-ō**. The imperfect tense uses **-m**, but the present tense uses **-ō**. The perfect tense uses **-ī**, but as you remember, the perfect tense has a special set of personal endings that it alone uses.

To put all this into practice, let's use the verb **portō**.

portō, portāre, portāvī, portātum (1) to carry

Person	Singular	Plural
First	portō	portā**mus**
Second	portā**s**	portā**tis**
Third	porta**t**	porta**nt**

N.B. The first-person singular is the only form where the stem of a first-conjugation verb doesn't have the theme vowel **ā**. There is a contraction: **ā + ō = ō**.

The English version of the chart above would be as follows.

I carry, to carry, I carried, carried portō (1)

Person	Singular	Plural
First	*I carry*	*we carry*
	I am carrying	*we are carrying*
	I do carry	*we do carry*
Second	*you carry*	*you carry*
	you are carrying	*you are carrying*
	you do carry	*you do carry*
Third	*he/she/it carries*	*they carry*
	he/she/it is carrying	*they are carrying*
	he/she/it does carry	*they do carry*

Written Practice 4-1

Conjugate the following verbs in present tense.

Person	Singular	Plural

1. **optō** (1) to desire, choose

First _____ _____

Second _____ _____

Third _____ _____

2. **postulō** (1) to ask, demand

First _____ _____

Second _____ _____

Third _____ _____

3. **clāmō** (1) to shout

First _____ _____

Second _____ _____

Third _____ _____

4. **stō, stāre, stetī, statum** to stand

First _____ _____

Second _____ _____

Third _____ _____

Written Practice 4-2

Translate each of the following verb forms in three different ways.

1. intrō (*to enter*) _____
   _____
   _____

2. optātis (*to choose*) _____
   _____
   _____

3. clāmant (*to shout*) _____
   _____
   _____

4. obstāmus (*to block*) _____
   _____
   _____

5. plaudat (*to applaud*) _____
   _____
   _____

Written Practice 4-3

Translate the following verb phrases into Latin.

1. we love _____
2. she is praising _____
3. he stands _____
4. I do ask _____
5. they are calling _____

Second Conjugation

The theme vowel of second-conjugation verbs for the present system is **ē**, as you can see in the infinitive (second principal part), which ends in **-ēre**. Only about half of second-conjugation verbs follow a standard pattern in their principal parts. You can see this pattern in the verb **habeō, habēre, habuī, habitum** (*to have*).

In order to form present tense in second conjugation, follow the same rules as for first conjugation.

Step 1: Go to the second principal part (the infinitive).

Step 2: Drop the **-re**.

Step 3: Add personal endings.

Person	Singular	Plural
First	-ō	-mus
Second	-s	-tis
Third	-t	-nt

Here is the full conjugation of the verb **habeō** in present tense.

habeō, habēre, habuī, habitum to have

Person	Singular	Plural
First	habeō	habēmus
Second	habēs	habētis
Third	habet	habent

Notice that unlike in first conjugation, the theme vowel **ē** does not contract with the personal ending **-ō**, so **ē** + **ō** = **eō**.

Written Practice 4-4

Conjugate the following verbs in present tense.

     Person   **Singular**   **Plural**

1. **maneō, manēre, mansī, mansum** to stay

   First   _____   _____

   Second _____   _____

   Third   _____   _____

2. **video, vidēre, vīdī, vīsum** to see

   First   _____   _____

   Second _____   _____

   Third   _____   _____

3. **teneō, tenēre, tenuī, tentum** to hold

   First   _____   _____

   Second _____   _____

   Third   _____   _____

4. **moveō, movēre, mōvī, mōtum** to move

   First   _____   _____

   Second _____   _____

   Third   _____   _____

5. **dēbeō, dēbēre, dēbuī, dēbitum** to owe, ought

   First   _____   _____

   Second _____   _____

   Third   _____   _____

Written Practice 4-5

Translate each of the following verb forms in three different ways.

1. dolēmus (*to feel pain*)   _____

                                  _____

                                  _____

2. manēs (*to stay*) _____

_____

_____

3. persuādet (*to persuade*) _____

_____

_____

4. mordeō (*to bite*) _____

_____

_____

5. haerent (*to stick*) _____

_____

_____

Written Practice 4-6

Translate the following verb phrases into Latin.

1. they do have _____
2. we see _____
3. you (*sg.*) are teaching _____
4. it is moving _____
5. I am holding _____

Third Conjugation

First and second conjugations show almost no differences besides their theme vowels of **ā** and **ē**. With third conjugation, you enter another world.

In third conjugation, the infinitive (second principal part) contains short **e**, as opposed to the second-conjugation infinitive, where you find long **ē**. For phonetic reasons, long vowels tend to be strong vowels. Short vowels, on the other hand, morph under the influence of prefixes and endings. In the imperfect, you may have noticed that third conjugation's short **e** strengthened to long **ē** before you attached the imperfect tense indicator **-ba-**. In present tense, that short **e** weakens.

The phenomenon of vowel weakening happens frequently. For example, the **a** in the stem of **capiō** shifts to **i** in **accipiō**, and the fourth principal part shifts from **captum** to **acceptum**.

Rather than strengthen to long **ē**, as it does in the imperfect tense, the short **e** of third conjugation weakens in the present tense. (It also weakens in the future tense, as you will see.) A certain unexpected vowel pattern emerges that you should pay close attention to. You'll see it again!

Here is the full conjugation of **agō, agere, ēgī, actum** (*to do*) in present tense. Watch how the stem vowel changes.

agō, agere, ēgī, actum to do

Person	Singular	Plural
First	agō	agi**mus**
Second	agis	agi**tis**
Third	agit	agu**nt**

For the first-person singular, the short **e** is swallowed up by the personal ending **-ō**, it changes to **u** in the third-person plural, and it weakens to **i** in the rest of the present tense forms. This is a very important pattern to remember!

Person	Singular	Plural
First	-ō	-imus
Second	-is	-itis
Third	-it	-unt

Written Practice 4-7

Conjugate the following verbs in present tense.

Person	Singular	Plural

1. **mittō, mittere, mīsī, missum** to send

First _____ _____

Second _____ _____

Third _____ _____

2. **intellegō, intellegere, intellexī, intellectum** to understand

First _____ _____

Second _____ _____

Third _____ _____

	Person	Singular	Plural

3. claudō, claudere, clausī, clausum to close

First _____ _____

Second _____ _____

Third _____ _____

4. tollō, tollere, sustulī, sublātum to raise

First _____ _____

Second _____ _____

Third _____ _____

5. surgō, surgere, surrexī, surrectum to rise

First _____ _____

Second _____ _____

Third _____ _____

Written Practice 4-8

Translate each of the following verb forms in three different ways.

1. lūdō (*to play*) _____

_____

_____

2. flectitis (*to bend*) _____

_____

_____

3. tendunt (*to stretch*) _____

_____

_____

4. sinimus (*to allow*) _____

_____

_____

5. tegit (*to cover*) _____

_____

_____

Written Practice 4-9

Translate the following verb phrases into Latin.

1. he does abandon _____
2. I say _____
3. you (*pl.*) are writing _____
4. they conquer _____
5. we are putting _____

Third Conjugation -*iō*

Third-conjugation -**iō** verbs are considered third conjugation because their infinitives end in -**ere**. You can distinguish them from regular third-conjugation verbs by their first principal part, which ends in -**iō**.

What characterizes -**iō** verbs is the persistence of **i** in all but a couple of forms in the present system, the infinitive being one of them. Except for the insertion of -**i**- between the stem and ending, they are formed just like regular third-conjugation verbs. The basic rule for -**iō** verbs is that any regular third-conjugation ending in a present system tense (i.e., the present, imperfect, or future) that doesn't already begin with -**i**- adds one before the ending.

iaciō, iacere, iēcī, iactum to throw

| Person | Present Tense | | Imperfect Tense | |
	Singular	Plural	Singular	Plural
First	iaciō	iacimus	iaciēbam	iaciēbāmus
Second	iacis	iacitis	iaciēbās	iaciēbātis
Third	iacit	iaciunt	iaciēbat	iaciēbant

Notice that the ending of the first-person singular in present tense is -**iō** instead of -**ō**, and that the ending of the third-person plural is -**iunt** instead of -**unt**. For the imperfect tense, -**i**- is inserted at the end of the stem and before the vowel -**ē**-, so instead of forms like **agēbam**, you have **iac*i*ēbam**, etc. When we get to the future tense, you will see -**iō** verbs do exactly the same thing.

Don't forget that perfect system tenses (i.e., the perfect, pluperfect, and future perfect) are formed in the same way for all verbs. Thus, third-conjugation -**iō** verbs behave just as any other verb does in the perfect tenses.

Written Practice 4-10

Conjugate the following verbs in present tense.

Person	Singular	Plural

1. **faciō, facere, fēcī, factum** to make, do

   First   _____   _____

   Second   _____   _____

   Third   _____   _____

2. **capiō, capere, cēpī, captum** to take, catch

   First   _____   _____

   Second   _____   _____

   Third   _____   _____

3. **fugiō, fugere, fūgī** to run away, flee

   First   _____   _____

   Second   _____   _____

   Third   _____   _____

Written Practice 4-11

Translate each of the following verb forms in three different ways.

1. dēficiunt (*to fall short, fail*)   _____

   _____

   _____

2. prōiciō (*to throw forward*)   _____

   _____

   _____

3. rapis (*to grab*)   _____

   _____

   _____

4. cupit (*to desire*)   _____

   _____

   _____

5. ēlicitis (*to lure*)   _____

                                         _____

                                         _____

Written Practice 4-12

Translate the following verb phrases into Latin.

1. we are running away   _____
2. he does welcome   _____
3. they are making   _____
4. you (*sg.*) catch   _____
5. I take   _____

Fourth Conjugation

If you have mastered third-conjugation **-iō** verbs, very little needs to be said about fourth-conjugation verbs. All fourth-conjugation verbs are **-iō** verbs. You can spot them by their infinitive (second principal part), which ends in **-īre**. Their theme vowel is **ī**, so you can be sure that this letter dominates these verb forms. Most forms are identical to those of third-conjugation **-iō** verbs, with a few exceptions. One difference, of course, is that the infinitive ends in **-īre** rather than **-ere**. Another is that in some of the present tense endings, the **-i-** is long where it is short for third-conjugation **-iō** verbs. (This is not crucial unless you are scanning poetry, where long and short vowels make a difference.)

Here is the model of a fourth-conjugation verb in the two present system tenses you've been introduced to.

feriō, ferīre to strike

Person	Present Tense Singular	Plural	Imperfect Tense Singular	Plural
First	feriō	ferīmus	feriēbam	feriēbāmus
Second	ferīs	ferītis	feriēbās	feriēbātis
Third	ferit	feriunt	feriēbat	feriēbant

A glance at the chart shows that the verb stem for the imperfect tense is identical to that for third-conjugation **-iō** verbs. Just pop an **i** in!

(Spoiler: The difference between third-conjugation **-iō** and fourth-conjugation verbs in present tense lies in the length of the **i** in the second-person singular and first- and second-person plural endings.)

Written Practice 4-13

Conjugate the following verbs in present tense.

Person	Singular	Plural

1. **sentiō, sentīre, sensī, sensum** to feel, perceive

First _____   _____

Second _____   _____

Third _____   _____

2. **veniō, venīre, vēnī, ventum** to come

First _____   _____

Second _____   _____

Third _____   _____

3. **serviō, servīre, servīvī, servītum** to be a slave

First _____   _____

Second _____   _____

Third _____   _____

Written Practice 4-14

Translate each of the following verb forms in three different ways. Some are fourth conjugation, and some are third conjugation **-iō**. Can you tell which is which?

1. sentiō (*to feel, perceive*)   _____

_____

_____

2. perveniunt (*to arrive*)   _____

_____

_____

3. iacitis (*to throw*) _____

_____

_____

4. subiciunt (*to toss under*) _____

_____

_____

5. servīmus (*to be a slave*) _____

_____

_____

Written Practice 4-15

Translate the following verb phrases into Latin. Some are fourth conjugation, and some are third conjugation **-iō**. Watch how little it matters!

1. we are taking _____
2. he welcomes _____
3. they hear _____
4. you (*sg.*) find _____
5. she sleeps _____

The Irregular Verb *sum, esse, fuī, futūrus*

The most important, most common, and most irregular verb in Latin is **sum** (*to be, exist*). As you can see in the chart below, it is highly irregular in English as well.

sum, esse, fuī, futūrus am, to be, was, been

Present Tense

sum	sumus	*I am*	*we are*
es	estis	*you are*	*you are*
est	sunt	*he/she/it is*	*they are*

The Latin verb **sum**, along with a few other irregular verbs, is called ***athematic*** because it lacks a theme vowel. For example, look at the infinitive, **esse**. There is no **-re** to drop to find the stem, and if you drop the **-se**, you have **es-** with no vowel to which you can attach the personal endings. The personal endings, however, are normal—it is the stem that is strange.

The imperfect of **sum** is also irregular. It shows a linguistic phenomenon common in Indo-European languages called ***rhotacism***. With rhotacism, an **s** that appears between two vowels changes to **r**. You can see this sometimes in English as well, e.g., the plural of *was* is *were*.

Here is how rhotacism manifests itself with the verb **sum**. As you know, the imperfect tense of regular verbs is formed by adding the tense indicator **-ba-** to the present stem and adding personal endings, resulting in **-bam, -bās, -bat**, and so on. **Sum** also uses these endings, but without the **b**, resulting in **-am, -ās, -at**, and so on. When these endings are attached to the athematic stem **es-**, the **s** gets trapped between two vowels and rhotacizes, so **esam** becomes **eram**.

Imperfect Tense

eram	erāmus	*I was*	*we were*
erās	erātis	*you were*	*you were*
erat	erant	*he/she/it was*	*they were*

Remember that the perfect tense is formed in the same way for all verbs, regardless of conjugation or other irregularities. Here is the conjugation of **sum** in perfect tense.

Perfect Tense

fuī	fuimus	*I have been*	*we have been*
fuistī	fuistis	*you have been*	*you have been*
fuit	fuērunt	*he/she/it has been*	*they have been*

A usage note: Be aware that when a third-person form of **sum** appears first or very early in a sentence, it is usually just pointing to the existence of something. English uses the phrase *there is/are* to express this idea.

Canis est.	*It's a dog.*
Est canis.	*There is a dog.*
Canēs sunt.	*They are dogs.*
Sunt canēs.	*There are dogs.*

Written Practice 4-16

Translate the following verb forms into English.

1. erat   _____
2. es   _____
3. erant   _____
4. fuistī   _____
5. sum   _____

Written Practice 4-17

Translate the following verb phrases into Latin.

1. you (*pl.*) have been   _____
2. there were   _____
3. to be   _____
4. he used to be   _____
5. they began to be   _____

Key Vocabulary

The vocabulary presented here includes both new verbs and ones from previous chapters, all sorted into their proper conjugations. Because you now know why it's important to be able to recognize conjugations and how to tell them apart, future chapters won't micro-organize the vocabulary as below.

First-Conjugation Verbs

amō (1) to love [amiable]
dō, dare, dedī, datum to give [data]
laudō (1) to praise [laudatory]
rogō (1) to ask, beg [interrogate]
servō (1) to save, keep, guard, protect [preserve]
stō, stāre, stetī, statum to stand, stay [stand]
vocō (1) to call, summon [convoke]

Second-Conjugation Verbs

doceō, docēre, docuī, doctum to teach [doctor] (*This verb usually has two accusative objects, one for the thing being taught, the other for the person it is being taught to.*)

habeō, habēre, habuī, habitum to have, hold; consider, regard

moveō, movēre, mōvī, mōtum to move

teneō, tenēre, tenuī, tentum to hold, have

valeō, valēre, valuī, valitum to be well/strong [valid]

videō, vidēre, vīdī, vīsum to see

Third-Conjugation Verbs

agō, agere, ēgī, actum to do, drive, lead; be busy [act] (*Basically, this verb refers to doing something that exhausts but that doesn't yield a tangible result. The verb* **faciō** *covers that type of action.*)

cadō, cadere, cecidī, cāsum to fall [cadence]

dīcō, dīcere, dixī, dictum to say, tell [diction]

dūcō, dūcere, duxī, ductum to take (someone/something somewhere), lead [conduct] (*In a military context, "to lead" is a good choice; otherwise,* **dūcō** *simply refers to getting someone or something somewhere.*)

legō, legere, lēgī, lectum to choose, pick, gather; read [election, legible] (*This verb refers to the act of looking around for things that seem worthwhile and picking them up, be they flowers in a meadow with your hands or letters off a page with your eyes.*)

mittō, mittere, mīsī, missum to send, throw [missile] (*Unlike* **dūcō**, *which refers to taking someone or something somewhere with assistance, the verb* **mittō** *gets someone or something somewhere under its own power.*)

petō, petere, petīvī, petītum to look for, ask; head for a place; attack [petition] (*The basic idea is to go somewhere for a reason.*)

pōnō, pōnere, posuī, positum to put, lay [position]

relinquō, relinquere, relīquī, relictum to abandon, leave (behind) [relinquish]

scrībō, scrībere, scripsī, scriptum to write, scratch, carve [inscribe]

vincō, vincere, vīcī, victum to conquer [victory]

Third-Conjugation *-iō* Verbs

accipiō, accipere, accēpī, acceptum to welcome, receive; take [accept]

capiō, capere, cēpī, captum to take, catch [capture]

faciō, facere, fēcī, factum to make, do [fact]

fugiō, fugere, fūgī to run away, flee, escape [fugitive]

Fourth-Conjugation Verbs

audiō, audīre, audīvī, audītum to hear, listen [audition]

inveniō, invenīre, invēnī, inventum to come upon, find [invention] (*Be careful with this verb. Students sometimes see the prefix* **in-** *and assume the verb must mean* to enter (come in). *It doesn't. The verb* **intrō** (1) *is used to show that idea.*)

veniō, venīre, vēnī, ventum to come [convention]

Irregular Verb

sum, esse, fuī, futūrus to be, exist

QUIZ

Choose the best translation for each of the following verb phrases.

1. I have
   (a) habeō
   (b) habēbam
   (c) habēbis
   (d) habuī

2. you (*sg.*) are calling
   (a) vocās
   (b) vocāvistī
   (c) vocārēs
   (d) vocāmus

3. we are putting
   (a) putāmus
   (b) pōnimus
   (c) pōnāmus
   (d) pūnīmus

4. they do conquer
   (a) vocant
   (b) vincunt
   (c) vincant
   (d) volunt

5. you (*pl.*) are writing
   (a) scrīberētis
   (b) scrībētis
   (c) scrībātis
   (d) scrībitis

6. he is
   (a) esset
   (b) fuit
   (c) est
   (d) estis

7. they praise
   (a) laudārent
   (b) laudent
   (c) laudant
   (d) laudat

8. he is finding
   (a) invēnit
   (b) invenit
   (c) invenīret
   (d) inveniēbat

9. they are holding
   (a) tenuērunt
   (b) tenērent
   (c) teneant
   (d) tenent

10. she reads
    (a) legēs
    (b) legit
    (c) legat
    (d) lēgit

CHAPTER 5

Building Up Basic Sentences with Modifiers

In this chapter, you will learn about:

Using Noun Cases as Modifiers

In earlier chapters, you read that the heart of a clause or sentence is the verb. The importance of understanding verbs is the reason you find yourself in Chapter 5 without having covered much of anything else! We will now build on that strong foundation.

You have learned how the verb is the main element of a sentence and how everything else in a sentence only serves to modify the verb. Nouns take case endings to show their relationship to the verb. Nominative case shows the subject of the verb. Accusative case shows where the action of the verb stops (i.e., the direct object).

Other cases modify the verb as well. Dative case shows someone or something that is indirectly affected by the verb. Ablative case can show where an action starts, where it takes place, or what accompanies it. All that considered, these cases convert nouns into adverbs, or at least words that act like adverbs. Genitive case, however, makes a noun act more like an adjective, and adjectives, as you know, modify nouns.

First of all, just what is a "modifier"? A modifier is something that limits possibilities.

Imagine that you and I are in the parking lot of a shopping mall on a Saturday afternoon and I suddenly turn to you and excitedly say, "is buying." You'd be puzzled. Who is buying? Anyone could be putting money down. Buying what? Anyone could be purchasing anything. Where? It could be in any of dozens of stores. The possible questions continue … From whom? For whom? Using what? For what purpose? Alone or with someone else? What kind of whatever is it? Whose was it to start with?

Clearly, just saying "is buying" opens a world of endless possibilities. More information (i.e., modifiers) would narrow down these endless possibilities. Watch how adding nouns in various cases can limit the possibilities. We'll use English examples of Latin cases to make sure you understand how cases work.

Nominative case	***Jim*** *is buying.* Buying what? Buy is a transitive verb and requires a direct object.
Genitive case	*Jim is buying **Andrew's**.* Still no direct object. Andrew's what?
Dative case	*Jim is buying Andrew's **for his son**.* Good for his son, but still no direct object. Andrew's what? House? Hamster?
Accusative case	*Jim is buying Andrew's **car** for his son.* Finally a sentence that makes sense! Is there any more information?

Original ablative case	*Jim is buying Andrew's car **from him** for his son.* Ah! That's where he's getting it from.
Old instrumental case	*Jim is buying Andrew's car **with the dent** from him for his son.* But Andrew has a few cars and they all have dents.
Old locative case	*Jim is buying Andrew's car with the dent **on the hood** from him* *for his son.* I remember that lemon!

Other Types of Modifiers

The examples in the chart above show how the various cases work as modifiers. There are other kinds of modifiers. Let's continue building on this example sentence as we add these new types to our repertoire. Some of them modify verbs, some modify nouns, some even modify each other! Here is a list of them with examples; over the course of this and the following chapters, we will examine each one. Relative clauses are provided as an example, but we will discuss them in depth in Chapter 11.

Predicate nominatives	*Jim is my **brother**.*
Appositives	*Jim, **my brother**, is buying Andrew's car.*
Adjectives	*Jim is buying Andrew's **red** car.*
Prepositional phrases	*Jim **down the street** is buying Andrew's car.*
Adverbs	*Jim is **foolishly** buying Andrew's car.*
Relative clauses	*Jim is buying Andrew's car, **which is still being repaired**.*

Using Predicate Nominatives as Modifiers

There are a few ways in which a noun can modify another noun. You have learned that the nominative case is used to show the subject of a sentence. You can also put a noun in the nominative in the predicate of a sentence—hence the grammatical term ***predicate nominative***—to equate something to the subject. (The predicate of a sentence is the part that isn't the subject, i.e., the verb and everything that goes after it in an English sentence.)

The verb most commonly found with this construction is a form of the verb **sum, esse, fuī, futūrus** (*to be*), which basically works like an equal sign.

Ego mīles sum.	*I am a soldier.*
Marcus est amīcus meus.	*Marcus is my friend.*
Puerī sunt molestī.	*The boys are pests.*

Using Appositives as Modifiers

Another way to use one noun to identify with another noun is ***apposition***. In this construction, the nouns can be in any case, and any kind of verb can be used. The following English sentence has three nouns in apposition. In English, we usually set appositives off with commas.

> *Jim, my **brother**, is buying a truck, a **Ford**, for his son **Paul**.*

The words in boldface italic are all appositives. The noun *Jim* is identified as *brother,* just as *truck* is identified as *Ford* and *son* is identified as *Paul.* A noun in apposition takes the same form (i.e., case) as the noun it modifies, which makes sense because both words refer to the same thing. If the sentence were in Latin, *Jim* would be in nominative case, since he is the subject; *my brother* would also be nominative. Since *truck* is the direct object, it would be accusative, and so would *Ford.* (If you are curious, *son* and *Paul* would be in dative case. You'll learn about the dative later in this chapter.)

Genitive Case

The genitive case allows a noun to modify another noun, but not in quite the same way as a noun in apposition does. The most basic function of the genitive case is to link two nouns without saying that they are the same thing. For example, in the phrase *the dog's bone, dog* is a noun, and so is *bone.* The genitive ending *'s* makes it clear that they are two separate things, and *dog's* is making clear which *bone* is being referred to.

As this example suggests, the most common use of the genitive case is to show possession, both in Latin and in English. It is also important to remember that English can express the idea behind genitive case in two ways. One is with *'s* (or *s'* in the plural), the other is with the preposition *of. The daughter of the farmer* means the same as *the farmer's daughter.* Possession isn't the only use of the genitive

case, though. Consider the phrase *hatred of shrimp. Hatred* and *shrimp* are different things and are not being equated. Nor does the shrimp own the hatred. For the
moment, however, concentrate on the use of the genitive to show possession.

As with most modifiers in Latin, words in the genitive usually follow the words
they modify.

The dictionary entry for nouns gives you the nominative, the genitive, the gender, and the meaning. If you learn your vocabulary thoroughly, you'll know that
remembering only the first entry, the nominative, and the first meaning given isn't
enough. The second form in the listing, the genitive, provides two crucial pieces of
information. One is the stem to which you attach all other case endings. The second, and even more important, thing it tells you is the declension the word belongs
to. Here are some refresher examples in which the genitive ending signals the
declension of the noun.

First declension	**sagitta, sagitt***ae f.* arrow
Second declension	**nummus, numm***ī m.* coin
Third declension	**lapis, lapid***is m.* stone

In these examples, the genitive **sagittae** for **saggita** shouldn't be surprising, nor
should **nummī** for **nummus**. The stem change from **lapis** to **lapid-**, however, is
crucial. You couldn't have known this unless you'd learned your vocabulary! Also
crucial is the ending **-is**. It signals that this is a third-declension word, which means
it takes third-declension endings.

The boldface endings in the charts below show what you have already learned,
plus the addition of genitive case.

Case	Singular	Plural
First Declension		
Nominative	**-a**	**-ae**
Genitive	**-ae**	**-ārum**
Dative	-ae	-īs
Accusative	**-am**	**-ās**
Ablative	-ā	-īs
Second Declension		
Nominative	**-us/-er**	**-ī/-rī**
Genitive	**-ī**	**-ōrum**
Dative	-ō	-īs
Accusative	**-um**	**-ōs**
Ablative	-ō	-īs

Case	Singular	Plural
Third Declension		
Nominative	*Wild card!*	-ēs
Genitive	**-is**	**-um**
Dative	-ī	-ibus
Accusative	**-em**	**-ēs**
Ablative	-e	-ibus

Written Practice 5-1

The following nouns are in accusative case. Write them in genitive case, keeping singular for singular and plural for plural. Then, identify the declension of each. You don't need to know what they mean in order to perform this exercise.

	Genitive Form	**Declension**
1. oculōs	_____	_____
2. aquam	_____	_____
3. mulierēs	_____	_____
4. principium	_____	_____
5. iuvenem	_____	_____
6. sermōnēs	_____	_____
7. animās	_____	_____
8. vēlōcitātem	_____	_____
9. hircōs	_____	_____
10. fāmam	_____	_____

Written Practice 5-2

Using the nouns you already know—and the new ones at the end of this chapter—translate the following phrases into English.

1. animus mīlitum _____
2. servī dominī _____
3. fīlius patris _____
4. vōcēs puellārum _____

5. cūrae mātris   _____

6. dominus nēminis   _____

7. equī virōrum   _____

8. hostēs Rōmae   _____

9. liber puerī   _____

10. animus hominis   _____

Written Practice 5-3

Translate the following phrases into Latin.

1. the boys' friend   _____

2. a master's slaves   _____

3. the courage of the soldiers   _____

4. the girl's dog   _____

5. the horses' eyes   _____

Possessive Adjectives

In Chapter 3, you were introduced to personal pronouns. It is important to know that their genitive forms are used to show many genitive case uses, but *not* possession. In order to show possession, there are special possessive adjectives. This is much like the difference in English between the phrase *of me* and the adjective *my*. Here are some examples.

Pars **meī** hīc manēre voluit.   *Part **of me** wanted to stay here.*

Pars **mea** erat inūtilis.   ***My** part was useless.*

The possessive adjectives are the following.

meus, mea, meum *my*
tuus, tua, tuum *your* (sg.)
noster, nostra, nostrum *our*
vester, vestra, vestrum *your* (pl.)

This only applies to first- and second-person singular and plural forms. For third person (i.e., *he, she, it,* and *they*), there are different arrangements, which you will learn in Chapter 11.

The list of possessive adjectives above shows how they appear in the dictionary. They are all first- or second-declension adjectives, which is a topic we'll go into in depth in the next chapter. For the moment, all you need to know is that the first form in the entry is the masculine nominative singular; it uses second-declension endings. The second form is the feminine nominative singular; it uses first-declension endings. The third form is the neuter.

The second form also shows whether or not the adjective has a stem change. Why is this important? In a nutshell, an adjective has to *agree*, which means that it must take the same form as the noun it modifies in gender, case, and number. Thus, the nominative plural of **servus meus** (*my slave*) would be **servī meī** (*my slaves*). Also, these adjectives take only first- or second-declension endings, even if the noun they are modifying is third declension, so *my dogs* would be **canēs meī**.

One other thing to be aware of is that references to possession are sometimes assumed in certain contexts. For instance, if I'm clearly writing about my father, I don't need to say **pater *meus*** every time I refer to him. Just **pater** will suffice.

Written Practice 5-4

Translate the following phrases into English.

1. dominus tuus   _____
2. servum nostrum   _____
3. cūrae meae   _____
4. vōcēs vestrās   _____
5. aqua tua   _____

Written Practice 5-5

Translate the following phrases into genitive case in Latin.

1. your (*sg.*) book   _____
2. our cares   _____
3. my master   _____
4. your (*pl.*) enemy   _____
5. my daughters   _____

Dative Case

Students often have a hard time getting a good conceptual grasp of the dative case. I admit that it is rather odd to think that a simple ending can convey such complex meaning. But as you have already seen, Latin can do a lot of things quite concisely that English can't.

The basic idea of the dative case is to show some sort of interest in the action of a verb—someone or something that might gain or lose because of the verb, gain advantage or disadvantage from it, or be affected in some way by the outcome. While the nominative case shows a verb's subject and the accusative shows the thing being directly acted upon, the dative case stands on the outside and is *indirectly* affected or referenced. Here are English examples of the different ways in which the dative is used in Latin.

*He sent **me** the money.*	He didn't send *me* anywhere. He [nominative subject] sent [verb] the money [accusative direct object] *to me* [dative] … so I profited.
*That toadstool was poisonous **for her**.*	It was the toadstool that was deadly, not *her*. The toadstool [nominative subject] was poisonous by nature [intransitive, state-of-being verb] … and it wasn't *to her advantage* [dative] to have eaten it.
*He made those cookies **for me**.*	He [nominative subject] made [verb] those cookies [accusative direct object] *for me* [dative] to enjoy.
*Is there a lid **to this jar**?*	*This jar* [dative] possessed a lid at some point!
*This job has to be done **by you**.*	*You* [dative] must do this job. It's in your interest to do it. (Otherwise, it's the breadline for you, buddy!)

Think about how all of those sentences make sense and consider them and the questions they prompt.

He sent the money. (To whom?)

That toadstool was poisonous. (For whom?)

He made those cookies. (To make whom happy?)

Is there a lid? (That fits what?)

This job has to be done. (Who will pay the consequences if it isn't?)

From a grammatical standpoint, the dative case adds information regarding whose interest, advantage, or disadvantage the sentence is about. This is interesting information, even if it only has gossip value, but note that the sentences above work grammatically *without* the dative.

Here are the dative case endings. Once you learn these, there's only the ablative case left to go, and its forms are amazingly easy!

Case	Singular	Plural
First Declension		
Nominative	-a	-ae
Genitive	-ae	-ārum
Dative	-ae	-īs
Accusative	-am	-ās
Ablative	-ā	-īs
Second Declension		
Nominative	-us/-er	-ī/-rī
Genitive	-ī	-ōrum
Dative	-ō	-īs
Accusative	-um	-ōs
Ablative	-ō	-īs
Third Declension		
Nominative	*Wild card!*	-ēs
Genitive	-is	-um
Dative	-ī	-ibus
Accusative	-em	-ēs
Ablative	-e	-ibus

DATIVE OF POSSESSION

Besides showing possession by using the genitive and possessive adjectives, you can use a noun in the dative to show a different kind of possession. The only real difference is a shift in emphasis. The first two ways put stress on the owner, while the third way, the dative, highlights the object owned.

Liber **Marcī** est.	*It's **Marcus'** book.*
Liber **meus** est.	*It's **my** book.*
Liber **mihi** est.	***The book** is mine (for me).*

DATIVE INDIRECT OBJECT

The term ***indirect object*** refers to a person or thing that is somehow affected indirectly by the action of the verb. Because you usually give something *to someone,* say something *to someone,* and so on, it is usually found with verbs of giving, telling, showing, entrusting, and the like.

In English, we have two ways of showing indirect objects. One way is to put it after the verb but before the direct object.

> *Gaius gave **the boy** a cookie.*

As you recall, English is an analytical language, so word order is important. Therefore, if we change the word order and say, *Gaius gave a cookie the boy,* it doesn't make much sense. If we change the word order in this manner, we have to add the preposition *to* or *for.*

> *Gaius gave a cookie **to the boy**.*

From a grammatical standpoint, you could put the indirect object first, but the result would be rather awkward: *Gaius gave **to the boy** a cookie.*

To show an indirect object, Latin uses the dative case, *never* a prepositional phrase. Here is the English example above translated into Latin.

> Gāius **puerō** crustulum dedit.
>
> **Puerō** dedit crustulum Gāius.

The first example has the word order you will see most often in Latin, with the dative coming before the accusative. Because Latin is an inflected language, the second example means the same thing. **Puerō** is clearly in the dative, **dedit** is the verb, **crustulum** is obviously accusative, and **Gāius** is nominative. The sentence couldn't mean anything else. If there is a difference, it is only in emphasis. The first example answers the question **Quid fēcit Gāius?** (*What did Gaius do?*) or **Quis puerō crustulum dedit?** (*Who gave the boy a cookie?*). The second example answers the question **Cui dedit crustulum Gāius?** (*To whom did Gaius give a cookie?*).

Written Practice 5-6

The following words are in random cases and declensions. Write each in dative case, keeping singular for singular and plural for plural. You should be able to recognize the declension each belongs to, even if you've never seen the word before and don't know what it means.

1. fundum   _____

2. gladius   _____

3. grātiārum   _____

4. rūpem   _____

5. equitum (*gen. pl.*)   _____

6. ūvās   _____

7. nectaris   _____

8. vallum   _____

9. falcēs   _____

10. lacrima   _____

Written Practice 5-7

Translate the following sentences into English.

1. Servī mīlitibus aquam dant.

2. Māter puerīs equōs monstrābat.

3. Liber mihi fuit.

4. Amīcus nōbīs erat Publius.

5. Pater amīcō Septimiō fīliam mandāvit.

Key Vocabulary

You should learn these important words, in addition to the possessive adjectives presented earlier in this chapter.

Nouns

animus, animī *m.* soul, mind; courage, spirit [animate]
aqua, aquae *f.* water [aqueous]
canis, canis *c.* dog [canine]
cūra, cūrae *f.* care, concern [cure]
fīlia, fīliae *f.* daughter [filial]
fīlius, fīliī *m.* son [filial]
nēmo, nēminis *c.* no one, nobody (*This word is a contraction of* **nē** (not) *and* **homō** (person).)
oculus, oculī *m.* eye [binoculars]
puella, puellae *f.* girl
servus, servī *m.* slave [servile]

Verbs

dōnō (1) to give [donate] (*This verb means to give as a gift, as opposed to* **dō**, *which means to give in general.*)
mandō (1) to entrust [mandate]
monstrō (1) to show [demonstrate]
narrō (1) to tell (*in story form*) [narrate]

QUIZ

Identify the case of each of the following nouns.

1. hominī
   (a) nominative
   (b) genitive
   (c) dative
   (d) agglutinative

2. librōs
   (a) nominative
   (b) genitive
   (c) dative
   (d) accusative

3. vox
   (a) nominative
   (b) genitive
   (c) dative
   (d) accusative

4. puerum
   (a) nominative
   (b) genitive
   (c) dative
   (d) accusative

5. equōrum
   (a) nominative
   (b) genitive
   (c) dative
   (d) accusative

6. nēminem
   (a) nominative
   (b) genitive
   (c) dative
   (d) accusative

7. fīliās
   (a) nominative
   (b) genitive
   (c) dative
   (d) accusative

8. amīcō
   (a) nominative
   (b) genitive
   (c) dative
   (d) accusative

9. puella
   (a) nominative
   (b) genitive
   (c) dative
   (d) accusative

10. mīlitibus
    (a) nominative
    (b) genitive
    (c) dative
    (d) accusative

PART ONE TEST

Choose the most appropriate answer to complete each statement.

1. Latin nouns are divided into groups called _____.
    (a) declensions
    (b) conjugations
    (c) accommodations
    (d) inflections

2. Latin verbs are divided into groups called _____.
    (a) declensions
    (b) conjugations
    (c) subjugations
    (d) inflections

3. The term for the type of word that shows a person, place, or thing is _____.
    (a) noun
    (b) interjection
    (c) jackal
    (d) conjunction

4. The abbreviation meaning *for the sake of example* is _____.
    (a) et al.
    (b) N.B.
    (c) i.e.
    (d) e.g.

5. The abbreviation meaning *note well* is _____.
    (a) et al.
    (b) N.B.
    (c) i.e.
    (d) e.g.

6. The term _____ refers to a change in word order to show grammatical function.

   (a) declension

   (b) conjugation

   (c) analysis

   (d) inflection

7. Subjunctive is an example of grammatical _____.

   (a) mood

   (b) tense

   (c) voice

   (d) case

8. Indicative is an example of grammatical _____.

   (a) mood

   (b) tense

   (c) voice

   (d) case

9. Dative is an example of grammatical _____.

   (a) mood

   (b) attitude

   (c) voice

   (d) case

10. Bottleneck is an example of grammatical _____.

   (a) mood

   (b) huh?

   (c) voice

   (d) case

Choose the best Latin translation for each English verb phrase.

11. they are hearing

    (a) audiēbant

    (b) audīvērunt

    (c) audiunt

    (d) audīverint

12. you (*sg.*) kept falling

    (a) cadēbās

    (b) cecidistī

    (c) cadō

    (d) cadēbātis

13. we are saying

    (a) dīximus

    (b) dīxērunt

    (c) dīcimus

    (d) dīcerēmus

14. we were giving

    (a) dōnābāmus

    (b) dedērunt

    (c) dedimus

    (d) damus

15. they have said

    (a) dīxērunt

    (b) duxērunt

    (c) dūcunt

    (d) dīcēbant

16. he is making

    (a) facit

    (b) fēcit

    (c) faciēbat

    (d) fēcistī

17. they used to have
    - (a) habēbant
    - (b) habuērunt
    - (c) habērent
    - (d) habuerant

18. you (*pl.*) looked for
    - (a) petis
    - (b) petēbās
    - (c) petīvistī
    - (d) petīvistis

19. I was coming
    - (a) veniō
    - (b) venture
    - (c) veniēbam
    - (d) vēnistī

20. I see
    - (a) videō
    - (b) vīdī
    - (c) vidērem
    - (d) vīderim

Complete each of the following statements with the most appropriate answer.

21. **Sum** _____.
    - (a) is a transitive verb
    - (b) is an intransitive verb

22. **Legō** _____.
    - (a) is a transitive verb
    - (b) is an intransitive verb

23. **Scrībō** _____.

 (a) is a transitive verb

 (b) is an intransitive verb

24. **Moveō** _____.

 (a) is a transitive verb

 (b) is an intransitive verb

25. **Vocō** _____.

 (a) is a transitive verb

 (b) is an intransitive verb

26. **Stō** _____.

 (a) is a transitive verb

 (b) is an intransitive verb

27. **Mandō** _____.

 (a) is a transitive verb

 (b) is an intransitive verb

28. **Amō** _____.

 (a) is a transitive verb

 (b) is an intransitive verb

29. **Valeō** _____.

 (a) is a transitive verb

 (b) is an intransitive verb

30. **Servō** _____.

 (a) is a transitive verb

 (b) is an intransitive verb

Choose the best Latin translation for each English verb phrase.

31. I did have

 (a) habeō

 (b) habēbam

 (c) habēbis

 (d) habuī

32. you (*sg.*) are teaching
    - (a) docēbās
    - (b) docuistī
    - (c) docēs
    - (d) docērēs

33. we were putting
    - (a) putāmus
    - (b) pōnēbāmus
    - (c) pōnimus
    - (d) pūnīmus

34. they will conquer
    - (a) vocābant
    - (b) vincunt
    - (c) vincant
    - (d) dunno!

35. you (*pl.*) are writing
    - (a) scrīberētis
    - (b) scrībētis
    - (c) scrībātis
    - (d) scrībitis

36. he used to be
    - (a) esset
    - (b) fuit
    - (c) est
    - (d) erat

37. they praised
    - (a) laudārent
    - (b) laudent
    - (c) laudant
    - (d) laudāvērunt

38. he is finding
    (a) invēnit
    (b) invenit
    (c) invenīret
    (d) inveniēbat

39. they are saving
    (a) servāvērunt
    (b) servāvissent
    (c) servant
    (d) servent

40. she reads
    (a) lēgerit
    (b) legit
    (c) legat
    (d) lēgit

Identify the case of each of the following nouns.

41. hominibus
    (a) nominative
    (b) genitive
    (c) dative
    (d) accusative

42. librum
    (a) nominative
    (b) genitive
    (c) dative
    (d) accusative

43. vōcum
   (a) nominative
   (b) genitive
   (c) dative
   (d) accusative

44. puerōs
   (a) nominative
   (b) genitive
   (c) dative
   (d) accusative

45. equīs
   (a) nominative
   (b) genitive
   (c) dative
   (d) accusative

46. nēminis
   (a) nominative
   (b) genitive
   (c) dative
   (d) accusative

47. fīliam
   (a) nominative
   (b) genitive
   (c) dative
   (d) accusative

48. amīcō
   (a) nominative
   (b) genitive
   (c) dative
   (d) accusative

49. puellārum
    (a) nominative
    (b) genitive
    (c) dative
    (d) accusative

50. mīlitis
    (a) nominative
    (b) genitive
    (c) dative
    (d) accusative

PART TWO

BUILDING ON FOUNDATIONS

CHAPTER 6

Adjectives

In this chapter, you will learn about:

Using Adjectives as Modifiers
First/Second-Declension Adjectives
Third-Declension Adjectives
Key Vocabulary

Using Adjectives as Modifiers

Adjectives are words that describe qualities of nouns, such as *tiny, thirteenth,* and *balding.* Like all modifiers, they narrow possibilities and make references clearer. They can also be piled up in an endless chain to pare possibilities almost infinitely. Watch how the following sentence increases in clarity and vividness with every adjective added.

> *Zack has **a** balloon.*
> *Zack has **a red** balloon.*
> *Zack has **a big red** balloon.*
> *Zack has **a deflated big red** balloon.*
> ***Poor** Zack has **a deflated big red** balloon.*
> ***Poor little** Zack has **a deflated big red** balloon.*

If we unleash all the other kinds of modifiers on this sentence, the clarity would be even greater.

> ***My best friend Betty's poor little son** Zack has **tightly in his hand a deflated big red** balloon, **which he was given by a very scary clown at the annual springtime carnival over at his elementary school the other day**.*

The original sentence, Subject-Verb-Object, is in lightface type. Everything else, shown in boldface, describes Zack, how he is holding the balloon, and the balloon itself.

ARTICLE ADJECTIVES

Go back up to the original sentence, *Zack has **a** balloon.* Notice how the word *a* is in boldface? The English words *a* (or *an* in front of a word beginning with a vowel, as in *an otter*) and *the* are special types of adjectives called ***article adjectives***. They play an important role in English. Consider the difference in meaning among these versions of our first example.

> *Zack has balloon.*
> *Zack has **a** balloon.*
> *Zack has **the** balloon.*

The first sentence doesn't work grammatically. It's Tarzan talk. (We could say, however, that he has *a* cold, but not that he has cold or that he has *the* cold.) The second sentence works grammatically, but all you really know is that he has some sort of balloon. (It would sound odd, however, if we said he has *a* pneumonia.) The third sentence, with the word *the,* makes an assumption that you know that it's not some random balloon, but one in particular that you are already acquainted with.

You have no doubt noticed that Latin has no article adjectives. Except in extreme circumstances, Latin leaves all understanding of these distinctions to context.

AGREEMENT

Latin adjectives must *agree* with the nouns they modify. Grammatical agreement means that they have the same gender, case, and number as the nouns they modify. For example, if **servum** (*slave*) is masculine accusative singular, to say *good slave,* the adjective **bonus** (*good*) also needs to be masculine accusative singular, resulting in **servum bonum**. *Pretty girl* in the nominative singular would be **puella pulchra**.

A long time ago, English was also an inflected language. It has retained only a few features from its adjective-noun agreement days. For gender, the adjective *blonde* is feminine, but *blond* (without the *e*) is masculine. For number, the plural of *this* is *these,* and the plural of *that* is *those.*

The examples of adjective-noun agreement above, **servum bonum** and **puella pulchra**, may be a bit misleading. These pairs happen to rhyme, but that's a coincidence. The rule is that adjectives must agree with their nouns in gender, case, and number. No one ever said anything about rhyming! For instance, the noun **vir** (*man*) is second-declension, masculine nominative singular, but *good man* is **vir bonus**. **Bonus** is the masculine nominative singular form of this adjective.

Don't forget that in second declension there are nouns that end in **-us** and some that end in **-r**. **Vir** happens to be an **-r** noun, and **bonus** happens to be an **-us** adjective, but both forms are masculine nominative singular. In grammatical agreement, only gender, case, and number matter. Like virtually all modifiers in Latin, the adjective tends to follow the word it modifies. An exception is adjectives that refer to size or quantity; they tend to precede the words they modify, so you'd see **multī hominēs** much more often than **hominēs multī**.

First/Second-Declension Adjectives

For the most part, adjectives in Latin fall into two declensional groups. There are *first/second-declension adjectives* and *third-declension adjectives*. Let's investigate these two groups one at a time.

First/second-declension adjectives are exactly what they sound like: They are adjectives that take their endings from first and second declension. The chart below is arranged in the traditional fashion, with the columns of second-declension masculine and neuter forms flanking the first-declension feminine forms. Ablative forms and neuter forms are italicized in the chart; these will be studied later. If you have already memorized the case endings that have been presented so far, there are no new forms for you to learn.

bonus, bona, bonum good

Singular	Masculine	Feminine	Neuter
Nominative	bonus	bona	*bonum*
Genitive	bonī	bonae	*bonī*
Dative	bonō	bonae	*bonō*
Accusative	bonum	bonam	*bonum*
Ablative	*bonō*	*bonā*	*bonō*

Plural	Masculine	Feminine	Neuter
Nominative	bonī	bonae	*bona*
Genitive	bonōrum	bonārum	*bonōrum*
Dative	bonīs	bonīs	*bonīs*
Accusative	bonōs	bonās	*bona*
Ablative	*bonīs*	*bonīs*	*bonīs*

As you can see, if you know your first- and second-declension noun endings, you already know the first/second-declension adjective endings as well.

Dictionaries provide the information you need to identify first/second-declension adjectives. The sample dictionary entry below is the first line of the declension chart above, which lists the masculine, feminine, and neuter forms, followed by the meaning.

bonus, bona, bonum good

However, since most first/second-declension adjectives work this way, you usually find them listed in shorthand as follows.

bonus, -a, -um good

Just as some second-declension nouns end in **-r** instead of **-us** in the nominative singular, there are some adjectives that do so as well. Some of the **-r** words have stem changes, while others don't. As with a dictionary entry for a noun, you can tell by the second form in the listing if there's a stem change.

No stem change   līber, lībera, līberum *free*
Stem change   pulcher, pulchra, pulchrum *beautiful, handsome*

Written Practice 6-1

Decline the following adjective in all its forms. So far you have only been tasked with the nominative, genitive, dative, and accusative cases, and masculine and feminine gender forms. Focus on those, but try all of them if you'd like!

ruber, rubra, rubrum red

Singular	Masculine	Feminine	Neuter
Nominative	_____	_____	_____
Genitive	_____	_____	_____
Dative	_____	_____	_____
Accusative	_____	_____	_____
Ablative	_____	_____	_____

Plural	Masculine	Feminine	Neuter
Nominative	_____	_____	_____
Genitive	_____	_____	_____
Dative	_____	_____	_____
Accusative	_____	_____	_____
Ablative	_____	_____	_____

Written Practice 6-2

Change the following Latin phrases from singular to plural or plural to singular, then translate the new phrases into English. Use the Key Vocabulary at the end of this chapter for adjectives you don't know.

	Changed Version	English Translation
servus malus	*servī malī*	*bad slaves*
1. hominēs Rōmānī	_____	_____
2. puellārum laetārum	_____	_____
3. canēs amīcōs	_____	_____

4. canēs amīcī   _____   _____

5. fīliōrum meōrum   _____   _____

Written Practice 6-3

Translate the following English phrases into Latin, using nominative case. Be sure that the noun and adjective agree.

1. good dogs   _____

2. handsome horse   _____

3. good water   _____

4. a small forest   _____

5. your (*pl.*) mother   _____

6. your (*sg.*) voice   _____

7. the happy girls   _____

8. the evil eye   _____

9. friendly soldiers   _____

10. our books   _____

Written Practice 6-4

Translate the following Latin sentences into English.

1. Erant multae silvae parvae.

   _____

2. Puerī laetī vōcēs magnās habēbant.

   _____

3. Nēmō virōs Rōmānōs capit.

   _____

4. Pater tuus mē accēpit.

   _____

5. Animus mīlitum nostrōrum erat magnus.

   _____

Written Practice 6-5

Translate the following English sentences into Latin.

1. Good mothers are caring for the small children.

   _____

2. The book was good.

   _____

3. I like your (*sg.*) friends.

   _____

4. Our soldiers have conquered many enemies.

   _____

5. We used to have many horses.

   _____

Third-Declension Adjectives

Most adjectives are first/second declension, but there are many that are third declension. As the name suggests, they take third-declension endings. A few endings are a little different from normal third-declension noun endings.

Third-declension adjectives are divided into three groups, called *terminations*. Termination refers to how many different nominative singular endings an adjective has across the genders. This is important, because, as you recall, the masculine and feminine forms of third-declension nouns are identical. This isn't the case for some third-declension adjectives.

THIRD-DECLENSION ADJECTIVES OF THREE TERMINATIONS

The adjective forms that vary from normal third-declension noun endings are underlined in the following chart, which gives all forms of a third-declension adjective of three terminations. As with the earlier first/second-declension adjective chart, you don't need to worry about the ablative forms or neuter forms at the moment, even though you will soon! Nevertheless, it would be worth your while to go ahead and learn the full chart anyway.

ācer, ācris, ācre sharp, keen, fierce

Singular	Masculine	Feminine	Neuter
Nominative	ācer	ācris	*ācre*
Genitive	ācris	ācris	*ācris*
Dative	ācrī	ācrī	*ācrī*
Accusative	ācrem	ācrem	*ācre*
Ablative	*ācrī*	*ācrī*	*ācrī*

Plural	Masculine	Feminine	Neuter
Nominative	ācrēs	ācrēs	*ācria*
Genitive	ācr**ium**	ācr**ium**	*ācr**ium***
Dative	ācribus	ācribus	*ācribus*
Accusative	ācrēs	ācrēs	*ācria*
Ablative	*ācribus*	*ācribus*	*ācribus*

The main differences between regular third-declension adjective forms and noun forms are the ablative singular in **-ī** rather than **-e**, and the addition of **-i-** in the genitive plural, so **-um** becomes **-ium**. The other departures are in the neuter gender forms, which we haven't gotten to yet. There, the nominative and accusative plurals also add **-i-**, making the usual **-a** into **-ia**.

Look at the nominative singular line in the chart above. The masculine is **ācer**, but the feminine is **ācris**, and the neuter is **ācre**. Since the adjective **ācer** has three different forms, one for each gender, it is formally called a ***third-declension adjective of three terminations***. The dictionary entry shows the following.

ācer, ācris, ācre sharp, keen, fierce

With this information, you can immediately tell that it is a third-declension adjective of three terminations. From the second word, the feminine nominative singular, you can also tell whether or not there is a stem change for the rest of the forms. For this adjective, there is a stem change, but there are also adjectives, like **celer, celeris, celere** (*quick, fast*) for which there aren't.

THIRD-DECLENSION ADJECTIVES OF TWO TERMINATIONS

The majority of third-declension adjectives are of two terminations. They are more like third-declension nouns, because they have the same form for both the masculine and the feminine in the nominative singular. Only the neuter nominative singular is different. Here's a sample dictionary listing.

omnis, -e all, every, whole

The first form, **omnis**, is the masculine and feminine nominative singular. The second form, **omne**, is the neuter nominative singular. Apart from the nominative singular, the forms of these adjectives are the same as those of third-declension adjectives of three terminations. As an added bonus, third-declension adjectives of two terminations never have a stem change.

Here is a full declension of an adjective of two terminations. Note how the only difference between it and that of third-declension adjectives of three terminations is in the nominative singular.

brevis, breve short

Singular	Masculine	Feminine	Neuter
Nominative	brev**is**	brev**is**	*breve*
Genitive	brev**is**	brev**is**	*brevis*
Dative	brev**ī**	brev**ī**	*brevī*
Accusative	brev**em**	brev**em**	*breve*
Ablative	*brevī*	*brevī*	*brevī*

Plural	Masculine	Feminine	Neuter
Nominative	brev**ēs**	brev**ēs**	*brevia*
Genitive	brev**ium**	brev**ium**	*brevium*
Dative	brev**ibus**	brev**ibus**	*brevibus*
Accusative	brev**ēs**	brev**ēs**	*brevia*
Ablative	*brevibus*	*brevibus*	*brevibus*

THIRD-DECLENSION ADJECTIVES OF ONE TERMINATION

You were correct if you guessed that the only difference between third-declension adjectives of one termination and those of two and three terminations is that the former share the same nominative singular form for all three genders. Apart from that, they decline the exact same way.

One way they do differ from their brethren is in the style of their dictionary listing.

ingens, ingentis huge

The first form is the nominative singular for the masculine, feminine, and neuter genders. The second form, however, is the *genitive* singular. It is there to let you know what the stem change is, if there is one; with third-declension adjectives of one termination, there almost always is a stem change.

ingens, ingentis huge

Singular	Masculine	Feminine	Neuter
Nominative	ingens	ingens	*ingens*
Genitive	ingent**is**	ingent**is**	*ingentis*
Dative	ingent**ī**	ingent**ī**	*ingentī*
Accusative	ingent**em**	ingent**em**	*ingens*
Ablative	*ingentī*	*ingentī*	*ingentī*

Plural	Masculine	Feminine	Neuter
Nominative	ingent**ēs**	ingent**ēs**	*ingentia*
Genitive	ingent**ium**	ingent**ium**	*ingentium*
Dative	ingent**ibus**	ingent**ibus**	*ingentibus*
Accusative	ingent**ēs**	ingent**ēs**	*ingentia*
Ablative	*ingentibus*	*ingentibus*	*ingentibus*

Written Practice 6-6

Decline the following adjective in all its forms. Focus on just the forms that you have been tasked with: the nominative, genitive, dative, and accusative cases for the masculine and feminine genders (not the ablative case forms and not the neuter gender forms).

omnis, omne all, every, whole

Singular	Masculine	Feminine	Neuter
Nominative	_____	_____	_____
Genitive	_____	_____	_____
Dative	_____	_____	_____
Accusative	_____	_____	_____
Ablative	_____	_____	_____

Plural	Masculine	Feminine	Neuter
Nominative	_____	_____	_____
Genitive	_____	_____	_____
Dative	_____	_____	_____
Accusative	_____	_____	_____
Ablative	_____	_____	_____

Written Practice 6-7

Change the following Latin phrases from singular to plural or plural to singular, then translate the new phrases into English. Use the Key Vocabulary at the end of this chapter for adjectives you don't know.

	Changed Version	**English Translation**
servus fortis	_servī fortēs_	_strong slaves_
1. cūrās difficilēs		
2. omnis mīles		
3. canum ingentium		
4. hostēs ācrēs (*nom.*)		
5. virōrum nōbilium		

Written Practice 6-8

Translate the following English phrases into Latin, using nominative case. Be sure that the noun and adjective agree.

1. short books   _____
2. swift horses   _____
3. sweet water   _____
4. every forest   _____
5. a serious concern   _____

Written Practice 6-9

Translate the following Latin sentences into English.

1. Nēminem timet homō fortis. (**timeō, -ēre, -uī** *to fear, be afraid of*)

   _____

2. Soror mea animum gravem habēbat.

   _____

3. Canēs ācrēs vīdimus.

   _____

4. Omnēs nōs accipiunt.

_____

5. Equus tuus celer est.

_____

Key Vocabulary

There are many vocabulary words in this chapter. Don't forget to use the derivatives or related words to help you remember them, but don't confuse the derivatives with the actual meanings. At times, some Latin words won't appear in notes or the vocabulary, because they should be very obvious. For example, can you guess what the adjective **Rōmānus, -a, -um** means?

First/Second-Declension Adjectives

amīcus, amīca, amīcum friendly [amicable] (*When this adjective is used as a noun, it refers to a friendly person, in other words,* **amīcus** *or* **amīca** friend.)

bonus, bona, bonum good [bonus]

laetus, laeta, laetum happy; fat

magnus, magna, magnum big, large; loud [magnificent]

malus, mala, malum bad, evil [malice]

multus, multa, multum much; (*plural*) **multī, multae, multa** many [multiply]

noster, nostra, nostrum our

parvus, parva, parvum little, small

pulcher, pulchra, pulchrum beautiful, handsome [pulchritude]

vester, vestra, vestrum your (*pl.*)

Third-Declension Adjectives

ācer, ācris, ācre sharp, keen, fierce [acrid]

brevis, breve short [brevity]

celer, celeris, celere quick, fast [accelerator]

difficilis, difficile difficult [difficulty]

dulcis, dulce sweet, pleasant [dulcet]

facilis, facile easy [facile]

fortis, forte strong; brave [fortitude]

gravis, grave heavy; serious [gravity]

ingens, ingentis huge

nōbilis, nōbile well-known, famous; of high birth [noble]

omnis, omne all, every, whole [omniscient]

    omnēs, omnium everyone

    omnia, omnium everything (**Omnia** *is the neuter plural of* **omnis**. *You haven't been introduced to neuters yet. For the moment, just remember that even though it looks feminine singular, it's really neuter plural; by the rules of subject-verb agreement, it takes a plural verb.*)

potens, potentis powerful, capable [potent]

Nouns

frāter, frātris *m.* brother [fraternity]

servus, servī *m.* slave [service] (*A* **servus** *is a slave,* **not** *a servant! Slaves are possessions, not employees. They don't get Wednesdays off, they can't quit, and they have to do windows whether they like it or not.*)

silva, silvae *f.* forest [*Transylvania (literally, "across the forest"—that forest being the Black Forest of Germany)*]

soror, sorōris *f.* sister [sorority]

QUIZ

Choose the correct plural form for each of the following noun-adjective pairs, retaining the case of the pair.

1. puella laeta
   (a) puellae laetārum
   (b) puellae laetae
   (c) puellīs laetīs
   (d) puellam laetam

2. mīlitī omnī
   (a) mīlitēs omnēs
   (b) mīlitum omnium
   (c) mīlitibus omnibus
   (d) mīlite omnī

3. canī parvō
   (a) canēs parvī
   (b) canum parvōrum
   (c) canibus parvīs
   (d) canēs parvōs

4. aquam dulcem
   (a) aquae dulcēs
   (b) aquārum dulcium
   (c) aquae dulcī
   (d) aquās dulcēs

5. oculum pulchrum
   (a) oculī pulchrī
   (b) oculōrum pulchrōrum
   (c) oculīs pulchrīs
   (d) oculōs pulchrōs

6. homō malus

   (a) hominēs malī

   (b) hominum malōrum

   (c) hominibus malīs

   (d) hominēs malōs

7. dominī gravis

   (a) dominī gravēs

   (b) dominōrum gravium

   (c) dominīs gravibus

   (d) dominōs gravēs

8. silvae ingentī

   (a) silvae ingentēs

   (b) silvārum ingentium

   (c) silvīs ingentibus

   (d) silvās ingentēs

9. magnae mātris

   (a) magnae mātrēs

   (b) magnārum mātrum

   (c) magnīs mātribus

   (d) magnās mātrēs

10. virum bonum

   (a) virī bonī

   (b) virōrum bonōrum

   (c) virīs bonīs

   (d) virōs bonōs

CHAPTER 7

Adverbs and the Ablative Case

In this chapter, you will learn about:

Using Adverbs as Modifiers

Adverbs are words that modify verbs, like *quickly, well, fast,* and *soon.* In Latin, they do not agree with the verbs they modify. In English, we can change adjectives into adverbs by adding *-ly,* as in *quickly* above. Not all adverbs, however, are made from adjectives by adding *-ly.* For example, the adverb of *good* is *well,* not *goodly.* Latin has its share of irregular adverbs, too. You should also note that not all Latin or English adverbs come from adjectives. The English adverbs *fast* and *soon* are examples.

Latin's equivalent of English's *-ly* is a little more complicated, but not by much. Basically, a first/second-declension adjective adds **-ē** to its stem to form an adverb. If the adjective has a stem change, you use the modified stem.

clārus, -a, -um	*clear*	clārē	*clearly*
līber, lībera, līberum	*free*	līberē	*freely*
pulcher, pulchra, pulchrum	*beautiful*	pulchrē	*beautifully*

A third-declension adjective adds **-iter** to its stem.

celer, celeris, celere	*quick*	celer**iter**	*quickly*
ācer, ācris, ācre	*fierce*	ācr**iter**	*fiercely*
brevis, -e	*short*	brev**iter**	*shortly*
potens, potentis	*powerful*	potent**er**	*powerfully*

As you can see, the rule for using the modified stem, if there is one, applies here as well. One exception: An adjective whose modified stem ends in **-nt-** only adds **-er**.

Since Latin adverbs don't decline, you never have to worry about making them agree with anything!

Here is a list of some of the more common irregularly formed adverbs with their adjective counterparts.

bonus, -a, -um	*good*	bene	*well*
malus, -a, -um	*bad*	male	*badly*
magnus, -a, -um	*great*	magnopere	*greatly*
multus, -a, -um	*much*	multum	*much, a lot*
parvus, -a, -um	*little*	parum	*little, not much*
difficilis, -e	*difficult*	difficile	*with difficulty*
facilis, -e	*easy*	facile	*easily*

Written Practice 7-1

Change the following adjectives to adverbs, then translate the new forms. You may find that some of the words have no adverbial counterpart in English. In these situations, you should process what the idea behind the Latin word is, then consider how we would express that idea in English as an adverb or adverbial phrase. Remember: A foreign language is not a code for English or a simple matter of word substitution; sometimes, there are no single words to substitute!

1. cōpiōsus, -a, -um   *abundant*   _____   _____
2. maestus, -a, -um   *sad*   _____   _____
3. tristis, -e   *sad*   _____   _____
4. fortis, -e   *brave*   _____   _____
5. saevus, -a, -um   *savage*   _____   _____
6. ingens, ingentis   *huge*   _____   _____
7. alacer, alacris, alacre *lively*   _____   _____
8. amīcus, -a, -um   *friendly*   _____   _____
9. negōtiōsus, -a, -um   *busy*   _____   _____
10. dīligens, dīligentis   *careful*   _____   _____

Neuter Gender

The neuter gender and the ablative case are the only elements left to fill out your noun and adjective charts. In this chapter, we will add them to your repertoire one at a time.

Neuter is a Latin word meaning *neither*. The neuter gender gets its name from the fact that its forms parallel neither masculine nor feminine forms precisely. Nevertheless, they don't represent a whole new set of endings for you to learn, since they are actually just variations on the masculine forms you already know. There are no neuter words in first declension, but there are many in second and third declensions. (There are also a few neuter words in fourth declension. Fourth and fifth declensions will be presented together in a later chapter.)

The best way to sum up these variations is with the **_double neuter rule_**.

1. Nominative and accusative endings are always the same.

2. The nominative plural ends in **-a**. (The accusative plural also does. See rule No. 1.)

Here are a couple of charts to help you compare masculine and neuter forms for second- and third-declension neuter nouns.

	Masculine	**Neuter**
Second Declension		
	liber, librī *m.* book	**templum, templī** *n.* temple
	Singular	**Singular**
Nominative	liber	templum ◄
Genitive	librī	templī
Dative	librō	templō
Accusative	librum	templum ◄
Ablative	librō	templō
	Plural	**Plural**
Nominative	librī	templa ◄
Genitive	librōrum	templōrum
Dative	librīs	templīs
Accusative	librōs	templa ◄
Ablative	librīs	templīs
Third Declension		
	pēs, pedis *m.* foot	**iter, itineris** *n.* route, way; journey
	Singular	**Singular**
Nominative	pēs	**iter** ◄
Genitive	pedis	itineris
Dative	pedī	itinerī
Accusative	pedem	**iter** ◄
Ablative	pede	itinere
	Plural	**Plural**
Nominative	pedēs	itinera ◄
Genitive	pedum	itinerum
Dative	pedibus	itineribus
Accusative	pedēs	itinera ◄
Ablative	pedibus	itineribus

The rules are simple enough, but there are a couple of tricky things that you have to keep in mind. First is that the ending **-a** doesn't look very plural. In fact, it looks like first declension, nominative singular. It might be helpful to remember that there are a few Latin neuter words that have come into English and retained their original Latin neuter plural. Some examples are *bacterium/bacteria, referendum/ referenda, memorandum/memoranda,* and *datum/data.* One germ is a *bacterium.* Two or more are *bacteria.* Notice the subject-verb agreement in those last two sentences.

The other potentially tricky thing is recognizing the accusative singular of third-declension neuter words. In second-declension neuter nouns, the nominative singular always ends in **-um**, and the accusative always does too. There's no danger there, since the masculine accusative singular also ends in **-um**. It's a different story for third-declension neuter nouns. As you recall, the third-declension nominative singular can end in any letter. Because of the double neuter rule, the nominative singular form repeats itself in the accusative singular. As always, be sure to learn your vocabulary thoroughly, and remember that **liber, librī** is second declension because its genitive ends in **-ī**, not because its nominative ends in **-r**. The noun **iter** also ends in **-r**, but it is third declension because its genitive ends in **-is**.

Neuter forms for adjectives follow the same rules. The only exceptions are for third-declension adjectives. Here, the neuter nominative plural ends in **-ia** instead of just **-a**, and the genitive plural ends in **-ium** rather than **-um**.

Written Practice 7-2

Decline the following noun-adjective pairs fully.

	Singular	Plural

1. **arvum lātum, arvī lātī** *n.* a wide field

   Nominative _____   _____

   Genitive _____   _____

   Dative _____   _____

   Accusative _____   _____

   Ablative _____   _____

2. **collum gracile, collī gracilis** *n.* a slender neck

   Nominative _____   _____

   Genitive _____   _____

   Dative _____   _____

   Accusative _____   _____

   Ablative _____   _____

	Singular	Plural
3. **tempus breve, temporis brevis** *n.* a short time		
Nominative	_____	_____
Genitive	_____	_____
Dative	_____	_____
Accusative	_____	_____
Ablative	_____	_____

Ablative Case

Ablative case is actually three different cases rolled into one: the original ablative case, which shows where an action starts; the instrumental case, which shows something that moves alongside the action from start to finish; and the locative case, which shows where an action takes place.

Original ablative	Ex Italiā vēnit.	*He came from Italy.*
Instrumental	Cum comitibus vēnit.	*He came with his buddies.*
Locative	In tabernā istōs invēnī.	*I found the creeps at a bar.*

Since the ablative case is the fusion of three different cases, it seems to have 1,001 uses. This really isn't anything to worry about, as long as you keep in mind its threefold origin. If you do, its bafflingly myriad, seemingly random uses will make sense.

Before delving into a few of the ablative's uses, let's review its forms.

	Singular	Plural
First Declension		
Nominative	-a	-ae
Genitive	-ae	-ārum
Dative	-ae	-īs
Accusative	-am	-ās
Ablative	**-ā**	**-īs**
Second Declension Masculine		
Nominative	-us/-r	-ī/-rī
Genitive	-ī	-ōrum
Dative	-ō	-īs
Accusative	-um	-ōs
Ablative	**-ō**	**-īs**

	Singular	Plural
Second Declension Neuter		
Nominative	-um	-a
Genitive	-ī	-ōrum
Dative	-ō	-īs
Accusative	-um	-a
Ablative	**-ō**	**-īs**
Third Declension Masculine and Feminine		
Nominative	*Wild card!*	-ēs
Genitive	-is	-um
Dative	-ī	-ibus
Accusative	-em	-ēs
Ablative	**-e**	**-ibus**
Third Declension Neuter		
Nominative	*Wild card!*	-a
Genitive	-is	-um
Dative	-ī	-ibus
Accusative	*Same as nominative*	-a
Ablative	**-e**	**-ibus**

The ablative singular forms are essentially the theme vowels of the declension: first declension, **ā**; second declension, **ō**; and third declension, short **e**. If you learned the dative plural endings, you're in luck—the ablative plural endings are identical! In fact, dative and ablative plural endings are always the same, no matter which declension the noun is.

The first/second-declension adjectives have the same endings as the nouns in ablative case. Third-declension adjectives, however, have **-ī** instead of the **-e** that you see in nouns.

Written Practice 7-3

Change the following nouns, whatever their forms, to ablative case, keeping singular for singular and plural for plural. This exercise is about form recognition, so it doesn't matter if you have never seen the words before or know what they mean. To make things a little more interesting, some might already be in ablative case!

1. ventus   _____

2. perīculum   _____

3. flammae (*pl.*) _____

4. iūre _____

5. arvōrum _____

6. mōrī (*third declension*) _____

7. cīvēs _____

8. crētā _____

9. creātiōnem _____

10. ūvārum _____

Using Prepositional Phrases as Modifiers

A **preposition** is a part of speech that helps show the relationship of one thing to another thing. Here are some English examples to help you get the idea.

> *the fool **on** the hill*
>
> *the dust bunnies **under** the couch*
>
> *the girl **from** Ipanema*

In Latin, all nouns have to be in the case that corresponds to their function in the sentence. Prepositions take (i.e., are followed by) nouns in either the accusative or ablative case. When you study your vocabulary, it is important to learn which case each preposition takes. There is, however, a simple trick to this. There are seven main prepositions that require the nouns that follow them to be in the ablative. If you learn which ones they are, you can assume all the other prepositions take the accusative.

ā (ab) *from, away from*
   Ab incendiō fūgimus.   *We fled away from the fire.*

ē (ex) *out (of), from*
   Tyrannum ex urbe expulērunt.   *They threw the tyrant out of the city.*

dē *down from, from; concerning, about*
   Dē monte descendērunt.   *They climbed down from the mountain.*
   Liber dē agricultūrā est.   *It is a book about agriculture.*

prō *on behalf of, for; in exchange for, instead of*
    quid prō quō   *something in exchange for something*

sine *without*
    Sine tē vīvere nōlō.   *I don't want to live without you.*

cum *with*
    Cum cane currēbat.   *He was running with his dog.*

prae *in front of, before*
    Prae iūdice stābās.   *You were standing in front of the judge.*

N.B. The preposition **ā** becomes **ab** when the next word begins with a vowel, e.g., **ā silvā** (*away from the forest*), but **ab aquā** (*away from the water*). Similarly, the preposition **ē** becomes **ex** in this situation, e.g., **ē silvā** (*out of the forest*), but **ex aquā** (*out of the water*). This works like the alternation between *a* and *an* in English, e.g., *a boy,* but *an apple.*

    There are, of course, a couple of exceptions to the accusative/ablative rule. The Latin prepositions **in** and **sub** can take either the accusative or ablative case, depending on how they are being used. To express motion toward something, they take the accusative. When they are showing location, they use the ablative. Here are some examples to show the subtle differences in these ideas.

Canēs **in** silv**am** currēbant.   *The dogs were running **into** the woods.*
                                    (They were outside, moved in the direction of the woods, and then entered the woods.)

Canēs **in** silv**ā** currēbant.   *The dogs were running **in** the woods.*
                                    (They were already in the woods and were running around inside it.)

Fēles **sub** mens**am** cucurrit.   *The cat ran under the table.*
                                    (It was somewhere else in the kitchen and scurried beneath the table.)

Fēles **sub** mens**ā** dormit.   *The cat is sleeping under the table.*
                                    (It is already there and snoozing away.)

Written Practice 7-4

Translate the following prepositional phrases into Latin. For this exercise, use the Key Vocabulary at the end of this chapter and the following word list.

Vocabulary

amīcitia, amīcitiae *f.* friendship
frīgidus, frīgida, frīgidum cold
Italia, Italiae *f.* Italy
lītus, lītoris *n.* shore
mons, montis *m.* mountain
unda, undae *f.* wave

1. about many dangers   _____
2. with all my friends   _____
3. among the unfortunate people   _____
4. out of the cold water   _____
5. without you (*pl.*)   _____
6. away from the huge waves   _____
7. in exchange for your (*sg.*) friendship   _____
8. at the foot of the tall mountain   _____
9. toward Italy's shore   _____
10. in front of the brave soldiers   _____

Ablative Case Uses

All case uses have formal, traditional names, for example, ***dative indirect object***, ***predicate nominative***, and ***genitive of possession***. The ablative case has many, many formal names for its many, many uses. You should learn these terms, so that when you read other books about Latin or talk with fellow Latin students, you'll be "in the know."

In English, prepositions do much of the work that the ablative case does in Latin. But not all ablative uses in Latin require a preposition. Keep in mind the three original ideas behind ablative case: source, accompaniment, and location.

ABLATIVE OF PLACE WHERE

There is nothing misleading about the name of this case use. The ***ablative of place where*** shows the place where something is located or is occurring. It is introduced by the prepositions **in**, **sub**, **prō**, or **prae**.

in casā	*in the hut*
sub monte	*at the foot of the mountain*
prō patriā	*for the fatherland*
prae omnibus	*in front of everyone*

When the place where something is located or is occurring is a city, town, or small island, no preposition is used. They don't require a preposition to show motion toward—or motion away from. Instead, a simple accusative or ablative will do, so **Rōmam** means *to Rome* and **Rōmā** means *from Rome*.

Likewise, no preposition is required for the words **domus** (*home*), **humus** (*the ground*), and **rūs** (*the countryside*). These words employ special forms, which are survivals of the old Indo-European locative case. The English word *home* is like this when expressing motion toward. You say you are *going home,* not *going to home.* We'll explore the details of these peculiar words in a later chapter.

ABLATIVE OF PLACE FROM WHICH

This is another ablative case use whose name does not need much explanation. It shows the place from which the action of the verb originates. It descends from the original Indo-European ablative case, whose basic concept is *source.* The prepositions that introduce this ablative are **ā**, **ē**, **dē**, and **sine**. **Sine** is in this group, because the idea of *source* doesn't just involve *motion away from.* It also bears a sense of *separation,* not to mention *cause,* i.e., the thing *from which* an action arises.

ab ōrīs	*away from the shores*
ex aedibus	*out of the house*
dē arbore	*down from the tree*
sine perīculō	*without danger*

ABLATIVE OF ACCOMPANIMENT

The *ablative of accompaniment* clearly reveals the influence of the Indo-European instrumental case. The original instrumental case identified something that goes along with the action of the verb. The preposition that introduces it in Latin is **cum**.

> Pictor parietem **cum fīliō** pinxit.   *The painter painted the wall **with his son**.*

When **cum** is used with first- and second-person singular and plural personal pronouns, it becomes an *enclitic*. Enclitics are particles that attach themselves to the ends of the words they go with.

> mēcum *with me*
> tēcum *with you* (sg.)
> nōbīscum *with us*
> vōbīscum *with you* (pl.)

ABLATIVE OF MEANS

The *ablative of means*, sometimes called the *ablative of means or instrument*, is by far the most common use of the ablative without a preposition. When you see a lone ablative form that isn't introduced by a preposition, your first hunch should be that it is an ablative of means. This use of the ablative identifies a tool, usually an inanimate object, that is used to accomplish the action of the verb.

> Publius lupum **lapidibus** reppulit.   *Publius drove the wolf off **with stones**.*

The stones were the tools, or means, by which our brave Publius saved the day.

ABLATIVE OF MANNER

The *ablative of manner* shows the manner in which something was done, using the preposition **cum**. It generally appears with a noun that expresses an abstract concept, such as love, happiness, or praise.

> Amīcōs nostrōs **cum gaudiō**   *We welcomed our friends **with joy**.*
> accēpimus.

When the noun in an ablative of manner phrase is modified by an adjective, the phrase has a peculiar construction. The adjective comes *before* the **cum** introducing the phrase, and the **cum** becomes optional in such a phrase. Whether it is there or not has no effect on the meaning. It is purely stylistic.

> Amīcōs nostrōs **magnō cum gaudiō** accēpimus. ⎫ *We welcomed our friends*
> Amīcōs nostrōs **magnō gaudiō** accēpimus. ⎬ *with great joy.*

Since ablatives of manner show the manner in which something happened, you can often translate them as if they were adverbs.

> Amīcōs nostrōs **cum gaudiō** accēpimus.   *We welcomed our friends **joyfully**.*

This is not an option with an ablative of means.

> Publius lupum **lapidibus** reppulit.   *Publius drove the wolf off **stonesfully**.*

Distinguishing Dative and Ablative Forms

Ablative uses that don't require a preposition can present a point of potential confusion, since ablative forms are identical to the dative forms in the singular for second-declension nouns and in the plural for all declensions. There are two things to remember if you find yourself in this situation. One is context; the dative is used in ways that the ablative isn't. Also, datives are usually "people words," while ablatives are usually "thing words." For example, let's say you're reading about a marriage and you run across the following sentence.

> Valerius fīliō aedēs ēmit. ⎰ *Valerius bought a house for his son.*
>   **(fīliō** as dative)**
>   *Valerius bought a house with his son.*
>   **(fīliō** as ablative of means)**

The first reading gives the young man a wedding present. The second reading suggests he's being sold off as a slave … or maybe worse!

Written Practice 7-5

For each of the following sentences, underline the noun or nouns that are dative or ablative. Identify them as dative or ablative; if ablative, give the ablative use shown in the sentence. Finally, translate the sentence.

Vocabulary

castra, castrōrum *n.pl.* camp
cornū with its horn
dens, dentis *m.* tooth
lupus, lupī *m.* wolf
nisi except
pompa, pompae *f.* parade
post *prep.* + *acc.* after
taurus, taurī *m.* bull
Tullus, Tullī *m.* Tullus (*N.B. When translating Latin names, always put them back into nominative case. They decline in Latin, but not in English!*)
urbs, urbis *f.* city
verberō (1) to beat
virga, virgae *f.* switch, green twig

Dē <u>arbore</u> cecidit. *ablative of place from which*
    He fell down out of the tree.

1. Iam in Āfricā diū manēbant. _____

_____

2. Heri ē castrīs celeriter fūgērunt. _____

_____

3. Hodiē in pompā multōs hominēs clārōs facile vīdimus.

_____

_____

4. Nōn erat Tullō magnum imperium. _____

_____

5. Dente lupus, cornū taurus petit. _____

_____

_____

6. Nihil nisi multa corpora ibi in mediō locō post bellum invēnistis.

_____

_____

7. Nunc servus puerōs magnā cum cūrā spectat.

_____

_____

8. Hominēs in urbe novā saepe tristēs sunt.

_____

_____

9. Dominus bonus servōs virgā numquam verberat.

_____

_____

Key Vocabulary

Adjectives

altus, alta, altum tall, high, deep [altitude] (_This word's meanings may seem to contradict one another, but for the Romans they didn't. Basically,_ **altus** _refers to an extreme vertical distance. Being in "deep water" is the same as being in "high water." Whether you are looking from the top down or the bottom up, the distance remains extreme._)

clārus, clāra, clārum clear, bright; famous; obvious [clarity]

medius, media, medium (the) middle (of) [median]

miser, misera, miserum unfortunate, unhappy, pitiful [miserable]

novus, nova, novum new, young; strange [novel]

tristis, triste sad, gloomy

Adverbs

N.B. Adverbs are notoriously difficult to learn, because there are virtually no derivatives to help as memory cues. For the most part, you have to memorize them as they are. Don't be afraid to create your own memory devices. In fact, the stranger you make your devices, the more likely you are to remember them!

bene well [benediction]

difficile with difficulty

diū for a long time
facile easily
heri yesterday
hīc here
hodiē today
iam now, already, at this point in time (*in a story; compare with* **nunc**)
ibi there
magnopere greatly
multum much, a lot
nōn not
numquam never
nunc now (*as in right now, as I am speaking*)
parum little, not much; not enough, too little
saepe often
semper always

Nouns

bellum, bellī *n.* war [belligerent]
corpus, corporis *n.* body [corpse]
imperium, imperiī *n.* power, command [imperial]
locus, locī *m.* place [location] (*The plural forms of this word have gender issues. When the reference is to individual, unconnected places, the masculine plural* (**locī**) *is used. If the reference is to connected areas, such as in a region or neighborhood, neuter plural forms* (**loca**) *are used.*)
nihil *n.* nothing [nil] (*This word is indeclinable, meaning that it belongs to no declension, takes no endings, and has no plural. It is sometimes contracted to* **nīl**.)
nōmen, nōminis *n.* name [nominate]
perīculum, perīculī *n.* danger [peril]

Prepositions That Take the Ablative

ā (ab) from, away from; by
cum with
dē down from, from; concerning, about
ē (ex) out (of), from
in (*showing location*) in, on
prae in front of, before
prō on behalf of, for; in exchange for, instead of; in front of
sine without
sub (*showing location*) under, beneath, at the foot of

Prepositions That Take the Accusative

ad to, toward, near, at
in (*showing motion toward*) in, into, onto, to, at, against

N.B. It is important to compare **in** *with* **ad**. *Both can sometimes be translated* to, *but in different senses. The preposition* **in** *implies motion toward and contact or penetration, while* **ad** *simply refers to heading in a certain direction.*)

Appius ad Graeciam iter fēcit.	*Appius made a trip to Greece.* (He was headed there, at least.)
Appius in Graeciam iter fēcit.	*Appius made a trip to Greece.* (He arrived and went within its borders.)
Puer pilam ad amīcum mīsit.	*The boy tossed the ball to his friend.* (He tossed it toward him.)
Puer pilam in amīcum mīsit.	*The boy tossed the ball to his friend.* (He hit him with the ball.)

inter between, among
per through, along; over; throughout; because of
sub (*showing motion toward*) under, beneath

Verb

spectō (1) to watch, look at [spectator]

QUIZ

Choose the correct grammatical description for each of the following Latin words.

1. perīcula
   - (a) nominative singular
   - (b) ablative singular
   - (c) accusative plural
   - (d) adverb

2. imperiī
   - (a) dative plural
   - (b) nominative plural
   - (c) genitive singular
   - (d) adverb

3. locō
   - (a) ablative singular
   - (b) nominative singular
   - (c) dative plural
   - (d) adverb

4. numquam
   - (a) accusative singular
   - (b) genitive plural
   - (c) nominative singular
   - (d) adverb

5. corpus
   - (a) accusative singular
   - (b) ablative plural
   - (c) genitive singular
   - (d) adverb

6. nōmine
   (a) ablative singular
   (b) nominative plural
   (c) dative singular
   (d) adverb

7. nihil
   (a) nominative plural
   (b) genitive singular
   (c) mahjong
   (d) adverb

8. clārē
   (a) ablative singular
   (b) accusative singular
   (c) accusative plural
   (d) adverb

9. puellae
   (a) ablative singular
   (b) dative singular
   (c) genitive plural
   (d) adverb

10. graviter
   (a) nominative singular
   (b) nominative plural
   (c) accusative singular
   (d) adverb

CHAPTER 8

The Future, Pluperfect, and Future Perfect Tenses

In this chapter, you will learn about:

Future Tense

The *future* is the final tense in the present system. You'll recall that the imperfect tense shows something in the process of happening before the time of speaking. The present tense expresses actions in progress—or in general—at the time of speaking. The future tense is much like the present, in that it also shows something in the midst of happening or in general, but *after* the time of speaking.

Canis lātrābit. {
  The dog will be barking. (in progress)
  The dog will bark. (in general)

Imperfect tense creates its forms using the tense indicator **-ba-**. In present tense, each conjugation has its own variation. Future tense is formed by two different methods—one for first- and second-conjugation verbs, and one for third- and fourth-conjugation verbs.

FIRST- AND SECOND-CONJUGATION FORMS FOR FUTURE TENSE

First- and second-conjugation verbs express future tense using a tense indicator that looks somewhat similar to the one used for the imperfect. Rather than a uniform syllable, however, the tense indicator for the future of these verbs follows a certain vowel pattern, which you should recognize immediately.

Step 1: Go to the second principal part: **habēre**.

Step 2: Drop the final **-re** to get the stem: **habē-**.

Step 3: Add the future tense indicator for first and second conjugation plus personal endings.

-bō	-bimus
-bis	-bitis
-bit	-bunt

Here are sample conjugations of the future tense in first and second conjugations.

First Conjugation amō, amāre, amāvī, amātum to love

Singular

First person	amābō	*I will love*
Second person	amābis	*you will love*
Third person	amābit	*he/she/it will love*

Plural

First person	amā**bimus**	*we will love*
Second person	amā**bitis**	*you will love*
Third person	amā**bunt**	*they will love*

Second Conjugation teneō, tenēre, tenuī, tentum to hold

Singular

First person	tenē**bō**	*I will hold*
Second person	tenē**bis**	*you will hold*
Third person	tenē**bit**	*he/she/it will hold*

Plural

First person	tenē**bimus**	*we will hold*
Second person	tenē**bitis**	*you will hold*
Third person	tenē**bunt**	*they will hold*

Does the **ō-i-u** vowel pattern look familiar to you? It is the very same pattern you learned for making the present tense forms for third-, third **-iō**, and fourth-conjugation verbs. The endings are the same as third-conjugation present tense, except they start with **b**. Also note that unlike in imperfect tense, the personal ending for the first-person singular of future tense is **-ō**, not **-m**.

Written Practice 8-1

Conjugate (i.e., put into all their forms) the following verbs in future tense and translate each form.

1. **portō, portāre, portāvī, portātum** to carry

   Singular

   First person   _____   _____

   Second person   _____   _____

   Third person   _____   _____

   Plural

   First person   _____   _____

   Second person   _____   _____

   Third person   _____   _____

2. **doceō, docēre, docuī, doctum** to teach
Singular
First person   _____   _____
Second person _____   _____
Third person   _____   _____
Plural
First person   _____   _____
Second person _____   _____
Third person   _____   _____

Written Practice 8-2

The following verb forms are in various tenses. Change each to future tense, retaining person and number, and translate the new form.

1. rogās   _____   _____
2. laudāmus   _____   _____
3. tenuistis   _____   _____
4. dōnābam   _____   _____
5. vocāvērunt   _____   _____
6. valet   _____   _____
7. monuistī   _____   _____
8. rīdēbāmus   _____   _____
9. stō   _____   _____
10. servāvit   _____   _____

THIRD-, THIRD -*iō*, AND FOURTH-CONJUGATION FORMS FOR FUTURE TENSE

As mentioned earlier, third-, third -**iō**, and fourth-conjugation verbs have a very different way of showing future tense. Instead of a tense indicator, they have a vowel shift from present tense. Here is the best approach to forming future tense for these verbs.

Step 1: Go to the first principal part: **pōnō**.

Step 2: Drop the final **-ō** to get the stem: **pōn-**.

Step 3: Add the special future tense endings for third-, third *-iō*, and fourth-conjugation verbs.

-am	-ēmus
-ēs	-ētis
-et	-ent

Here are sample conjugations of the future tense in third, third **-iō**, and fourth conjugations.

Third Conjugation **pōnō, pōnere, posuī, positum** to put

Singular

First person	pōn**am**	*I will put*
Second person	pōn**ēs**	*you will put*
Third person	pōn**et**	*he/she/it will put*

Plural

First person	pōn**ēmus**	*we will put*
Second person	pōn**ētis**	*you will put*
Third person	pōn**ent**	*they will put*

Third Conjugation *-iō* **faciō, facere, fēcī, factum** to make, do

Singular

First person	faci**am**	*I will make*
Second person	faci**ēs**	*you will make*
Third person	faci**et**	*he/she/it will make*

Plural

First person	faci**ēmus**	*we will make*
Second person	faci**ētis**	*you will make*
Third person	faci**ent**	*they will make*

Fourth Conjugation sentiō, sentīre, sensī, sensum to feel, perceive

Singular

First person	senti**am**	*I will feel*
Second person	senti**ēs**	*you will feel*
Third person	senti**et**	*he/she/it will feel*

Plural

First person	senti**ēmus**	*we will feel*
Second person	senti**ētis**	*you will feel*
Third person	senti**ent**	*they will feel*

The thing to remember with these verbs is that rather than **-bō, -bi-, -bu-,** they have "an **a** and five **es**." You should also note that instead of **-ō**, these verbs use **-m** for the first-person singular ending.

Written Practice 8-3

Conjugate the following verbs in future tense and translate each form.

1. **caedō, caedere, cecīdī, caesum** to cut

   Singular

   First person   _____   _____

   Second person   _____   _____

   Third person   _____   _____

   Plural

   First person   _____   _____

   Second person   _____   _____

   Third person   _____   _____

2. **īciō, īcere, īcī, ictum** to strike

   Singular

   First person   _____   _____

   Second person   _____   _____

   Third person   _____   _____

Plural

First person _____ _____

Second person _____ _____

Third person _____ _____

3. **perveniō, pervenīre, pervēnī, perventum** to arrive

Singular

First person _____ _____

Second person _____ _____

Third person _____ _____

Plural

First person _____ _____

Second person _____ _____

Third person _____ _____

Written Practice 8-4

The following verb forms are in various tenses. Change each to future tense, retaining person and number, and translate the new form.

1. cadis _____ _____

2. fūgimus _____ _____

3. cēpī _____ _____

4. legēbant _____ _____

5. vēnērunt _____ _____

6. mīsistī _____ _____

7. inveniēbāmus _____ _____

8. agō _____ _____

9. dixit _____ _____

10. relīquistī _____ _____

DISTINGUISHING PRESENT AND FUTURE TENSES

You may have noticed that five out of six future tense endings for third-, third **-iō**, and fourth-conjugation verbs are identical to second-conjugation present tense endings.

Third-Conjugation Future	Second-Conjugation Present
dūcō, dūcere	maneō, manēre
dūcam	maneō
dūcēs	manēs
dūcet	manet
dūcēmus	manēmus
dūcētis	manētis
dūcent	manent

So, how can you distinguish between present and future tense? All you can do is know your vocabulary thoroughly. That is to say, you need to remember all the principal parts of a verb included in a dictionary listing, not just the meaning!

THE FUTURE OF *sum*

Just as **sum** is irregular in imperfect tense, it follows a similar pattern in its future tense forms.

	Singular	Plural
First person	erō	erimus
Second person	eris	eritis
Third person	erit	erunt

These forms have the same endings as the first and second conjugation, **-bō, -bis, -bit**, etc. They are only missing the **b**.

Written Practice 8-5

Translate the following verb forms into English. They might come from any conjugation or tense, so pay close attention!

1. timet　　　　_____

2. docēbāmus　_____

3. rapient _____

4. reddunt _____

5. dōnābimus _____

6. scrībis _____

7. agam _____

8. rogāvistis _____

9. vidētis _____

10. petō _____

Function of the Pluperfect and Future Perfect Tenses

These are the last two tenses for you to learn. The pluperfect and future perfect tenses are grouped together for presentation because they perform essentially the same function. They indicate that one action is completed before another action takes place. The pluperfect denotes this in past time, while the future perfect does so in future time.

Following is a time line showing the relationship of all the tenses to one another.

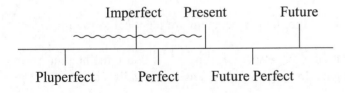

The pluperfect happens before the perfect.

Ubi pervēnimus, omnēs iam **discesserant.**	*When we arrived, everyone **had** already **left**.*

The future perfect happens before the future.

Ubi perveniēmus, omnēs iam **discesserint.**	*When we arrive, everyone **will have** already **left**.*

Since the pluperfect and future perfect tenses refer to an action relative to another action, you will usually see them in complex sentences. Pluperfect forms appear fairly often. The future perfect is among the least common of the tenses.

As you may recall from Chapter 2, all perfect system tenses are formed in the same way for all verbs, regardless of conjugation. Even the irregular verbs behave themselves. That being the case, we can pick any verb at random to serve as our example.

Pluperfect Tense

Since the pluperfect is a perfect system tense, the first thing you need is the perfect stem.

Step 1: Go to the third principal part: **discessī**.

Step 2: Drop the final **-ī** to get the stem: **discess-**.

Step 3: Add the pluperfect tense indicator, **-era-**: discess**era**-.

Step 4: Add the personal endings.

discesseram	discesser**āmus**
discesser**ās**	discesser**ātis**
discesser**at**	discesser**ant**

Notice that the endings you add to the perfect stem are identical to the imperfect forms of **sum**.

The only way to translate the pluperfect into English is to use the helping verb *had* with the past participle. In English, this tense is usually called the past perfect.

discesseram	*I **had** left*
discesser**ās**	*you **had** left*
etc.	

Future Perfect Tense

Formation of the future perfect in Latin is the same as formation of the pluperfect, with only two exceptions.

Step 1: Go to the third principal part: **discessī**.

Step 2: Drop the final **-ī** to get the stem: **discess-**.

Step 3: Add the future perfect tense indicator, **-eri-**: discess**eri-**.

Step 4: Add the personal endings.

discesser**ō**	discesser**imus**
discesser**is**	discesser**itis**
discesser**it**	discesser**int**

The first difference in pluperfect and future perfect tense formation is the tense indicator: **-eri-** for the future perfect, **-era-** for the pluperfect. The second difference lies in the first-person singular of the future perfect. Here the **-i-** of the tense indicator disappears and the personal ending is **-ō** rather than **-m**.

You might have noticed a similarity between these endings and the future tense forms of **sum**. They are identical except in one form, the third-person plural. There you have **-erint** (with an **i**) instead of **erunt** (with a **u**). Remember that the ending **-ērunt** is already in use for the third-person plural of the regular perfect tense.

In English grammar, we also call this tense the future perfect. It is traditionally translated with the helping verb *will have* and the past participle. English, however, is often sloppy in constructions that involve this tense, and this affects how you should translate it in sentences in which it appears. Let's take a closer look at that earlier example.

Ubi perveniēmus [Latin future tense], omnēs iam **discesserint**.	*When we arrive* [English present tense], *everyone **will have** already left*.

Latin is strict about such matters. Future events require future tense. In English, with the future perfect verb in the other clause, *will* gets dropped, and even though the reference is to a future event, there is a shift to present tense. Doesn't "When we *will arrive*, everyone will have already left" sound awkward?

Written Practice 8-6

Conjugate the following verb in pluperfect tense and translate each form.

sum, esse, fuī, futūrus to be

Singular

First person _____ _____

Second person _____ _____

Third person _____ _____

Plural

First person _____ _____

Second person _____ _____

Third person _____ _____

Written Practice 8-7

Conjugate the following verb in future perfect tense and translate each form.

crēdō, crēdere, crēdidī, crēditum to believe

Singular

First person _____ _____

Second person _____ _____

Third person _____ _____

Plural

First person _____ _____

Second person _____ _____

Third person _____ _____

Written Practice 8-8

Translate the following sentences into English.

Vocabulary

eīs to them (*dative*)
impedimenta, impedimentōrum *n.pl.* baggage
praedō, praedōnis *m.* mugger
tōtum diem for the entire day

1. Crās mīlitēs nostrī in Germāniam pervēnerint.

   _____

2. Fuerant ibi magna perīcula.

   _____

3. Dē hostibus ācribus vōbīs monuerāmus.

   _____

4. Postquam in Forum vēnerō, amīcī meī mē salūtābunt.

   _____

5. Multōs hominēs miserōs heri occiderant.

   _____

6. Mīlitēs in castra cum impedimentīs tristēs ambulāverint.

   _____

7. Servī laetī erunt postquam dominus eīs lībertātem dederit.

   _____

8. Praedō pecūniam virī rapuerat antequam in turbam cucurrit.

   _____

9. Mātrem tuam mox vidēbis.

   _____

10. Fīlius cum patre tōtum diem manserit.

    _____

Key Vocabulary

Adverbs

crās tomorrow
mox soon

Conjunctions

antequam before
postquam after

Nouns

castra, castrōrum *n.pl.* camp (*military*)
lībertās, lībertātis *f.* freedom [liberty]
turba, turbae *f.* crowd, mob

Verbs

ambulō (1) to walk [ambulatory]
discēdō, discēdere, discessī, discessum to leave, go away
maneō, manēre, mansī, mansum to stay [remain]
moneō, monēre, monuī, monitum to warn, advise [monitor]
occīdō, occīdere, occīdī, occīsum to kill
parō (1) to prepare, get ready [prepare]
perveniō, pervenīre, pervēnī, perventum to arrive
properō (1) to hurry
rapiō, rapere, rapuī, raptum to seize, grab, take (*forcefully*) [rape]
timeō, timēre, timuī to be afraid of, fear [timid] (*This verb has no fourth principal part.*)

QUIZ

Identify the tense of each of the following verb forms.

1. discessimus
   (a) perfect
   (b) pluperfect
   (c) future perfect
   (d) present

2. scrībō
   (a) future
   (b) present
   (c) imperfect
   (d) future perfect

3. ambulāverant
   (a) pluperfect
   (b) imperfect
   (c) future perfect
   (d) perfect

4. properābam
   (a) present
   (b) imperfect
   (c) pluperfect
   (d) future perfect

5. laudāverint
   (a) future perfect
   (b) pluperfect
   (c) present
   (d) perfect progressive

6. rogābit
   - (a) future perfect
   - (b) imperfect
   - (c) future
   - (d) present

7. cadunt
   - (a) perfect
   - (b) pluperfect
   - (c) future
   - (d) present

8. fūgerō
   - (a) future
   - (b) pluperfect
   - (c) future perfect
   - (d) imperfect

9. vincēs
   - (a) future
   - (b) present
   - (c) future perfect
   - (d) pluperfect

10. habēs
   - (a) future
   - (b) present
   - (c) future perfect
   - (d) pluperfect

CHAPTER 9

When, Whither, Whence, and Where

In this chapter, you will learn about:

Talking About Time

Apart from adverbs that make reference to time, such as **hodiē** (*today*), **crās** (*tomorrow*), **heri** (*yesterday*), **māne** (*in the morning*), and **noctū** (*at night*), Latin describes time in two ways, one of which uses the accusative case, and the other, the ablative.

Before moving into the grammar involved, there is a cultural note that you may find interesting. The smallest unit of time the Romans recognized was the **hōra**. We translate this word as "hour," but it was not what we think of as an hour, i.e., a period of 60 minutes. Instead, the Romans divided the daylight—sunrise to sunset—into 12 equal units, each of which was a **hōra**, which meant that the length of an hour varied from day to day. Rome is roughly at the same latitude as Boston (about 42° N), so there is considerably less daylight in the winter than there is in the summer. As a consequence, winter **hōrae** were far shorter than summer ones. Imagine the difference between one-twelfth of a cupcake and one-twelfth of a wedding cake! Sunrise marked the beginning of **hōra prīma**, the first hour.

The night was divided into four **vigiliae** (*vigils*). At dusk, the Romans marked which star or constellation was in the east. When it had risen a quarter of the way up, that was the end of **vigilia prīma** and the start of **vigilia secunda**. **Vigilia tertia** began when it had reached its zenith, as high as it would get before descending toward the west. That was literally midnight. Then, when the star or constellation was halfway between there and the western horizon, it became **vigilia quarta**.

The modern equivalent to cloudy nights would be when your watch battery dies and you have to guess what time it is!

ACCUSATIVE OF EXTENT

The accusative case can be used to show a span of time during which something takes place. Unlike the English way of expressing this idea, the ***accusative of extent*** does not require a preposition.

quinque diēs	*for five days*
multās hōrās	*for many hours*

The accusative of extent can also show an expanse of space.

pauca mīlia passuum	*for a few miles*
duōs pedēs	*for two feet*

ABLATIVE OF TIME WHEN OR WITHIN WHICH

The ***ablative of time when or within which*** is much like the ablative of place where; it shows a location in time rather than in space. That the Romans conceived of time and space similarly is also reflected in the conjunction **ubi**, which can mean both *when* and *where*. Unlike the ablative of place where, however, and unlike the way English expresses the concept, the ablative of time when or within which does not use a preposition.

brevī tempore	*in a short time*
sex diēbus	*within six days*
tertiā hōrā	*at the third hour*

Motion Toward, Away, and in Places

In our discussion of prepositions and of the ablative case, you learned several things about the grammar involving places. Now is the time to review those things and embellish them. Movement toward, movement from, and action simply occurring in a place each deserves separate consideration.

SHOWING MOTION TOWARD A PLACE

Heading toward or going into or onto a place calls for the accusative case. It shows the limit or stopping point of an action. The main prepositions used to convey the idea of motion toward are **ad** and **in**.

Ad Āfricam nāvigāvimus.	*We sailed to Africa.* (We headed in that general direction, anyway.)
In Āfricam nāvigāvimus.	*We sailed to Africa.* (We actually landed and went ashore.)

With some nouns, a preposition isn't necessary. A good English counterpart is the word *home. Going home* has a different sense than *going to the house,* and certainly a different sense than *going to the home*!

In Latin, the names of cities, towns, and small islands don't need a preposition to show motion toward them. Being in accusative case is sufficient.

Rōmam	*to Rome*
Athēnās	*to Athens*

There are a few other special words that fall into this category.

domum	*home* (homeward bound)
domus, -ūs *f.* house	
humum	*to the ground* (as an apple falls)
humus, -ī *f.* ground	
rūs	*to the country* (away from the city)
rūs, rūris *n.* country (*as opposed to the city or town*)	

SHOWING MOTION AWAY FROM A PLACE

The central concept behind the original Proto-Indo-European ablative case is source. The ablative case use called ***ablative of place from which*** is the most literal expression of this idea. It is usually introduced by the prepositions **ā**, **ē**, and **dē**.

ā silvā	*away from the forest*
ē silvā	*out of the forest*
dē silvā	*down from the forest*

Just as the names of cities, towns, and small islands and the nouns **domus**, **humus**, and **rūs** don't use a preposition to show motion toward them—being in accusative case is sufficient—motion away from those same places only requires putting them in the ablative case.

Rōmā	*from Rome*
Athēnīs	*from Athens*
domō	*from home*
humō	*from the ground*
rūre	*from the country*

Although the noun **domus, -ūs** is usually considered fourth declension, it is treated as a second-declension noun when it means *home* rather than simply *house*.

What defines a small island as being "small" is somewhat tricky. In general, an island is small when it is so small that it has only one or two towns and the name of the main town is the same as the name of the island.

LOCATIVE CASE

The original Proto-Indo-European locative case wasn't entirely absorbed into Latin's ablative case. For the most part, the ablative of place where uses a preposition, especially **in** or **sub**.

in lectō	*on the bed*
sub lectō	*under the bed*

With the names of cities, towns, and small islands, however, a special rule applies. This is where the old locative case survived.

The rules for formation of the locative case are quite simple. If a place's name is first- or second-declension singular, the locative form looks just like its genitive. Otherwise, it looks like its ablative form.

Rōmae   *at/in Rome*
   Rōma, -ae *f.* Rome (first-declension singular)

Athēnīs   *at/in Athens*
   Athēnae, -ārum *f.pl.* Athens (first-declension plural)

The nouns **domus, humus,** and **rūs** have their own special locative case forms.

domī	*at home*
humī	*on the ground*
rūrī	*in the country*

N.B. This signature ī appears in various other place words, such as **hīc** (*here, in this place*).

Occasionally, you will find singular place names whose locative ending is -ī. The locative form of the city of Carthage is almost always **Carthāginī**.

Written Practice 9-1

Complete the following chart, using the words below.

Vocabulary

Aegyptus, Aegyptī *f.* Egypt
Corinthus, Corinthī *f.* Corinth
Delphī, Delphōrum *m.pl.* Delphi
Fīdēnae, Fīdēnārum *f.pl.* Fidenae
Graecia, Graeciae *f.* Greece
insula, insulae *f.* island
Mediolānum, Mediolānī *n.* Milan
oppidum, oppidī *n.* town
patria, patriae *f.* fatherland, native country
Perusia, Perusiae *f.* Perugia
Sicilia, Siciliae *f.* Sicily
Tībur, Tīburis *n.* Tibur
urbs, urbis *f.* city
Vēiī, Vēiōrum *m.pl.* Veii
vīcus, vīcī *m.* village

	Motion Toward	Place Where	Motion Away From
1. Egypt			
2. Corinth			
3. Delphi			
4. Fidenae			
5. Greece			
6. island			
7. Milan			
8. town			
9. fatherland			
10. Perugia			
11. Sicily			
12. Tibur			
13. city			

	Motion Toward	Place Where	Motion Away From
14. Veii	_____	_____	_____
15. village	_____	_____	_____

Third-Declension *i*-Stem Nouns

There is a small group of third-declension nouns called *i*-stems that exhibit certain peculiarities in their forms. You were introduced to these peculiarities when you learned third-declension adjectives in Chapter 6, so there really isn't very much new to learn about them. They fall into three groups, which will make them instantly identifiable to you when you run across them in your vocabulary study. First, we will learn how to recognize them before moving on to see what makes them peculiar.

PARISYLLABICS

These are third-declension nouns that have two syllables in the nominative ending in **-is** (or occasionally in **-ēs**). Their nominative and genitive forms are usually identical. They are the most common type of third-declension **i**-stem nouns.

cīvis, cīvis *c.* citizen

nāvis, nāvis *f.* ship

nūbēs, nūbis *f.* cloud

MONOSYLLABICS

As their name suggests, these words have one syllable in the nominative, but they have stems that end in at least two consonants.

urbs, urbis *f.* city

nox, noctis *f.* night

Don't forget that the stem must end in more than one consonant. There are some third-declension words that have one syllable in the nominative, but whose stem ends in only one consonant, such as **rex, rēgis** (*m.* king).

NEUTERS ENDING IN *-al, -ar,* AND *-e*

These third-declension **i**-stem nouns vary the most from regular third-declension nouns. In fact, they show the same departures from the norm as third-declension adjectives.

> **animal, animālis** *n.* animal
>
> **exemplar, exemplāris** *n.* model, example
>
> **mare, maris** *n.* sea

FORMS FOR THIRD-DECLENSION *i*-STEM NOUNS

In regular third declension, the masculine and feminine forms are identical. This is also the case with third-declension **i**-stem nouns; their only variation is in the genitive plural, which ends in **-ium** rather than **-um**. The accusative plural can also end in **-īs** instead of the usual **-ēs**, but you're more likely to find that alternative in poetry, so you shouldn't worry about it at the moment.

The neuter forms have several points of departure from the norm, but, as stated earlier, if you learned third-declension adjective forms, you already know them.

In the following declension charts, the endings that deviate from regular third declension are in boldface type.

	Singular	Plural
nāvis, nāvis *f.* ship		
Nominative	nāvis	nāvēs
Genitive	nāvis	nāv**ium**
Dative	nāvī	nāvibus
Accusative	nāvem	nāvēs OR nāv**īs**
Ablative	nāve	nāvibus
nox, noctis *f.* night		
Nominative	nox	noctēs
Genitive	noctis	noct**ium**
Dative	noctī	noctibus
Accusative	noctem	noctēs OR noct**īs**
Ablative	nocte	noctibus

	Singular	Plural

iubar, iubaris *n.* beam of light

	Singular	Plural
Nominative	iubar	iubar**ia**
Genitive	iubaris	iubar**ium**
Dative	iubarī	iubaribus
Accusative	iubar	iubar**ia**
Ablative	iubarī	iubaribus

Written Practice 9-2

Identify which type of third declension **i**-stem each of the following nouns is, and then decline the noun fully.

	Singular	**Plural**

1. **fulgur, fulguris** *n.* flash of lightning   Type: _____

Nominative	_____	_____
Genitive	_____	_____
Dative	_____	_____
Accusative	_____	_____
Ablative	_____	_____

2. **classis, classis** *f.* fleet   Type: _____

Nominative	_____	_____
Genitive	_____	_____
Dative	_____	_____
Accusative	_____	_____
Ablative	_____	_____

3. **ars, artis** *f.* art, skill, method   Type: _____

Nominative	_____	_____
Genitive	_____	_____
Dative	_____	_____
Accusative	_____	_____
Ablative	_____	_____

	Singular	Plural
4. **calcar, calcāris** *n.* spur		Type: _____
Nominative	_____	_____
Genitive	_____	_____
Dative	_____	_____
Accusative	_____	_____
Ablative	_____	_____

Fourth Declension

Fourth declension is aptly named, since it is the fourth most common declension of nouns you will run across. Many, but not all, of the words belonging to this declension are related to verbs, for example, **ēventus** (*outcome*), **cāsus** (*fall*), and **exitus** (*act of going out*). You can recognize these nouns by their genitive singular form, which ends in **-ūs**. In fact, **ū** is the theme vowel of this declension.

The predominant gender in fourth declension is masculine, although some words, such as **manus** (*hand*) and **domus** (*house*), are feminine. There are also a few neuter words in this declension, the most common being **cornū** (*horn*) and **genū** (*knee*).

	Singular	Plural
situs, sitūs *m.* location		
Nominative	situs	sitūs
Genitive	sitūs	situum
Dative	situī	sitibus
Accusative	situm	sitūs
Ablative	sitū	sitibus
cornū, cornūs *n.* horn		
Nominative	cornū	cornua
Genitive	cornūs	cornuum
Dative	cornū	cornibus
Accusative	cornū	cornua
Ablative	cornū	cornibus

Fifth Declension

It is rather ironic that Latin's least populated declension contains two of the most common words in the language, namely **diēs** (*day*) and **rēs**, which is the catchall, "whatchamacallit" word of the language. All fifth-declension nouns are feminine, with the exception of **diēs** (*day*) and its compound **merīdiēs** (*noon*), which are masculine. The theme vowel in fifth declension is **ē**.

	Singular	Plural
speciēs, speciēī *f.* sight, appearance		
Nominative	speciēs	speciēs
Genitive	speciēī	speciērum
Dative	speciēī	speciēbus
Accusative	speciem	speciēs
Ablative	speciē	speciēbus

Written Practice 9-3

Decline the following nouns fully.

	Singular	Plural
1. **aciēs, aciēī** *f.* edge; battleline		
Nominative	_____	_____
Genitive	_____	_____
Dative	_____	_____
Accusative	_____	_____
Ablative	_____	_____
2. **morsus, morsūs** *m.* bite		
Nominative	_____	_____
Genitive	_____	_____
Dative	_____	_____
Accusative	_____	_____
Ablative	_____	_____

Substantive Use of Adjectives

An adjective is a word that modifies a noun. It describes a certain quality of a noun, so it really has no substance itself. A **substantive** is an adjective that is treated as a noun, and the noun it would have agreed with is understood. In English, we do this by placing an article adjective in front of the adjective. For example, the word *poor* is an adjective, as in *that* **poor** *child.* If you add *the,* though, and include no noun after *poor,* the adjective itself becomes a noun: *Give to the* **poor.** Poor what? People. The noun *people* is understood.

The same principle applies in Latin, except that in Latin there is the benefit of gender distinctions.

bonus	*a good man* (*man* is understood, because the ending is masculine singular)
bona	*a good woman*
bonum	*a good thing*
bonī	*good men*
bonae	*good women*
bona	*good things* (or *goods,* as the English substantive would have it)

If you see an adjective with no noun beside it with which to agree or that it could modify, you can pretty safely assume it is a substantive. **Multī** means *many people.* **Nostrī** (especially in a military context) means *our men.*

Conjunctions

Conjunctions are little words, such as *and, or, but,* and *because,* that join words, groups of words, or clauses. Sometimes they merely link things: *They fight like cats* **and** *dogs.* At other times, they describe a special relationship between the things they are joining: *He was running very quickly,* **because** *a dog was chasing him.*

You will find a list of the most common conjunctions in the Key Vocabulary at the end of this chapter.

Written Practice 9-4

Now that you have a fair amount of grammar and vocabulary under your belt, you will find bits of connected prose rather than just stray sentences to practice your Latin on.

Translate the following little passage, and don't fret over how "Dick and Jane" it might sound—we all had to learn to read starting somewhere! You can find a list of vocabulary for this passage following the reading.

Abhinc multōs annōs erat bellum longum et difficile inter Graecōs Trōiānōsque. Causa bellī fuit Helena, uxor Menelāī. Helena erat fīlia Lēdae, virginis pulchrae, et Iovis, rēgis omnium deōrum. Menelāus fratrem habēbat nomine Agamemnonem. Agamemnon habitābat Mycēnīs, quae urbs dīves et antīqua in Graeciā erat, et ibi regnābat. Quādam nocte Helena Mycēnās atque Menelāum relīquerat et trans mare Trōiam cum Paride, iuvene cuius pater erat rex Trōiae, nāvigāverat. Māne Menelāus uxorem invenīre nōn poterat. Ubi erat? Quō discesserat?

Trōia nōn oppidum parvum, sed urbs vetus et magna prope mare in Asiā erat. Menelāus fratrī suō appropinquāvit et ab eō auxilium petīvit. Statim vocāvit aliōs rēgēs potentēs et ūnā multīs nāvibus ē Graeciā Trōiam nāvigāvērunt. Omnēs cīvēs Trōiānī valdē timēbant atque portās urbis clausērunt et Graecōs nōn accēpērunt.

Vocabulary

abhinc ago
Agamemnon, Agamemnonis *m.* Agamemnon
Asia, Asiae *f.* Asia
causa, causae *f.* cause, reason
claudō, claudere, clausī, clausum to close
cuius whose
dīves, dīvitis wealthy
eō him (*ablative sg.*)
Graecia, Graeciae *f.* Greece
Graecus, Graeca, Graecum Greek
Helena, Helenae *f.* Helen
Iuppiter, Iovis *m.* Jupiter
Lēda, Lēdae *f.* Leda
Menelāus, Menelāī *m.* Menelaus
Mycēnae, Mycēnārum *f.pl.* Mycenae (pronounced meye-SEE-nee)
nomine by the name of, named

Paris, Paridis *m.* Paris
porta, portae *f.* gate
poterat could
quādam nocte on a certain night
quae which
quō to what place, where
regnō (1) to be king, rule
Trōia, Trōiae *f.* Troy
Trōiānus, Trōiāna, Trōiānum Trojan
ūnā together
valdē very, very much

Synopsis

So far, the verb charts that you have seen and been filling in are called ***conjugations***. They show all the different persons and numbers of a verb in the same tense. There is another type of verb chart, called a ***synopsis***. A synopsis is a verb chart that turns things around—it shows all the tenses of a verb in the same *person* and *number*.

Here is a sample synopsis.

capiō, capere, cēpī, captum *3pl.* (*third-person plural*)

Present	**capiunt**
Imperfect	**capiēbant**
Future	**capient**

Perfect	**cēpērunt**
Pluperfect	**cēperant**
Future Perfect	**cēperint**

The dividing line is a signal for you to change verb stems. Above the line, you need the first two principal parts. Below the line, the last two parts come into play.

This is actually a partial synopsis chart. Over time, it will grow to occupy most of a page! Not to fear, though. At this point, you will find that everything else there is to learn about the Latin language is nothing more than variations on what you have already mastered.

Written Practice 9-5

Here are a few practice synopses. When you have finished, check your work in the Answer Key. It is very important that you don't "cheat" by looking up things as you go. This exercise, like all quizzes, is an opportunity for you to see what you do and do not have down yet. Whatever errors you may find are indications of what you ought to review. It is very important to fill any gaps in your foundation!

1. **iaciō, iacere, iēcī, iactum** *1sg.* (*first-person singular*)

    Present   _____

    Imperfect   _____

    Future   _____

                     _____

    Perfect   _____

    Pluperfect   _____

    Future Perfect   _____

2. **dīcō, dīcere, dixī, dictum** *2sg.* (*second-person singular*)

    Present   _____

    Imperfect   _____

    Future   _____

                     _____

    Perfect   _____

    Pluperfect   _____

    Future Perfect   _____

3. **sum, esse, fuī, futūrus** *2pl.* (*second-person plural*)

    Present   _____

    Imperfect   _____

    Future   _____

                     _____

    Perfect   _____

    Pluperfect   _____

    Future Perfect   _____

4. **teneō, tenēre, tenuī, tentum** *3pl. (third-person plural)*

Present _____

Imperfect _____

Future _____
_____

Perfect _____

Pluperfect _____

Future Perfect _____

5. **sentiō, sentīre, sensī, sensum** *1pl. (first-person plural)*

Present _____

Imperfect _____

Future _____
_____

Perfect _____

Pluperfect _____

Future Perfect _____

6. **habitō, habitāre, habitāvī, habitātum** *3sg. (third-person singular)*

Present _____

Imperfect _____

Future _____
_____

Perfect _____

Pluperfect _____

Future Perfect _____

Key Vocabulary

Adjectives

antīquus, antīqua, antīquum old, old-fashioned, ancient [antique]
iuvenis, iuvene young [juvenile]
līber, lībera, līberum free [liberty]
paucī, paucae, pauca few [paucity]
vetus, veteris old [veteran]

Adverbs

cōtīdiē every day, daily [quotidian]
hīc here
ibi there
māne in the morning
noctū at night [nocturnal]
quoque also, too
statim immediately (*You often hear this Latin word abbreviated to* stat *over hospital P.A. systems when someone's presence is required without delay.*)

Conjunctions

atque (ac) and, and so, and even (*This word joins things implying that one is a logical consequence of the other, as in* We were hungry and we ate.)
aut or
   aut … aut either … or
et and, also, too, even
   et … et both … and
 neque (nec) and … not, nor
   neque … neque neither … nor
-que and (*This word is an enclitic, a particle that conveys meaning but can't stand alone like a regular word. Instead, it needs to be attached to the end of a word. This word is peculiar, because it attaches to the* second *of the two things being joined, e.g.,* **puerī puellaeque** (boys and girls). *It usually joins things that are natural pairs or that, when joined, make a whole, such as* salt and pepper *and* top and bottom.)
quia since, because
sed but, rather
ubi where; when

Nouns

annus, annī *m.* year [annual]
auxilium, auxiliī *n.* help [auxiliary]
cīvis, cīvis *c.* citizen [civic]
dea, deae *f.* goddess [deity]
deus, deī *m.* god [deity]
diēs, diēī *m.* day [diurnal]
domus, domūs *f.* house, home [domestic]
hōra, hōrae *f.* hour [hour]
humus, humī *f.* ground, soil [humus]
insula, insulae *f.* island; apartment building [insular]
manus, manūs *f.* hand; band of men, posse [manual]
mare, maris *n.* sea [marine]
mensis, mensis *m.* month [menstruation]
merīdiēs, merīdiēī *m.* noon, midday [A.M. (ante meridiem),
   P.M. (post meridiem)]
nāvis, nāvis *f.* ship [naval]
nox, noctis *f.* night [nocturnal]
oppidum, oppidī *n.* town
pēs, pedis *m.* foot [pedal]
Pompēiī, Pompēiōrum *m.pl.* Pompeii
rēgīna, rēgīnae *f.* queen
rēs, reī *f.* thing; matter, affair, situation, problem, trouble ... [reify]
   (*This is Latin's catch-all, thingamajig word.*)
rex, rēgis *m.* king [regal]
rūs, rūris *n.* the country, countryside [rural]
tempus, temporis *n.* time [temporal]
urbs, urbis *f.* city [urban]
uxor, uxōris *f.* wife [uxorious]
virgō, virginis *f.* young woman [virgin]

Prepositions

prope (+ *accusative*) near [propinquity]
trans (+ *accusative*) across, over [transport]

Verbs

habitō (1) to live (*in a place*), dwell, inhabit [habitat]
nāvigō (1) to sail [navigate]

QUIZ

Choose the best translation for each of the following Latin words or phrases.

1. domī
   - (a) in a home
   - (b) at home
   - (c) from home
   - (d) homeward bound

2. in vīcum
   - (a) in the village
   - (b) from the village
   - (c) to the village
   - (d) concerning the village

3. Rōmā
   - (a) from Rome
   - (b) to Rome
   - (c) around Rome
   - (d) in Rome

4. Pompēiōs
   - (a) in Pompeii
   - (b) to Pompeii
   - (c) from Pompeii
   - (d) near Pompeii

5. rūrī
   - (a) toward the country
   - (b) from the country
   - (c) in the country
   - (d) by means of the country

6. in Galliam
   (a) toward Gaul
   (b) into Gaul
   (c) from Gaul
   (d) near Gaul

7. ā Siciliā
   (a) toward Sicily
   (b) from Sicily
   (c) to Sicily
   (d) in Sicily

8. in urbem
   (a) to the city
   (b) near the city
   (c) from the city
   (d) ain't the city

9. Mediolānī
   (a) from Milan
   (b) in Milan
   (c) for Milan
   (d) to Milan

10. humō
    (a) to the ground
    (b) toward the ground
    (c) from the ground
    (d) in the ground

CHAPTER 10

Irregular Verbs

In this chapter, you will learn about:

Irregular Verbs

In comparison with other languages, Latin has surprisingly few irregular verbs. The most common and important ones are presented in this chapter. All but one of these are called *athematic verbs*, i.e., verbs without a theme vowel. For example, you can recognize first-conjugation verbs by their infinitive ending in **-āre**, second-conjugation verbs by **-ēre**, etc. The irregular verbs in this chapter, such as **ferō ferre tulī lātum**, have infinitives without theme vowels.

The Irregular Verb *possum, posse, potuī*

One of the most fundamental verbs in Latin or any language is the verb that expresses ability. In English, we have not only *can,* but also *to be able.* It is critical that English have two ways to express this idea, since *can* is what is called a *defective verb*. A defective verb is one that is missing forms. As an example, *can* has no infinitive (*to can?*), no participles (*I am canning? I have canned?*), and no future tense (*I will can?*). In fact, it has only two forms: a present (*can*) and a simple past (*could*).

(As an aside, there is a verb *to can,* but that verb has to do with pickles and tomatoes, not ability. To complicate matters, you can say *I can can,* to announce your ability to preserve fruits and vegetables, but then you could also be saying that you are dancing a certain French dance.)

English gets around the deficiencies of the verb *can* by using the phrase *to be able*: *I am able, I have been able, I will be able,* etc.

Latin also had a single verb to express ability, **queō**, but it had become rather archaic by the time of Classical Latin, which is what we are studying. (*Classical Latin* refers to a stage in the language's development, roughly from the late first century B.C.E. to the early/mid-first century C.E.) By this point, a Latin parallel to English's *to be able* had appeared: a combination of the words **potis** (*able*) and **sum** (*to be*). Those two words contracted into the irregular verb **possum**.

If you have learned the irregular present, imperfect, and future tense forms of the verb **sum**, **possum** will be a piece of cake. Here are the formation rules. (Keep in mind that it is a contraction of the words **potis** and **sum**. The word **potis** loses its **-is**, so the contraction is actually between **pot-** and **sum**.)

1. When **pot-** appears before a form of **sum** that begins with **s-**, the **t** changes to **s**.

2. When **pot-** appears before **f-**, the **f** disappears.

3. The infinitive **posse** marches to a different linguistic drum and is best memorized as it is: **posse**.

Given these rules,

> **pot-** + **sum** becomes **possum**
> *but* **pot** + **est** becomes **potest**
> *and* **pot** + **erant** becomes **poterant**.

N.B. In my personal experience of teaching Latin, learners of the language sometimes confuse the perfect system tense forms of **possum** with those of **pōnō** (*to put*). The perfect stems are **potu-** and **posu-**, respectively, so **potuit** (*he was able*) is often mixed up with **posuit** (*he put*). Please be mindful of this potential trap—let the **t** of **pot-** be your guide, if you are not sure.

These formation rules may be clearer with charts showing how the verb appears in the various tenses. As always, the tenses of the perfect system, i.e., the perfect, pluperfect, and future perfect, are formed the same way, regardless of which conjugation they belong to, even if they are irregular.

possum, posse, potuī to be able

Present Tense

possum	possumus
potes	potestis
potest	possunt

Perfect Tense

potuī	potuimus
potuistī	potuistis
potuit	potuērunt

Imperfect Tense

poteram	poterāmus
poterās	poterātis
poterat	poterant

Pluperfect Tense

potueram	potuerāmus
potuerās	potuerātis
potuerat	potuerant

Future Tense

poterō	poterimus
poteris	poteritis
poterit	poterunt

Future Perfect Tense

potuerō	potuerimus
potueris	potueritis
potuerit	potuerint

Written Practice 10-1

Translate the following verb phrases into Latin.

1. they had been able   _____

2. they will have been able   _____

3. you (*pl.*) could   _____

4. you (*sg.*) will be able   _____

5. they used to be able   _____

6. we can   _____

7. you (*sg.*) had been able   _____

8. I can   _____

9. they are able   _____

10. he will be able   _____

Using Infinitives

Infinitives are peculiar verb forms. They express the general idea behind a verb, but don't (**in-** (*no*)) have personal endings (**-fin-** (*ending*)). In other words, they don't show any possible person to whom they may be applying—the possibilities are infinite (which is where we get the word *infinitive*).

Infinitives in Latin are also peculiar, because they come in three tenses that are really not tenses at all. The ***present infinitive***, which is the only one you have seen so far, actually does not show present time. English usually, but not always, forms it by placing *to* in front of the simple present tense form of a verb. For example, the present infinitive of *make* is *to make*.

The present infinitive refers to something happening at the same time as the main verb of a sentence. It should really be called the "same time" infinitive. It is called "present" merely because it is a member of the present system of verb forms.

If you are curious as to what the other two Latin infinitives might be, they are the ***perfect infinitive*** (e.g., *to have made*), which refers to an act completed before the main verb, and the ***future infinitive***, which denotes something happening after the main verb. There really isn't anything even remotely close to a future infinitive in English; the closest you can come to a standardized translation of a Latin future infinitive might be *to be about to make,* or *to intend to make.*

We will explore these other infinitives in greater depth in a later chapter. For the moment, we will stay with the present infinitive, which you have learned to recognize as a verb's second principal part.

Complementary Infinitives

There are four main infinitive uses in Latin, three of which are presented in this chapter. Among the most common of these uses is the ***complementary infinitive***. Complementary infinitives get their name from the fact that they ***complete*** the notion expressed by the main verb.

    Nunc optō.   *I want now.*

Want what? This sentence doesn't really make much sense as it is. Because transitive verbs require direct objects, this sentence leaves the options wide open. You might expect a noun in the accusative. But what if the desire is an action rather than a person, place, thing, or idea? How do you put a *verb* into the accusative!?

Enter the complementary infinitive. It completes the idea and answers the aforementioned question.

    Nunc **īre** optō.   *I want **to go** now.*

When put together, the verbs **īre** and **optō** express a ***complete*** thought. When talking about grammar, the word *complement* refers to something that fills a linguistic slot, which an infinitive can do when the main verb is seeking an action as its direct object. **Īre optō** (*I want to go*) is as linguistically valid as **Dulcia optō** (*I want candy*).

Written Practice 10-2

Translate the following sentences into English.

Vocabulary

hoc this
illud that
libenter gladly
litterae, litterārum *f.pl.* literature, letters (*of the alphabet*)
madidus, madida, madidum drunk
natō (1) to swim
nimis too much
plānē obviously, clearly

1. Omnia facere possunt.

   _____

2. Titus hoc intellegere coepit.

   _____

3. Natāre nesciō ego nam aquam timeō.

   _____

4. Mihi auxilium ferre nōn poterant.

   _____

5. Libenter aut hoc vīnum aut illud bibere optāmus.

   _____

6. Litterās Latīnās legere discere dēbētis. (*There's a double complementary infinitive in this one!*)

   _____

7. Litterās Graecās scrībere sciēbant.

   _____

8. Crās domum pervenīre poteris.

   _____

9. Quintus, fīlius Marcī, bonus esse nescit.

   _____

10. Nimis vīnī bibere coepī itaque iam plānē madidus sum.

    _____

The Irregular Verb *volō, velle, voluī*

The basic idea behind the verb **volō** is *to be willing*. You can see this quite easily in the English derivative *volunteer*. When you volunteer to do something, you are expressing willingness, not necessarily desire. Nevertheless, by extension **volō** can also mean *to wish (for)* or *want*.

The present tense of **volō** is very strange. Its vowel pattern is unlike that of any other verb, and so its forms just have to be memorized. The imperfect and future tense forms, however, behave themselves fairly well. They look like regular third-conjugation verbs. The perfect system tenses are formed normally.

volō, velle, voluī to be willing, want

Present Tense

volō	volumus
vīs	vultis
vult	volunt

Imperfect Tense

volēbam	volēbāmus
volēbās	volēbātis
volēbat	volēbant

Future Tense

volam	volēmus
volēs	volētis
volet	volent

N.B. There is another verb that you might be tempted to confuse with **volō, velle**, namely **volō, volāre**. This second **volō**, however, is first conjugation, so it has the thematic vowel **ā**. An even better clue to help you tell them apart is context, since this other **volō** means *to fly*!

The Irregular Verb *nōlō, nolle, nōluī*

The verb **nōlō** is the opposite of **volō**. It is a contraction of **nōn** and **volō** and means *to be unwilling* or *not to want*. If you compare the following chart with the one for **volō** above, you'll notice that only forms of **volō** with **o** in the first syllable contract.

nōlō, nolle, nōluī to be unwilling, not to want

Present Tense

nōlō	nōlumus
nōn vīs	nōn vultis
nōn vult	nōlunt

Imperfect Tense

nōlēbam	nōlēbāmus
nōlēbās	nōlēbātis
nōlēbat	nōlēbant

Future Tense

nōlam	nōlēmus
nōlēs	nōlētis
nōlet	nōlent

Written Practice 10-3

Translate the following verb phrases into Latin.

1. I have wanted   _____
2. you (*pl.*) will be willing   _____
3. he doesn't want   _____
4. they used to want   _____
5. you (*sg.*) are not willing   _____
6. we had wanted   _____
7. they will not have been willing   _____
8. you (*pl.*) do not want   _____
9. I was unwilling   _____
10. she will want   _____

Objective Infinitives

Earlier in this chapter, you learned about complementary infinitives. That's when the infinitive works together with the main verb to express a complete idea, and both actions refer to the subject of the main verb.

> Gāius cēnam parāre vult.   *Gaius wants to prepare dinner.*

In this example, Gaius is the one wanting (**vult**). He is also the one who would be preparing (**parāre**).

The *objective infinitive* construction works much the same way, but with one important difference—and that difference is what gives the construction its name. In this instance, the infinitive goes with the *direct object* of the main verb. Here is an example.

> Gāius tē cēnam parāre vult.   *Gaius wants you to prepare dinner.*

Gaius is still the one wanting (**vult**), but *you* would be the one preparing dinner (**tē cēnam parāre**). **Tē** is in the accusative case, because it is the direct object of the main verb **vult**. **Cēnam** is in the accusative, because it is the direct object of **parāre**.

Another way to look at this grammatical construction is the following.

> [Gāius   (tē cēnam parāre)   vult.]
> SUBJECT   DIRECT OBJECT   VERB

This is classic Latin word order: The verb goes at the end. **Gāius** is the subject of **vult**, and **tē-cēnam-parāre** is what he **vult**. In this sentence, rather than just a direct object in the accusative, there is a string of words working as a unit to express what is ultimately the direct object.

This string of words acting as a single unit is called an *infinitive phrase*. An infinitive phrase consists of an accusative subject and an infinitive, and sometimes additional words, which are located between the accusative subject and the infinitive. Let's take a closer look at this infinitive phrase itself.

> … tē   cēnam   parāre …
>   SUBJECT   DIRECT OBJECT   VERB

Once again, you see classic Latin word order. The phrase is actually a sort of sub-sentence within the main sentence.

If you are alarmed at a verb having an accusative subject, don't be. Infinitives always require a subject in the accusative. They do in English as well! For example, are you more likely to say *Joe wants **he** to prepare dinner* or *Joe wants **him** to prepare dinner?* In English, *he* is nominative while *him* is accusative.

Written Practice 10-4

Identify which infinitive use (complementary or objective) is demonstrated in each of the following sentences, and then translate the sentence into English.

Vocabulary
avunculus, avunculī *m.* uncle (*mother's brother*)
bōs, bovis *c.* ox, cow
hāc this
illō that
iussus, iussūs *m.* order, command
Mīsēnum, Mīsēnī *n.* Misenum (*a town on the bay of Naples*)
proelium, proeliī *n.* battle
sinō, sinere, sīvī, situm to allow, endure
texō, texere, texuī, textum to weave

1. Illō diē Caesar mīlitēs in proelium mittere vōluit. _____

   _____

2. Marcus nōbīscum in Forō convenīre nōn vult. _____

   _____

3. Servīlia Octāviam texere docēre optāvit. _____

   _____ (*There are two infinitives in this sentence.*)

   _____

4. Omnēs in domum coēgī. _____

   _____

5. Lūcium hoc intellegere cōgere coepī. _____

   _____

   _____

6. Stultus bovēs per silvam agere optāvit. _____

   _____

7. Tunc Plīnius cum avunculō Mīsēnō habitābat. _____

_____

8. Tē in hāc urbe manēre nōn sinam. _____

_____

9. Servōs ē domū exīre sine iussū vetābit. _____

_____

10. Gnaeus vōs hīc numquam adesse iam iussit. _____

_____

Impersonal Verbs

There is a small group of verbs in Latin called *impersonal verbs*. These peculiar verbs take some getting used to. In form, they almost always occur in the third-person singular, even though their subject is not a "person" at all. This is why they are called *impersonal*.

For the most part, impersonal verbs employ one of two constructions. The first group takes an accusative to show the person affected and a genitive to show the source of whatever the verb denotes. Of these verbs, perhaps the most common is **taedet, -ēre**, which means *it bores* or *makes tired*. We get the word *tedious* from this Latin word. Rather than be able to come right out and say your friend bores me, **taedet** takes the long way around.

Mē taedet amīcī tuī.   LITERALLY: *It tires me of your friend.*
                                   BETTER: *Your friend tires me.*
                                   BETTER YET: *I am tired of your friend.*

Notice that there is no nominative subject in the Latin sentence.

Here are a few other impersonal verbs that behave this way.

paenitet, paenitēre, paenituit *it causes regret, makes one feel sorry*
    Mē paenitet matris tuae.   LITERALLY: *It causes me regret of your*
                                   mother.
                                   BETTER: *I'm sorry about your mother.*

piget, pigēre, piguit *it annoys, irritates, disgusts*
    Mē piget illius puerī.   LITERALLY: *It annoys me of that boy.*
                                   BETTER: *That kid bugs me.*

pudet, pudēre, puduit *it causes shame*

 Mē pudet fīliī meī.   LITERALLY: *It shames me of my son.*
            BETTER: *I am ashamed of my son.*

The second group of impersonal verbs mostly uses dative case to show the person affected and usually has an infinitive phrase for the subject. This brings us to our third infinitive use.

Subjective Infinitives

If you want to use a verb as the subject of a sentence, you can't put it in nominative case. Instead, you use an infinitive. We do this in English as well, although you see other constructions more often. You are probably familiar with the following expression, albeit not in the original Latin.

 Errāre est hūmānum.   *To err is human.*

More common English constructions to express this would be *Erring is human* or, even more common, *It is human to err.*

Clearly, the subject of **est** in this sentence is the infinitive **errāre**; hence, we use the term ***subjective infinitive***.

As mentioned above, there is a second group of impersonal verbs that uses infinitives as subjects. The most frequently seen is **licet, -ēre** (*it is allowed, may*). (Incidentally, **licet** is also how Romans said "okay.")

 Nunc nōbīs discēdere licet.   LITERALLY: *It is allowed for us to leave now.*
             BETTER: *We may leave now.*

Here are several other impersonal verbs that have a dative for the person affected.

oportet, oportēre, oportuit *it is proper; should, ought*

 Nunc nōbīs discēdere oportet.   LITERALLY: *It is proper for us to leave now.*
             BETTER: *We ought to leave now.*

placet, placēre, placuit *it is pleasing*

 Nunc nōbīs discēdere placet.   LITERALLY: *It is pleasing to us to leave now.*
             BETTER: *We'd like to leave now.*

necesse est *it is necessary*

Nunc nōbīs discēdere necesse
est.

LITERALLY: *It is necessary for us to leave
now.*
BETTER: *We have to leave now.*

One impersonal verb prefers to use an accusative to refer to the person
affected.

decet, decēre, decuit *it is right/suitable; should*

Nunc discēdere nōs decet.

LITERALLY: *It is suitable that we leave now.*
BETTER: *We should leave now.*

Written Practice 10-5

Translate the following sentences into English.

Vocabulary

adventus, adventūs *m.* arrival
aliquandō sometimes
commissātiō, commissātiōnis *f.* party
eum him
factum, factī *n.* deed, action
hanc (*f. accusative sg.*) this
illius (*m. genitive sg.*) of that person
quid what
suus, sua, suum his/her/its/their

1. Factōrum suōrum eum nōn pudet.

   _____

2. Iam tē redīre nōn licet.

   _____

3. Eum amāre aliquandō difficile est.

   _____

4. Quid tibi ad cēnam placuit?

   _____

5. Nihil mē paenitet.

   _____

6. Adventūs Titī Lūcium valdē piget.

_____

7. Publium in commissātiōne relinquere nōs nōn decuit.

_____

8. Illius hominis mē taedet.

_____

9. Caesarī hanc epistulam statim legere necesse erat.

_____

10. Apud mē pernoctāre tibi oportet.

_____

The Irregular Verb _eō, īre, iī (īvī), itum_

The poor little irregular verb **eō** (_to go_), when conjugated, looks like a verb ending in search of a stem. The best it gets in that search, however, is an array of prefixes. As a consequence, when you see what appears to be a prefix with verb endings, it is most likely a compound verb of **eō**. If **eō** is _I go,_ **redeō** is _I go back,_ **adeō** is _I go toward,_ and so on. The last section of this chapter discusses prefixes.

The verb **eō** has a unique vowel pattern in present tense. In the imperfect and future, the verb stem is **ī-**. This is the only verb for which this is true. It is also the only irregular verb that uses the **-bō, -bi-, -bu-** approach to forming future tense. All the other irregular verbs form future tense like third-conjugation verbs.

eō, īre, iī (īvī), itum to go

Present Tense		Perfect Tense	
eō	īmus	iī	iimus
īs	ītis	iistī (OR istī)	iistis (OR istis)
it	eunt	iit	iērunt

Imperfect Tense		Pluperfect Tense	
ībam	ībāmus	ieram	ierāmus
ībās	ībātis	ierās	ierātis
ībat	ībant	ierat	ierant

Future Tense

ībō	ībimus	ierō	ierimus
ībis	ībitis	ieris	ieritis
ībit	ībunt	ierit	ierint

Future Perfect Tense

Written Practice 10-6

Translate the following verb phrases into Latin.

1. we are going   _____
2. I have gone   _____
3. they will go   _____
4. you (*sg.*) had gone _____
5. you (*pl.*) used to go _____
6. he will have gone   _____
7. I do go   _____
8. they had gone   _____
9. you (*pl.*) will go   _____
10. she went   _____

The Irregular Verb *ferō, ferre, tulī, lātum*

Like the irregular verb **volō** (*to be willing*), **ferō** (*to carry, bring, bear*) is athematic. You can see this quite clearly by its infinitive **ferre**, where the theme vowel is lacking. As with most irregular verbs, **ferō** has irregular forms only in present tense. The imperfect and future tenses are formed as if it were a regular third-conjugation verb.

The real trick with this verb is getting used to its strange principal parts. When you come across **tulī**, your mind will take a while to make an immediate association between it and **ferō**. The same will be true when you're learning what to do with the fourth principal part, **lātum**.

The truth of the matter is that the forms of **ferō** are cobbled together from three different verbs. We also have this phenomenon in English. For example, the English forms *is, was,* and *been* are from three separate verbs. The past tense we use for *to go* (i.e., *went*) is actually the past tense of the verb *to wend*.

ferō, ferre, tulī, lātum to carry, bring, bear

Present Tense

ferō	ferimus
fers	fertis
fert	ferunt

Perfect Tense

tulī	tulimus
tulistī	tulistis
tulit	tulērunt

Imperfect Tense

ferēbam	ferēbāmus
ferēbās	ferēbātis
ferēbat	ferēbant

Pluperfect Tense

tuleram	tulerāmus
tulerās	tulerātis
tulerat	tulerant

Future Tense

feram	ferēmus
ferēs	ferētis
feret	ferent

Future Perfect Tense

tulerō	tulerimus
tuleris	tuleritis
tulerit	tulerint

Written Practice 10-7

Translate the following verb phrases into Latin.

1. it carried   _____
2. you (*sg.*) will bring   _____
3. they had brought   _____
4. you (*pl.*) carry   _____
5. we used to bring   _____
6. I will have carried   _____
7. you (*sg.*) are bringing   _____
8. they do carry   _____
9. we will bring   _____
10. to bring   _____

Prefixes

The word *prefix* comes from Latin **prae** (*in front*) and **fixus** (*attached*). A prefix is an extra syllable or two attached to the beginning of a word in order to make its meaning more precise. In Latin, most prefixes are also used as prepositions. There are a few, however, that never appear independently.

The most common prefixes are listed below, but before we take a look at them, there are a couple of important phonetic rules you should be aware of.

The first of these rules is *assimilation*. Some prefixes that end in a consonant alter that consonant to match the first consonant of the word they are being attached to. For example, when the prefix **ad-** is added to **ferō**, the result is **afferō**.

The second phonetic rule is *vowel weakening*. Here, the vowel in the first syllable of the main word can shift a little. If you add **re-** to **teneō**, you get **retineō**; adding **dis-** to **facilis** results in **difficilis**.

Prefix	English Meaning	Latin Example(s)
ā-, ab-	*away, from*	absum *to be away*
ad-	*to, toward, near*	adeō *to go toward*, appōnō *to put near*
circum-	*around*	circumeō *to go around*
dē-	*down, from, off*	dēiciō *to throw down*
dis-/dī-	*apart, not*	discēdō *to go away*, difficilis *not easy*
ē-, ex-	*out*	ēdūcō *to lead out*
in-	*in, into, on, against*	inclūdō *to shut in*, immittō *to send in*
in-	*not*	immortālis *not mortal*
inter-	*between, among*	interveniō *to come between*
ob-	*opposite, against*	occurrō *to run into*
prae-	*in front of, before*	praemittō *to send ahead*
praeter-	*past, beyond*	praetereō *to go past*
prō-	*in front, ahead*	prōvideō *to see ahead*
re-	*back, again*	redeō *to go back*, reficiō *to do again*
sub-	*under, a little bit*	suppōnō *to put under*, subrīdeō *to grin*
super-	*above, over*	supersedeō *to sit above*
trans-	*across, over*	transmittō *to send across*, trādō *to hand over*

Other prefixes can also serve double duty. Not only do they function as their corresponding prepositions suggest, but they also serve as *intensifiers*. Intensifying prefixes do what their name suggests: They make things more intense. The most common of these are **con-** and **per-**.

The prefix **con-** is related to the preposition **cum** (*with*); used in this sense, there are words like **conveniō** (*to come together*). **Con-** can also be used as an intensifying prefix, as in **compleō** (*to fill up completely*).

Per- is probably the most common intensifying prefix. As a preposition, it means *through*, as in **perdūcō** (*to lead through*). As an intensifying prefix, **per-** means *thoroughly*. If **territus** means *afraid*, **perterritus** means *scared to death*. This prefix can also change a verb's meaning in surprising ways. For example, **perveniō** can mean *to come through*, but it usually means *to arrive* (to come so close that you can't come any closer). The verb **pereō** literally means *to go through*, but most of the time it is a nice way of saying *to die*, similar to the English expression *to pass away*.

Written Practice 10-8

See if you can guess what these words mean.

1. supersum   _____
2. circumveniō   _____
3. illicet   _____
4. interstō   _____
5. referō   _____
6. convocō   _____
7. perficiō   _____
8. oppōnō   _____
9. reclūdō   _____
10. irrevocābilis   _____

Key Vocabulary

Learn the following new words, in addition to the irregular and impersonal verbs presented in this chapter.

Adjectives

necesse necessary
stultus, stulta, stultum stupid, foolish [stultify]

Adverb

valdē very, very much, really, strongly [valid]

Conjunctions

itaque and so, therefore
nam because, since, for

Nouns

epistula, epistulae *f.* letter [epistle]
proelium, proeliī *n.* battle
vīnum, vīnī *n.* wine [vineyard]

Verbs

cōgō, cōgere, coēgī, coactum to compel, force, drive, gather [cogent]
intellegō, intellegere, intellexī, intellectum to understand [intelligent]
iubeō, iubēre, iussī, iussum to order [jussive]
placeō, placēre, placuī, placitum to please, be pleasing (*This verb is not always used impersonally.*)
vetō, vetāre, vetuī, vetitum to forbid [veto]

QUIZ

Choose the best translation for each of the following verbs or sentences.

1. tulerat

    (a) she is boring

    (b) he will have taken

    (c) it carries

    (d) he had brought

2. Tibi hoc vetāre oportēbit.

    (a) He will bring this old man to you.

    (b) It was proper that you denied this.

    (c) To forbid this will be the right thing for you to do.

    (d) You have the chance to say no to this.

3. periit

    (a) he is going through

    (b) he was perishing

    (c) he died

    (d) she has regretted

4. Nihil Titum pudēbat.

    (a) Titus was ashamed of nothing.

    (b) Titus could do nothing.

    (c) Nothing bored Titus.

    (d) Nothing disgusted Titus.

5. nōluimus

    (a) we were unwilling

    (b) we had to

    (c) we don't want

    (d) we won't

6. Quid mē facere voluerant?

    (a) Why do they want me to do (this)?

    (b) What had they wanted me to do?

    (c) Who wants pizza?

    (d) What will I want to do?

7. Quid facere poterās?

    (a) What are you ashamed to do?

    (b) What did you used to be able to do?

    (c) What can you do?

    (d) What will you do?

8. Nihil facere tibi nōn decuit.

    (a) It wasn't right for you to do nothing.

    (b) It isn't right for you to do nothing.

    (c) It won't be right for you to do nothing.

    (d) It's right for you to have done nothing.

9. Lūciī mē pigēbat.

    (a) Lucius used to bore me.

    (b) Lucius used to annoy me.

    (c) I was ashamed of Lucius.

    (d) Lucius felt sorry for me.

10. Servōs omnia parāre iusserit.

    (a) She ordered the slaves to get everything ready.

    (b) She will have ordered the slaves to get everything ready.

    (c) She had ordered the slaves to get everything ready.

    (d) She will order the slaves to get everything ready.

PART TWO TEST

Choose the option that best describes each of the following words, phrases, and sentences.

1. puellīs laetīs
   (a) nominative
   (b) genitive
   (c) accusative
   (d) ablative

2. mīlitis omnis
   (a) nominative
   (b) genitive
   (c) accusative
   (d) ablative

3. canī parvō
   (a) nominative
   (b) dative
   (c) genitive
   (d) ablative

4. aquā dulcī
   (a) nominative
   (b) genitive
   (c) accusative
   (d) ablative

5. oculōrum pulchrōrum
   (a) nominative
   (b) genitive
   (c) accusative
   (d) ablative

6. hominēs malōs
    (a) nominative
    (b) genitive
    (c) accusative
    (d) ablative

7. dominī gravis
    (a) nominative
    (b) genitive
    (c) accusative
    (d) ablative

8. silvārum ingentium
    (a) nominative
    (b) genitive
    (c) accusative
    (d) ablative

9. magna māter
    (a) nominative
    (b) genitive
    (c) accusative
    (d) ablative

10. virīs bonīs
    (a) nominative
    (b) genitive
    (c) accusative
    (d) ablative

11. perīculum
    (a) nominative singular
    (b) ablative singular
    (c) accusative plural
    (d) adverb

12. imperia
    (a) dative plural
    (b) nominative plural
    (c) genitive singular
    (d) adverb

13. hodiē
    (a) ablative singular
    (b) nominative singular
    (c) dative plural
    (d) adverb

14. numquam
    (a) accusative singular
    (b) genitive plural
    (c) nominative singular
    (d) adverb

15. corporum
    (a) accusative singular
    (b) genitive plural
    (c) genitive singular
    (d) adverb

16. corpore
    (a) ablative singular
    (b) nominative plural
    (c) dative singular
    (d) adverb

17. perīcula
    (a) nominative singular
    (b) genitive singular
    (c) accusative plural
    (d) adverb

18. clārō

    (a) ablative singular

    (b) accusative singular

    (c) accusative plural

    (d) adverb

19. puella

    (a) ablative singular

    (b) nominative singular

    (c) genitive plural

    (d) adverb

20. gravis

    (a) nominative singular

    (b) nominative plural

    (c) accusative singular

    (d) adverb

21. intulimus

    (a) perfect

    (b) pluperfect

    (c) future perfect

    (d) present

22. manēbō

    (a) future

    (b) present

    (c) imperfect

    (d) future perfect

23. ambulāverint

    (a) pluperfect

    (b) imperfect

    (c) future perfect

    (d) perfect

24. properābis
    (a) present
    (b) imperfect
    (c) pluperfect
    (d) future

25. laudāvērunt
    (a) future perfect
    (b) pluperfect
    (c) present
    (d) perfect

26. rogant
    (a) future perfect
    (b) imperfect
    (c) future
    (d) present

27. cadunt
    (a) perfect
    (b) pluperfect
    (c) future
    (d) present

28. fugiunt
    (a) future
    (b) pluperfect
    (c) present
    (d) imperfect

29. vincis
    (a) future
    (b) present
    (c) future perfect
    (d) pluperfect

30. habēbātis
    (a) future
    (b) present
    (c) imperfect
    (d) pluperfect

31. domum
    (a) in the house
    (b) at home
    (c) from home
    (d) homeward bound

32. ā vīcō
    (a) in the village
    (b) from the village
    (c) to the village
    (d) concerning the village

33. Rōmae
    (a) from Rome
    (b) to Rome
    (c) around Rome
    (d) in Rome

34. Pompēiōs
    (a) in Pompeii
    (b) to Pompeii
    (c) from Pompeii
    (d) near Pompeii

35. rūs
    (a) toward the country
    (b) from the country
    (c) in the country
    (d) by means of the country

36. in Germāniam

   (a) toward Germany

   (b) into Germany

   (c) from Germany

   (d) near Germany

37. ad Sardiniam

   (a) toward Sardinia

   (b) from Sardinia

   (c) to Sardinia

   (d) in Sardinia

38. in oppidum

   (a) to the town

   (b) near the town

   (c) from the town

   (d) on the town

39. Athēnās

   (a) from Athens

   (b) in Athens

   (c) at Athens

   (d) to Athens

40. humī

   (a) to the ground

   (b) toward the ground

   (c) from the ground

   (d) on the ground

41. fert

   (a) she does

   (b) he will have taken

   (c) it carries

   (d) he had brought

42. Nōbīs hīc manēre oportet.

    (a) He is bringing us here this morning.

    (b) We ought to stay here.

    (c) We had to stay here.

    (d) We regret to have to warn you of this.

43. perveniēs

    (a) you will arrive

    (b) you arrived

    (c) you will have arrived

    (d) you will regret

44. Nihil Titum piget.

    (a) Titus is ashamed of nothing.

    (b) Titus can eat nothing.

    (c) Nothing annoys Titus.

    (d) Nothing bores Titus.

45. nōlumus

    (a) we are unwilling

    (b) we are warning

    (c) we want

    (d) we won't

46. Tē hoc facere nōlent.

    (a) They won't want you to do this.

    (b) They don't want you to do this.

    (c) This needed to be done by you.

    (d) They will forbid you to do this.

47. Quid facere potes?

    (a) What are you ashamed to do?

    (b) What can you do?

    (c) What will you be able to do?

    (d) What will you regret doing?

48. conveniēmus

    (a) we gathered

    (b) we were getting together

    (c) we will have come together

    (d) we will meet

49. Lūciī mē taedet.

    (a) Lucius used to bore me.

    (b) Lucius used to annoy me.

    (c) I am tired of Lucius.

    (d) Lucius felt sorry for me.

50. Rōmam īre tibi necesse erit.

    (a) You have to go to Rome.

    (b) You had to go away from Rome.

    (c) You won't be able to head for Rome.

    (d) You will have to go to Rome.

PART THREE

ADVANCED GRAMMAR

CHAPTER 11

Pronouns

In this chapter, you will learn about:

More About Personal Pronouns
Demonstrative Adjectives/Pronouns
Reflexive Pronouns
Intensive Adjectives/Pronouns
Relative Pronouns
Key Vocabulary

More About Personal Pronouns

You were introduced to personal pronouns in Chapter 3, but only those for first and second person, singular and plural. As a refresher, here they are again.

	First Person		**Second Person**	
	Singular	**Plural**	**Singular**	**Plural**
Nominative	ego	nōs	tū	vōs
Genitive	meī	nostrī	tuī	vostrī
Dative	mihi	nōbīs	tibi	vōbīs
Accusative	mē	nōs	tē	vōs
Ablative	mē	nōbīs	tē	vōbīs

The nominative case forms for these pronouns are not necessary, since the personal endings on verbs make it quite clear who the subject is. An **-ō** ending is *I,* and I am I. Period. The nominative forms for these personal pronouns only provide emphasis.

Crās Rōmam redībō.	*I am returning to Rome tomorrow.*
Ego crās Rōmam redībō.	*I* (as opposed to someone else) *am returning to Rome tomorrow.*

Pronouns for third-person singular and plural are not as simple as they are in English. In Latin, they get complicated. They are quite specific as to who this other person is. For example, there are five different ways to say *he,* depending on just which "he" you are referring to. The same goes for *she, it,* and *they.*

Hic is *he* referring to this guy over here near me, the speaker.

Iste is *he* referring to that guy near you, the person I am speaking to.

Ille is *he* referring to that guy over there not near either of us.

Is is *he* referring to the guy we were just talking about.

Ipse is an emphasized sort of *he* referring to him and him alone, as in *he himself.*

Actually, these words really aren't pronouns at all. The first four are ***demonstrative adjectives*** being used as substantives. A substantive, as you may recall, is an adjective that acts like a noun. For example, **bonus** can mean *a good man,* even though the word **vir** isn't there. *Man* is understood, since the form **bonus** is masculine.

Demonstrative Adjectives/Pronouns

Demonstrative adjectives are so named because they demonstrate or point something out. There are two demonstrative adjectives in English: *this* and *that.* Incidentally, these are the only two adjectives left in English that change forms to agree in number. Their plurals are *these* and *those.*

Latin has four demonstrative adjectives, each pointing out something from the vantage point of the speaker. You might think of them as corresponding to the grammatical person of verbs. For example, first person (*I*) refers to the speaker, and **hic** (*this*) refers to something near the speaker, and so on. Let's explore each of these four in turn.

hic, haec, hoc "this"

This adjective finds a direct correspondence to the English demonstrative *this,* although it can also refer to *the latter* of two things. All demonstrative adjectives have a distinct declension pattern, but the chart for **hic** is extremely idiosyncratic.

hic, haec, hoc this, the latter

		Masculine	Feminine	Neuter
Singular	Nominative	hic	haec	hoc
	Genitive	huius	huius	huius
	Dative	huic	huic	huic
	Accusative	hunc	hanc	hoc
	Ablative	hōc	hāc	hōc
Plural	Nominative	hī	hae	haec
	Genitive	hōrum	hārum	hōrum
	Dative	hīs	hīs	hīs
	Accusative	hōs	hās	haec
	Ablative	hīs	hīs	hīs

If you look closely, especially at the plural forms, you will recognize first- and second-declension forms that you already know. In the singular, the ablative has the usual vowels despite the pesky **c**. You'll notice that in the accusative, the normal **m** changes to **n** in front of the **c**. This is only to make the word easier to pronounce.

Written Practice 11-1

Change each of the following adjective-noun pairs from singular to plural or from plural to singular, and then identify the case. If more than one case is possible, give the forms for and identify both cases.

1. hoc vīnum   _____   _____

2. hāc epistulā   _____   _____

3. hī deī   _____   _____

4. hārum noctium   _____   _____

5. hīs rēgibus   _____   _____

6. haec tempora   _____   _____

7. huic virginī   _____   _____

8. hic puer   _____   _____

9. hās rēs   _____   _____

10. huius librī   _____   _____

iste, ista, istud and *ille, illa, illud* "that"

Originally, **iste** referred to something near you (i.e., the person being spoken to) or something of yours. By the late first century B.C.E., however, it had picked up a negative connotation and began referring to something the speaker didn't like. You won't run across it very often.

    Ille, along with **hic**, is quite common. It corresponds to the English demonstrative adjective *that*. It can mean *the former* of two things. Sometimes, it even has a positive spin and can be translated as *that famous*.

    Iste and **ille** are declined in the exact same way. The only difference in form is that one begins with **ist-**, while the other begins with **ill-**. Therefore, looking at just one of them should suffice.

ille, illa, illud that, the former, that famous

		Masculine	Feminine	Neuter
Singular	Nominative	ille	illa	illud
	Genitive	illius	illius	illius
	Dative	illī	illī	illī
	Accusative	illum	illam	illud
	Ablative	illō	illā	illō

		Masculine	**Feminine**	**Neuter**
Plural	Nominative	illī	illae	illa
	Genitive	illōrum	illārum	illōrum
	Dative	illīs	illīs	illīs
	Accusative	illōs	illās	illa
	Ablative	illīs	illīs	illīs

The nominative singular is unique. The genitive has **-ius** all the way across; this is the same **-ius** you just saw in **huius**. The dative **-ī** is third declension. After those three cases, all the rest of the endings are the same as for first and second declension.

Written Practice 11-2

Change each of the following adjective-noun pairs from singular to plural or from plural to singular, and then identify the case. If more than one case is possible, give the forms for and identify both cases.

1. illōrum equōrum _____   _____
2. illa maria _____   _____
3. illius mātris _____   _____
4. illī locō _____   _____
5. illae rēs _____   _____
6. illō mīlite _____   _____
7. illīs virginibus _____   _____
8. illōs cīvēs _____   _____
9. illius templī _____   _____
10. illa puella _____   _____

is, ea, id

Whether you translate this little word as *this* or as *that,* you will be wrong. But since English has no better word for it, *this* or *that* is as close as we can come. Rather than refer to something near me, or you, or over there not near either of us, **is** points toward something just mentioned. It is very common, and you will see it more often used as a pronoun than as an adjective, especially meaning *he, she, it,* or *they.*

| Līvia erat uxor Augustī. Ea duōs fīliōs iam habēbat. | *Livia was Augustus' wife. She* (that woman we were just talking about) *already had two sons.* |

is, ea, id this, that

		Masculine	**Feminine**	**Neuter**
Singular	Nominative	is	ea	id
	Genitive	eius	eius	eius
	Dative	eī	eī	eī
	Accusative	eum	eam	id
	Ablative	eō	eā	eō
Plural	Nominative	eī	eae	ea
	Genitive	eōrum	eārum	eōrum
	Dative	eīs	eīs	eīs
	Accusative	eōs	eās	ea
	Ablative	eīs	eīs	eīs

As you can see, the forms correspond mostly to those of **ille**, with **e-** instead of **ill-**. The nominative singular varies, but the other forms follow the **ille** pattern.

Reflexive Pronouns

Reflexive pronouns are used when a verb refers back to the subject. In English, we use the suffix *-self* or *-selves*. In Latin, for the first and second persons singular and plural, the forms are the same as those of personal pronouns—minus the nominative forms. (The subject can't help but refer to itself, so there is no need for a nominative form!)

In the following sentence, the subject and direct object are different.

| Tū mē in speculō vīdistī. | *You saw me in the mirror.* |

Now let's look at another sentence.

| Ego mē in speculō vīdī. | *I saw myself in the mirror.* |

When the subject is the same as the direct object, English changes the personal pronoun *me* to the reflexive pronoun *myself.* Even though the Latin forms don't change, we translate them differently if the subject is the same as the direct object, as in the second sentence above (**ego** and **mē**). For the third person, there is a special reflexive pronoun, whose forms are not the same as for the personal pronoun.

Nominative	—
Genitive	suī
Dative	sibi
Accusative	sē
Ablative	sē

N.B. The preposition **cum** becomes enclitic when it is used with the third-person reflexive pronoun, so you will see **sēcum**, just like **mēcum**, **nōbīscum**, etc.

The third-person reflexive pronoun has no nominative form, for the reason stated above. The rest of the forms look just like the forms for **tū**, except that they begin with **s-** rather than **t-**. As an added bonus, third-person singular and plural forms of the reflexive pronoun are the same.

Lūcius sē in speculō vīdit.   *Lucius saw himself in the mirror.*

Compare this to the following sentence.

Lūcius eum in speculō vīdit.   *Lucius saw him in the mirror.*

In the second sentence, **eum** does not refer back to the subject (*Lucius*), but to some other guy that we were just talking about.

The concept can get a bit confusing with possession. Recall that with the personal pronouns, the genitive case is never used to show ownership. Instead, the possessive adjectives **meus**, **tuus**, **noster**, and **vester** are used. *My arrival* is **adventus meus.** **Adventus meī** would mean *an arrival of me,* which doesn't make much sense.

For the third person, you can use the genitive of **is**, **hic**, **iste**, or **ille**. If the possessor is the same as the subject, there is a special reflexive possessive adjective: **suus, sua, suum.**

Marcus canem **suum** amat.	*Marcus loves **his** dog.*
Marcus canem **eius** amat.	*Marcus loves **his** dog.*
Marcus canem **huius** amat.	*Marcus loves **his** dog.*
Marcus canem **illius** amat.	*Marcus loves **his** dog.*

These four sentences translate the same into English, but they refer to different dogs. In the first example, the reflexive possessive adjective **suum** informs us that Marcus' affection is for his own dog. In the second, the dog belongs to whatever other person has recently been spoken of (**eius**). In the third, this guy over here (**huius**) owns the dog. In the fourth, the dog is the property of that guy over there (**illius**).

Written Practice 11-3

Translate the following sentences into English.

1. Illā nocte clāmor turbae eōs terruit.

   _____

2. Id sibi retinuit.

   _____

3. Domum suum iam vendiderat.

   _____

4. Fīnēs eōrum tūtī nōn sunt.

   _____

5. Fīnēs suī tūtī nōn sunt.

   _____

6. Caesar suōs aciem istōrum oppugnāre iussit.

   _____

7. Amīcōs omnēs eius in hōc itinere sēcum dūcēbant.

   _____

8. Ubi nuntius pervēnerit, eī omnia scient.

   _____

9. Et haec et illa numquam consensērunt.

   _____

10. Dē hōc tamen heri vōbīs docuī.

    _____

Intensive Adjectives/Pronouns

Intensive adjectives intensify, i.e., emphasize, whatever it is that they are in grammatical agreement with. To put it differently, they serve much the same function as our use of boldface, italics, or underlining—something that occurs frequently as a result of computers.

ipse, ipsa, ipsum "-self"

The greatest challenge with this adjective is that English expresses the same idea that it does with reflexive pronouns, namely, the *-self* suffix. **Ipse** doesn't exactly fit with the earlier group of demonstrative adjectives that also serve as third-person pronouns; it can emphasize any noun or pronoun, even when neither of those is present and a personal ending is your only clue to the subject. Consider these examples.

Eōs audīvī.	*I heard them.*
Ego eōs audīvī.	*I heard them.*
Ipse eōs audīvī.	*I **myself** heard them.*
Ego ipse eōs audīvī.	*I **MYSELF** heard them.*
Eōs audīvī.	*I heard **them**.*
Eōs ipsōs audīvī.	*I heard **them themselves**.*

This adjective/pronoun introduces important distinctions and nuances to the language. This is a major benefit of learning another language: It opens a window to another linguistic world, which, in turn, opens a window onto our own.

īdem, eadem, idem "the same"

Have you ever seen the abbreviation *ibid.*? It is used to refer you back to the last work cited in a bibliography or list of footnotes. It is short for *ibidem,* which means *in the same place.* You already know that **ibi** means *there, in that place.* The **-dem** suffix carries the idea of *the same.* Thus, **ibidem** means *in the same place.* The adjective **īdem** works on the same principle; essentially, it is **is** plus the suffix **-dem.** Don't be fooled by the fact that it appears to decline in the middle—the **-dem** part is only a suffix!

īdem, eadem, idem the same

		Masculine	Feminine	Neuter
Singular	Nominative	īdem	eadem	idem
	Genitive	eiusdem	eiusdem	eiusdem
	Dative	eīdem	eīdem	eīdem
	Accusative	eundem	eandem	idem
	Ablative	eōdem	eādem	eōdem
Plural	Nominative	eīdem	eaedem	eadem
	Genitive	eōrundem	eārundem	eōrundem
	Dative	eīsdem	eīsdem	eīsdem
	Accusative	eōsdem	eāsdem	eadem
	Ablative	eīsdem	eīsdem	eīsdem

Once again, the nominative just has to be memorized as is. Like **hic,** the expected **m** in the accusative singular and genitive plural changes to **n** in front of **-dem,** simply for ease of pronunciation. You will see this linguistic phenomenon again in the next intensive adjective.

quīdam, quaedam, quoddam "a certain, a particular, the"

Previously, you learned that Latin has no words for *a, an,* and *the.* You might have wondered how Latin could get along without them, seeing that *the* is the most common word in the English language. Well, the statement is only half true. The Latin intensive adjective **quīdam** appears in places where English uses *the* to show emphasis.

Consider the difference between these two sentences.

I almost hit a goose on the way to work today.

I almost hit the goose on the way to work today.

In the first sentence, there was just some stray goose. In the second sentence, a certain goose is implied: no random goose, but a particular, maybe even special one. That is the role of *the* in English, and the role of **quīdam** in Latin.

Not unlike **īdem, quīdam** is the relative pronoun **quī, quae, quod** with the suffix **-dam** attached. As with **īdem, quīdam** also appears to decline in the middle rather than the end, which can make its case difficult to identify. Although you haven't learned relative pronouns yet—they are next—here is a chart just to show what **quīdam** looks like.

quīdam, quaedam, quoddam a certain, a particular, the

		Masculine	Feminine	Neuter
Singular	Nominative	quīdam	quaedam	quoddam
	Genitive	cuiusdam	cuiusdam	cuiusdam
	Dative	cuidam	cuidam	cuidam
	Accusative	quendam	quandam	quoddam
	Ablative	quōdam	quādam	quōdam
Plural	Nominative	quīdam	quaedam	quaedam
	Genitive	quōrundam	quārundam	quōrundam
	Dative	quibusdam	quibusdam	quibusdam
	Accusative	quōsdam	quāsdam	quaedam
	Ablative	quibusdam	quibusdam	quibusdam

Relative Pronouns

At this point, you have learned about several types of modifiers for nouns.

Adjectives	*The **brown** dog is snoozing.*
Appositives	*My dog, **a border collie**, is snoozing.*
Prepositional phrases	*The dog **in the yard** is snoozing.*
Genitives	***Fred's** dog is snoozing.*

Relative clauses are another type of modifier. These clauses are introduced by certain words, which include relative pronouns. In fact, the second half of the preceding sentence is a relative clause introduced by the word *which*. Let's look at another example.

*My dog, **who adores me**, is snoozing.*

The relative clause is in boldface. As you can see, it has a subject and a verb. Nevertheless, it cannot stand alone. What do we mean by that? Grammatically, a clause can't stand alone if it depends on something else in order to convey its intended meaning (which is why relative clauses are also dependent clauses). For instance, if we write *Who adores me* as a separate sentence, there's nothing to indicate that the *who* refers to my dog (or anything else, for that matter). Perhaps it will be clearer if we disentangle our example sentence. There are actually two (yes, two!) messages that the sentence is communicating.

My dog adores me.   *My dog is snoozing.*

Rather than say *my dog* twice, the two sentences can be joined. Because pronouns replace nouns, a pronoun is needed to stand in for what is being replaced. Therefore, *my dog* needs to be replaced by a relative pronoun.

My dog adores me.   *My dog who is snoozing.*

Here is a Latin translation of this sentence.

Canis meus, quī mē adōrat, dormit.

The two sentences that comprise this sentence are the following.

Canis meus mē adōrat.   Canis meus dormit.

And so …

Canis meus mē adōrat.   Canis meus quī dormit.

Latin pays far more attention to gender, case, and number than English does, so these factors have to be taken into consideration. The formula is simple. Relative pronouns are called *relative,* because they relate to something else in the sentence. Thus, their *gender* and *number* must agree with the word or phrase that they're modifying (literally, the word or phrase they're related to). Relative pronouns also play a role within the clause they introduce, and this is what determines their *case*.

Let's put this all together by returning to our sleeping canine.

Canis meus	dormit.	
NOMINATIVE SUBJECT	VERB	

Canis meus	mē	adōrat.
NOMINATIVE SUBJECT	ACCUSATIVE DIRECT OBJECT	VERB

And so …

Canis meus,	quī	mē
NOMINATIVE SUBJECT [,]	NOMINATIVE SUBJECT	ACCUSATIVE DIRECT OBJECT

adōrat,	dormit.
VERB [,]	VERB

The relative pronoun form **quī** is masculine singular, because it is related to **canis meus**, which is masculine singular. It is nominative case, because it is acting as the subject in its own clause.

Like virtually all modifiers in Latin, relative clauses follow the words they modify. The word the relative pronoun replaces (i.e., the word it is related to) is called an ***antecedent*** (**ante-** (*before*) + **-cedent** (*goes*)). A relative pronoun agrees in gender and number with its antecedent, but its case depends on its use in its own clause.

The declension of the relative pronoun **quī** is a unique mix of first-, second-, and third-declension endings.

quī, quae, quod who, which, that

		Masculine	Feminine	Neuter
Singular	Nominative	quī	quae	quod
	Genitive	cuius	cuius	cuius
	Dative	cui	cui	cui
	Accusative	quem	quam	quod
	Ablative	quō	quā	quō
Plural	Nominative	quī	quae	quae
	Genitive	quōrum	quārum	quōrum
	Dative	quibus	quibus	quibus
	Accusative	quōs	quās	quae
	Ablative	quibus	quibus	quibus

Written Practice 11-4

Imagine each of the following sentences in Latin, then underline the English relative pronoun and identify its case and number if it were Latin.

1. We saw many bodies that had washed up on the shore from the shipwreck.

   _____

2. Mike, whose son was in the hospital, is getting better now.

   _____

3. My husband just bought a book that I think is silly.

   _____

4. That's the house in which I was born.

   _____

5. That charity to which I contribute appears to be doing work that is good.

   _____

6. I'm afraid of the same dangers that you fear.

   _____

7. They went to the flea market with folks whom I haven't met yet.

   _____

8. I don't know anyone whose bank account is bigger than his.

   _____

9. He did the job with what he had to work with.

   _____

10. Ben wasn't sure to whom he should entrust his future.

    _____

Written Practice 11-5

Translate the following passage into English.

Ubi Graecī pervēnerant, prope mare extrā mūrōs urbis Trōiae castra posuērunt. Eī circum mūrōs urbis cōtīdiē circumībant, sed cōtīdiē omnis porta, quam invēnērunt, semper clausa stetit et Trōiānī eās aperīre nōlēbant. Itaque hoc bellum, quod nōs Bellum Trōiānum appellāmus, decem annōs gerēbant. Erant multa et ācria proelia, in quibus complūrēs virī fortēs prō patriā suā fortiter pugnāvērunt periēruntque. Post eōs decem annōs, tamen, neque Graecī neque Trōiānī vīcerant, atque et hī et illī valdē dēfessī atque miserī erant. Omnēs istud bellum conficere volēbant.

Ulixēs, tamen, quem aliī virum callidum, at aliī scelestum habuērunt, tandem quoddam consilium novum, quod erat et callidum et scelestum, cēpit. Volēbat is enim equum ligneum, ingentem et vacuum, aedificāre, in quō paucī mīlitēs furtim sē cēlāre poterant, deinde, dōnō—immō, dolō—cīvibus Trōiae, hunc equum ad portās urbis afferre atque ibi relinquere.

Mīsērunt Graecī nuntium ad Priamum, rēgem Trōiānōrum, cui ille dixit: "Ō rex, ego ad tē vēnī et tē pauca verba mea audīre volō, sī mihi licet. Vōs superāre nōn possumus nōs nec umquam poterimus. Hoc bene scīmus. Itaque domum redīre aut mox aut quam prīmum volumus. Nunc nostrī magnam statuam dōnō vōbīs aedificant. Cum hanc confēcerimus, in nāvēs nostrās ingrediēmur, et hoc dōnum extrā mūrōs vestrōs, in quōdam locō ubi nōs vōbīs id relīquerimus, inveniētis." Postquam ea verba dolōsa dixit, discessit, ad castra sua rediit, et omnia quae dixerat suīs rettulit.

Vocabulary

callidus, -a, -um clever
clausus, -a, -um closed [close]
complūrēs = **multī**
dolō as a trick (*dative of purpose*)
dolōsus, -a, -um tricky, deceitful
dōnō as a gift (*dative of purpose*) [donate]
habuērunt considered (*from* **habeō**)
ingrediēmur we will get on board
ligneus, -a, -um wooden [ligneous]
Priamus, -ī *m.* Priam (*king of Troy*)
quam prīmum as soon as possible
scelestus, -a, -um evil
Ulixēs, Ulixis *m.* Ulysses
vacuus, -a, -um hollow, empty [vacuum]

Key Vocabulary

Adjectives

alius, alia, aliud another [alias]
　　aliī ... aliī some ... others
dēfessus, -a, -um tired

Adverbs

furtim secretly, stealthily [furtive]
immō actually, on the contrary, rather
tandem finally, at last (*Be careful not to confuse this word with the conjunction* **tamen**.)
umquam ever (*Here is a good memory trick for this one:* **numquam** = n*ever*.)

Conjunctions

enim because, since, you see (*This word is used like the expression* you see *when we're about to explain something that had just been said and needs some clarification. You see, we're not always clear in what we say!*)
sī if
tamen nevertheless, anyway, yet (*Be careful not to confuse this word with the adverb* **tandem**.)

Nouns

bellum gerere to wage war

castra pōnere to pitch camp

consilium, consiliī *n.* plan, advice, consultation; assembly [counsel]
    consilium capere to adopt a plan

mūrus, -ī *m.* wall [mural] (*This word refers to exterior or city walls. The word for interior walls is* **pariēs, parietis** *m.*)

nuntius, nuntiī *m.* messenger; message [announce]

patria, -ae *f.* fatherland, native country [patriotic]

porta, -ae *f.* gate [port]

statua, -ae *f.* statue [statue]

verbum, -ī *n.* word [verb]

Preposition

extrā (+ *acc.*) outside (of) [extra]

Verbs

aedificō (1) to build [edifice]

aperiō, -īre, aperuī, apertum to open, uncover [aperture]

appellō (1) to call (*often by name*) [appellation]

cēlō (1) to hide [conceal]

conficiō, -ere, confēcī, confectum to finish [confection]

gerō, -ere, gessī, gestum to carry; wage (*war*); accomplish; wear (*clothes*) [gestate]

pereō, -īre, periī, peritum to die [perish]

pugnō (1) to fight [pugnacious]

referō, referre, rettulī, relātum to bring back; report; reply [relate]

sciō, scīre, scīvī, scītum to know (*a fact*) [science]

QUIZ

Choose the form of the adjective that agrees with each noun.

1. mūrō
   - (a) huic
   - (b) hic
   - (c) hoc
   - (d) hāc

2. nuntium
   - (a) ille
   - (b) illōrum
   - (c) illud
   - (d) illum

3. statuārum
   - (a) eam
   - (b) eum
   - (c) eārum
   - (d) id

4. patriā
   - (a) illa
   - (b) illā
   - (c) illī
   - (d) illius

5. verbum
   - (a) quīdam
   - (b) quaedam
   - (c) quondam
   - (d) quoddam

6. portās

   (a) eandem

   (b) eaedem

   (c) eundem

   (d) eāsdem

7. mīlitis

   (a) ipsīs

   (b) ipsī

   (c) ipse

   (d) ipsius

8. annō

   (a) hoc

   (b) hic

   (c) hōc

   (d) hunc

9. mātre

   (a) illud

   (b) illī

   (c) illā

   (d) illa

10. maria

   (a) ipsa

   (b) ipsum

   (c) ipsā

   (d) ipse

CHAPTER 12

Passive Voice

In this chapter, you will learn about:

Grammatical Voice

In grammar, the term *voice* refers to the relationship between a verb and its subject. So far, you have only learned ***active voice***. In active voice, the subject performs the action of the verb. ***Passive voice*** turns things around, so that the subject receives the action. In other words, what would have been an accusative direct object is suddenly a nominative subject, but it remains the recipient of the verb's action.

| Active voice | *The mother **is calling** her children.* |
| Passive voice | *The children **are being called** by their mother.* |

Only transitive verbs can be expressed in the passive voice. Transitive verbs, as you know, must have a direct object. Intransitive verbs illustrate a state of being, and therefore do not—cannot—have direct objects.

In English, passive voice is constructed with a form of the verb *to be* plus the past participle. Latin employs two different approaches, one for present system tenses and another for perfect system tenses. The examples above look like this when translated into Latin.

| Active voice | Māter līberōs suōs vocat. |
| Passive voice | Līberī ā mātre suā vocantur. |

Notice how Latin forms passive voice. The subject is in nominative case, but the active personal ending **-t** of **vocat** (*she is calling*) changes to the passive personal ending **-ntur**, resulting in **vocantur** (*they are being called*).

Passive Voice: Present System Tenses

Latin shows passive voice in the present system tenses using a set of personal endings distinct from the ones used for active voice. This chart shows both sets, so you can compare the two.

Active		Passive	
-ō/-m	-mus	-or/-r	-mur
-s	-tis	-ris	-minī
-t	-nt	-tur	-ntur

PRESENT SYSTEM PASSIVE FORMS FOR FIRST- AND SECOND-CONJUGATION VERBS

For the most part, these new passive personal endings replace the old active ones. There are only a few forms where this is not true. The following chart shows the passive voice forms for present system tenses in first- and second-conjugation verbs.

First Conjugation		Second Conjugation	
Present Passive			
portor	portāmur	moneor	monēmur
portāris	portāminī	monēris	monēminī
portātur	portantur	monētur	monentur
Imperfect Passive			
portābar	portābāmur	monēbar	monēbāmur
portābāris	portābāminī	monēbāris	monēbāminī
portābātur	portābantur	monēbātur	monēbantur
Future Passive			
portābor	portābimur	monēbor	monēbimur
portā**beris**	portābiminī	monē**beris**	monēbiminī
portābitur	portābuntur	monēbitur	monēbuntur

In this chart, the second-person singular forms in the future tense have a vowel shift, shown in boldface. The active **-bis** becomes passive **-beris**, with the expected **i** changing to **e**. You will see this vowel pattern again in the present passive of third-conjugation verbs.

Written Practice 12-1

Translate the following verb forms, write the active form of a passive form or the passive form of an active form, and then translate the new form.

1. cēlātis   _____   _____   _____

2. aedificābantur   _____   _____   _____

3. damus   _____   _____   _____

4. docēris   _____   _____   _____

5. habētur   _____   _____   _____

6. laudābit   _____   _____   _____

7. moveō   _____   _____   _____

8. poterant   _____   _____   _____

9. tenēberis   _____   _____   _____

10. amābō   _____   _____   _____

PRESENT SYSTEM PASSIVE FORMS FOR THIRD-CONJUGATION, THIRD-CONJUGATION -*iō,* AND FOURTH-CONJUGATION VERBS

As in active voice, these verb groups stand apart from first- and second-conjugation verbs. In passive voice, third-conjugation **-iō** verbs actually have one form where they behave like regular third-conjugation verbs rather than fourth-conjugation verbs.

The special passive voice personal endings still apply, with only a few stem vowel shifts.

Third Conjugation   **Third Conjugation** -*iō*

Present Passive

agor	agimur	capior	capimur
ag**eris**	agiminī	cap**eris**	capiminī
agitur	aguntur	capitur	capiuntur

Imperfect Passive

agēbar	agēbāmur	capiēbar	capiēbāmur
agēbāris	agēbāminī	capiēbāris	capiēbāminī
agēbātur	agēbantur	capiēbātur	capiēbantur

Future Passive

agar	agēmur	capiar	capiēmur
agēris	agēminī	capiēris	capiēminī
agētur	agentur	capiētur	capientur

Fourth Conjugation

Present Passive

audior	audīmur
audīris	audīminī
audītur	audiuntur

Imperfect Passive

audiēbar	audiēbāmur
audiēbāris	audiēbāminī
audiēbātur	audiēbantur

Future Passive

audiar	audiēmur
audiēris	audiēminī
audiētur	audientur

The important aberration in these conjugations is in the second-person singular ending in present tense. There, for third-conjugation and third-conjugation **-iō** verbs, you find **e** where you would have expected **i**.

Passive Voice: Perfect System Tenses

The perfect system tenses form passive voice in a radically different way. But like the rest of the perfect system tradition, passives are formed in the same way for all verbs, regardless of conjugation or irregularity.

The rules for passive formation in Latin are quite simple. Plus, you finally get to learn a use for the fourth principal part! English constructs its perfect system passive tenses by combining a form of the verb *to be* with the past participle. So does Latin, though in Latin grammar the past participle is called the ***perfect passive participle***. You already know the forms of the irregular verb **sum** (*to be*).

The perfect participle is created on the stem of a verb's fourth principal part, which is actually a form called the ***supine***, which will be discussed in a later chapter. The supine provides the required stem once the final **-um** is dropped. Essentially, all that needs to be done in order to form the perfect passive participle is to take this stem, add **-us**, and treat it like a first/second-declension adjective, which, in fact, it is. (Recall that all participles are verbal adjectives.)

agō, agere, ēgī, act*um* to drive

Perfect passive participle   act**us**, act**a**, act**um** *driven*

Latin being Latin, there is a little more to the story. This chart compares the English and Latin forms.

Perfect Passive (Masculine)

I was driven	*we were driven*	actus sum	actī sumus
you were driven	*you were driven*	actus es	actī estis
he/she/it was driven	*they were driven*	actus est	actī sunt

Pluperfect Passive (Masculine)

I had been driven	*we had been driven*	actus eram	actī erāmus
you had been driven	*you had been driven*	actus erās	actī erātis
he/she/it had been driven	*they had been driven*	actus erat	actī erant

Future Perfect Passive (Masculine)

I will have been driven	*we will have been driven*	actus erō	actī erimus
you will have been driven	*you will have been driven*	actus eris	actī eritis
he/she/it will have been driven	*they will have been driven*	actus erit	actī erunt

Gender has not been an issue with verbs until now. Notice how the participles below agree with the nouns they modify in gender, case, and number.

Equus actus est.	*The horse was driven.*
Equī actī sunt.	*The horses were driven.*
Epistula scripta est.	*The letter was written.*
Epistulae scriptae sunt.	*The letters were written.*
Templum aedificātum est.	*The temple was built.*
Templa aedificāta sunt.	*The temples were built.*

Another thing to pay attention to is the tense of the verb **sum** that is used in each of the perfect tenses. For perfect tense, you find the present tense of **sum**. In the pluperfect, the imperfect tense of **sum** is used, which is a bonus since the tense indicator for the pluperfect active is also **-era-**. Likewise, the tense indicator **-eri-** for the future perfect active appears in the future perfect passive, where the future of **sum** is used.

There is something dissonant (**dis-** (*off*) + **-sonant** (*sounds*)) that will take getting used to. Look again at English and Latin forms in perfect tense.

*he **was** driven*	(*was* = past tense of the verb *to be* in English)
actus est	(**est** = present tense of the verb **sum** in Latin)

Notice anything that sounds a bit off? At this point in your studies, when you see **est**, your knee-jerk reaction is to translate it as *is,* not *was.* Over time, you will grow accustomed to the fact that the perfect passive looks like present active tense—but isn't.

Written Practice 12-2

Translate the following verb forms, write the active form of a passive form or the passive form of an active form, and then translate the new form.

1. audīvistī (*m.*) _____ _____ _____
2. posuerat (*n.*) _____ _____ _____
3. relictus sum _____ _____ _____
4. occīsī erunt _____ _____ _____
5. cēpistis (*m.*) _____ _____ _____
6. facta erant _____ _____ _____
7. coēgimus (*m.*) _____ _____ _____
8. aperuit (*n.*) _____ _____ _____
9. accepta est _____ _____ _____
10. rapuī (*f.*) _____ _____ _____

Passive Infinitives

In Chapter 10, you were introduced to infinitives. An infinitive expresses the idea of a verb without the use of personal endings. The meaning it conveys is that of an action in general. Latin has six different infinitives—three tenses in both voices. The only one that you know so far is the present active infinitive, e.g., **amāre** (*to love*). The present passive infinitive is **amārī** (*to be loved*).

The chart below shows how the present passive infinitive is formed in each conjugation. The endings themselves appear in boldface.

	Active	Passive
First conjugation	am**āre**	am**ārī**
Second conjugation	mon**ēre**	mon**ērī**
Third conjugation	dūc**ere**	dūc**ī**
Third conjugation **-iō**	cap**ere**	cap**ī**
Fourth conjugation	aud**īre**	aud**īrī**

The rules for formation are simple. The final **e** of the active infinitive changes to **ī**. In the case of third conjugation, since the whole ending is basically short **e**, the whole ending changes to **ī**, so **-ere** becomes **-ī**. Also, note that **-iō** verbs behave like regular third-conjugation verbs. These third-conjugation present passive infinitives can be very difficult to recognize if you are accustomed to seeing **-r-** as a cue.

Written Practice 12-3

Write the active and passive infinitives for each of the following verbs, then translate each of the infinitives. Don't forget that intransitive verbs have no passive forms.

1. pōnō _____ _____ _____ _____
   _____ _____ _____ _____

2. dīcō _____ _____ _____ _____
   _____ _____ _____ _____

3. portō _____ _____ _____ _____
   _____ _____ _____ _____

4. aperiō _____ _____ _____ _____
   _____ _____ _____ _____

5. iaciō _____ _____ _____ _____
   _____ _____ _____ _____

6. appellō _____ _____ _____ _____
   _____ _____ _____ _____

7. habeō _____ _____ _____ _____
   _____ _____ _____ _____

8. sentiō _____ _____ _____ _____
_____ _____ _____ _____

9. nōlō _____ _____ _____ _____
_____ _____ _____ _____

10. inveniō _____ _____ _____ _____
_____ _____ _____ _____

Passive of *ferō*

The only transitive irregular verb that you have learned so far is **ferō**. Its passive forms are only irregular in present tense; the other passive forms follow the rules for third conjugation.

ferō, ferre, tulī, lātum to carry, bring

Present Passive
feror   ferimur
ferris   feriminī
fertur   feruntur

Imperfect Passive
ferēbar   ferēbāmur
ferēbāris   ferēbāminī
ferēbātur   ferēbantur

Future Passive
ferar   ferēmur
ferēris   ferēminī
ferētur   ferentur

Present Passive Infinitive
ferrī

Ablative of Agent

Before we put all of the above information about passive voice into practice with sentences, you need to know about the *ablative of agent*.

 This ablative case use is peculiar to sentences with passive verbs. It is introduced by the preposition **ā**, which usually translates as *from* or *away from*. In this ablative use, however, it translates as *by*. It shows the person *by whom* a passive verb's action was done and is used only with people words; otherwise, you use an ablative of means, which doesn't take any preposition.

  Servus **baculō** verberātus est.   *The slave was beaten **with a stick***.

  Servus **ā dominō** verberātus est.   *The slave was beaten **by his master***.

In passive voice, it is not grammatically necessary to identify who or what performed the action. **Servus verberātus est** (*The slave was beaten*) is a complete sentence all on its own. The ablative of agent or means merely provides additional information.

 N.B. When the preposition **ā** is followed by a people word, it is not necessarily an ablative of agent. A passive verb must also be involved. In the following sentence, the verb is active, so the prepositional phrase with **ā** is not an ablative of agent.

  Caesar arma ab hostibus rapuit.   *Caesar took the weapons away from the enemy.*

Written Practice 12-4

Translate the following sentences into English.

Vocabulary

 carcer, carceris *m.* prison
 excitō (1) to awaken
 iam diū for a long time now
 leō, leōnis *m.* lion
 optimus, -a, -um excellent, very good
 sollicitus, -a, -um worried
 Tiberius, Tiberiī *m.* Tiberius
 trīclīnium, trīclīniī *n.* dining room

1. Mox puerī ā mātre suā, quae semper sollicita est, domum revocābuntur, et tristēs erunt quia redīre nōlent.

_____

_____

2. Illī captīvī, quī in carcere etiam manēbant, līberārī cupiēbant.

_____

3. Hī hominēs tamen crās pūnientur.

_____

4. Post multōs annōs, Germānī, quī ā Tiberiō ācriter oppugnātī erant, vincī poterant.

_____

_____

5. Tandem leōnēs, quōs nōs omnēs exspectābāmus, in arēnam ductī sunt.

_____

_____

6. Fīliae miserae eius occīsae erunt antequam reveniet Athēnīs.

_____

7. Illā nocte, ego ipse strepitū, quī ab omnibus audīrī potuit, nōn excitātus sum.

_____

_____

8. Omnia ea perīcula, quae effugere coepimus, etiam valdē timēmus.

_____

_____

9. Cēna optima, quam vōs iam diū exspectātis, mox in trīclīnium nōbīs ā servīs inferētur.

_____

_____

10. Lūcius Tarquinius Superbus rex ā populō Rōmānō numquam creātus est, sed regnum ā patre rapuit, itaque iste ā nēmine amābātur.

_____

_____

Middle Voice

Proto-Indo-European, Latin's mother language, had a third voice called *middle voice,* of which Latin retained a few vestiges. The idea behind middle voice is that the subject performs an action like active voice, but performs it on itself or for its own benefit, or is somehow involved at some deep, personal level with the action.

Active voice   lavat   *he is washing* (an object in the accusative)
Passive voice   lavātur   *he is being washed* (by an ablative of agent or means)
Middle voice   lavātur   *he is bathing* (i.e., *washing himself*)

Notice any potential issue here?

Active and passive voices are distinguished by having their own unique set of personal endings. There is **-ō/-m, -s, -t**, etc., and **-or/-r, -ris, -tur**, etc. Middle voice also announces itself with personal endings. Unfortunately, those endings and forms are identical to those of passive voice. This wouldn't be such an issue if it weren't for the fact that verbs in middle voice *look* passive, but are *translated* as active.

Latin, however, found a way around this dilemma.

Deponent Verbs

In Latin, most of the verbs that employed middle voice were put aside. This class of verbs is called deponent (**dē** (*down, aside*) + **pōn-** (*put*)). They have passive-looking forms, but are translated in the active voice.

Most deponents have regular verb equivalents, but the subtle difference between active and middle voice lies in their sense. For example, the verb **temptō** means *to try,* but **cōnor** means *to try real hard because you have a personal investment in the outcome.* These nuances are easily lost in translation.

A deponent verb is recognized by its principal parts. Let's use these verbs meaning *to try* as examples to illustrate this point (and as a refresher for principal parts).

temptō, temptāre, temptāvī, temptātum to try

temptō	first-person singular, present active
temptāre	present active infinitive
temptāvī	first-person singular, perfect active
temptātum	supine, source of perfect passive participle

cōnor, cōnārī, cōnātus sum to try

cōnor	first-person singular, present passive (*in apparent form*)
cōnārī	present passive infinitive (*in apparent form*)
cōnātus sum	first-person singular, perfect passive (*in apparent form*)

There is no need for a fourth principal part, because these verbs already contain a perfect passive participle in their third principal part.

Most Latin textbooks make deponent verbs into a major production. But if you already know passive voice forms, there is no need to create special charts for them. At minimum, simply remember that deponent verbs have passive-looking forms with active-sounding meanings. The most important and common of these verbs are listed in the Key Vocabulary at the end of this chapter.

Semi-Deponent Verbs

There are four verbs in Latin that can't decide which side of the fence they are on. They are regular in the present system tenses, but deponent in the perfect system tenses. This is why they are called *semi-deponent*.

audeō, audēre, ausus sum to dare

fīdō, fīdere, fīsus sum to trust

gaudeō, gaudēre, gāvīsus sum to rejoice, be happy

soleō, solēre, solitus sum to often/usually (do something), be accustomed to / in the habit of (doing something)

The Irregular Verb *fīō, fierī, factus sum*

This is easily one of the strangest verbs in the Latin language. It is semi-deponent in a way, and yet it is not. It can be translated in almost countless ways, as the noun **rēs** can. Let's look at its forms first. The present system tenses are the ones you need to learn. The perfect system tenses are from the verb **faciō**.

Present

fīō	fīmus
fīs	fītis
fit	fīunt

Imperfect

fīēbam   fīēbāmus
fīēbās   fīēbātis
fīēbat   fīēbant

Future

fīam   fīēmus
fīēs   fīētis
fīet   fīent

The verb **fīō** is more irregular in meaning than in form. In the present system tenses, it looks active, but can translate into English as an active or passive verb. Sometimes, it even has a sort of middle-voice feel to it. The same is true for its perfect system tense forms.

The most basic idea of this verb has to do with coming into being. It can translate not only as *to be made* or *be done,* but also as *to be, become, come into being,* or *happen.* A Roman proverb illustrates this sense of the word: **Cito fit quod dī volunt.** *What the gods want happens quickly.*

Written Practice 12-5

Using the Key Vocabulary at the end of this chapter, translate the following verbs and verb phrases from Latin to English or from English to Latin.

1. experiēbantur   _____

2. verita sum   _____

3. persecūtus eris   _____

4. cōnāminī   _____

5. vīsum erat   _____

6. ēgrediētur   _____

7. they dared (*m.*)   _____

8. we will become   _____

9. she waited   _____

10. she died   _____

11. you (*sg.*) were following   _____

12. I am happy   _____

Written Practice 12-6   Synopsis

Congratulations! Now that you have learned all the tenses and voices, it is time to expand your synopsis chart. There are many more verb forms to come, but if you have mastered all you have encountered so far, you will find that these others are merely variations.

In these new synopsis charts, an extra column has been added to accommodate passive voice. The T shape will help you remember which principal parts are involved in that area. For the forms above the horizontal line, the first two principal parts give you all the information you need. The first principal part tells you whether or not it is an **-iō** verb. The second principal part lets you know which conjugation the verb belongs to. At this point in your study, you know what a crucial piece of information that is! Below the horizontal line, the perfect system tenses are divided into two parts by a vertical line. The forms at the left require the third principal part. The forms at the right (the passive forms) need the fourth principal part.

Remember that as you are writing the forms, when you cross a line, it is time to look to a different principal part for the stem. Also remember that deponent verbs have no active forms, and that semi-deponent verbs are only active above the line, then only passive below it.

1. **legō, legere, lēgī, lectum** *1pl., masculine*

	Active	Passive
Present	_____	_____
Imperfect	_____	_____
Future	_____	_____
Perfect	_____	_____
Pluperfect	_____	_____
Future Perfect	_____	_____

2. **videō, vidēre, vīdī, vīsum** *2sg., feminine*

	Active	Passive
Present	_____	_____
Imperfect	_____	_____
Future	_____	_____
Perfect	_____	_____
Pluperfect	_____	_____
Future Perfect	_____	_____

3. **nascor, nascī, nātus sum** *3pl., masculine*

	Active	Passive
Present	_____	_____
Imperfect	_____	_____
Future	_____	_____
Perfect	_____	_____
Pluperfect	_____	_____
Future Perfect	_____	_____

4. **ferō, ferre, tulī, lātum** *3sg., neuter*

	Active	Passive
Present	_____	_____
Imperfect	_____	_____
Future	_____	_____
Perfect	_____	_____
Pluperfect	_____	_____
Future Perfect	_____	_____

5. **audeō, audēre, ausus sum** *2pl., feminine*

	Active	Passive
Present	_____	_____
Imperfect	_____	_____
Future	_____	_____
Perfect	_____	_____
Pluperfect	_____	_____
Future Perfect	_____	_____

Key Vocabulary

Adverb

etiam still, yet, even, also

Conjunction

quamquam although, even though

Nouns

cēna, -ae *f.* dinner
regnum, -ī *n.* royal power, kingdom, kingship [interregnum]
strepitus, -ūs *m.* noise, ruckus

Verbs

cōnor, cōnārī, cōnātus sum to try, attempt [conative]
creō (1) to create; elect [create]
cupiō, cupere, cupīvī, cupītum to desire, long for, want [Cupid]
experior, experīrī, expertus sum to try, test, prove [experience]
exspectō (1) to wait for [expect]
gradior, gradī, gressus sum to step, go [gradient] (*This verb itself is not very common, but its compounds are. Here is a list of the ones you are likely to encounter.*)
    aggredior, aggredī, aggressus sum to attack, step toward [aggression]
    ēgredior, ēgredī, ēgressus sum to go out, leave [egress]
    ingredior, ingredī, ingressus sum to step in, enter; begin [ingress]

    prōgredior, prōgredī, prōgressus sum to go forward, advance [progress]

    regredior, regredī, regressus sum to go back, return [regression]

līberō (1) to set free [liberate]

loquor, loquī, locūtus sum to talk, speak [loquacious]

mīror, mīrārī, mīrātus sum to wonder at, marvel, be amazed [miracle]

morior, morī, mortuus sum to die [mortuary]

moror, morārī, morātus sum to delay, wait, kill time [moratorium]

nascor, nascī, nātus sum to be born [nativity]

oppugnō (1) to attack [pugnacious]

orior, orīrī, ortus sum to rise [orient]

proficīscor, proficiscī, profectus sum to depart, set out (*on a journey*)

pūniō, pūnīre, pūnīvī, pūnītum to punish [punitive]

sequor, sequī, secūtus sum to follow [sequence]

    consequor, consequī, consecūtus sum to follow closely, pursue, catch up to [consequence]

    persequor, persequī, persecūtus sum to pursue, overtake [persecute]

vereor, verērī, veritus sum to fear, be afraid

videor, vidērī, vīsus sum to seem, appear, be seen (*This verb is actually just the passive of* **videō** *and not a deponent. While it can have the passive meaning* to be seen, *it usually has a more active meaning, like* to seem.*)

QUIZ

Choose the best translation for each of the following verb forms.

1. creātus est
   - (a) he is a creature
   - (b) he was elected
   - (c) he is being elected
   - (d) it has been chosen

2. ēgrediuntur
   - (a) they are being attacked
   - (b) they are leaving
   - (c) they will depart
   - (d) they will be forced

3. nāta erat
   - (a) she had been born
   - (b) they arose
   - (c) she was a dwarf
   - (d) she was giving birth

4. they used to follow
   - (a) secūtī sunt
   - (b) sequēbant
   - (c) sequentur
   - (d) sequēbantur

5. it will seem
   - (a) vidēbitur
   - (b) fīet
   - (c) proficiscentur
   - (d) lasagna

6. oriētur

   (a) he is creating

   (b) she will be chosen

   (c) it has risen

   (d) it will rise

7. mīror

   (a) I see myself

   (b) to be seen

   (c) it's incredible

   (d) I am amazed

8. pūnīrī

   (a) to punish

   (b) to be punished

   (c) you are punished

   (d) you will be punished

9. līberātis

   (a) for the children

   (b) you are free

   (c) you are being freed

   (d) you are setting free

10. ausae sunt

   (a) they were dared

   (b) they dare

   (c) they dared

   (d) they will have been dared

CHAPTER 13

Comparison of Adjectives and Adverbs

In this chapter, you will learn about:

Comparison of Adjectives

Comparison of Adverbs

Ablative of Comparison

Ablative of Degree of Difference

The Adverb quam *with Adjectives and Adverbs*

The Irregular Verb mālō, malle, māluī

Numerals

Adjectives of Special Declension

Key Vocabulary

Comparison of Adjectives

Adjectives describe a quality of something, such as *good* and *quick*. Most adjectives can also show a level of intensity. For example, something can be *good, pretty good,* or *really good*. This is what the grammatical term ***comparison*** refers to. In English, this is expressed by adding words, such as *pretty, rather, too, very, extremely, incredibly,* and so on. When something is being directly compared to something else, however, English adds endings to the adjective, namely, *-er* and *-est* (e.g., *quick, quicker, quickest*).

Latin also has forms for adjectives that express degrees of intensity. **Celer** is *quick*. **Celerior** is *pretty quick*. **Celerrimus** is *incredibly quick*.

Most of the time when you see these adjectival forms in Latin, they are merely showing the intensity of a certain quality.

Titus est fortis.	*Titus is brave.*
Titus est fortior.	*Titus is pretty brave.*
Titus est fortissimus.	*Titus is extremely brave.*

If, however, a direct comparison is being made, then the endings behave more like the English comparative endings *-er* and *-est*.

Titus est fortior quam Gnaeus.	*Titus is braver than Gnaeus.*
Titus est fortissimus omnium mīlitum.	*Titus is the bravest of all the soldiers.*

In Latin, first/second- and third-declension adjectives make their comparative forms in the same way, although adjectives ending in **-er** vary a little from the norm. Some are like the English adjective *fun,* which has no comparative forms and use adverbs to express comparison instead (e.g., *more fun* rather than *funner*). There are also a few adjectives that are completely irregular in the forms they use to express intensity. English has some of these; for instance, the comparative of *bad* is *worse,* not *badder*.

The grammatical term for these levels of intensity is ***degree***. There are three degrees: positive, comparative, and superlative. The ***positive degree*** is the dictionary listing of an adjective. The ***comparative degree*** is used to show comparison or a mid-level of intensity. The ***superlative degree*** is for an extreme level of intensity.

COMPARISON OF REGULAR ADJECTIVES

Comparative and superlative forms are made in the same way for both first/second- and third-declension adjectives.

Positive	Comparative	Superlative
First/Second Declension		
stultus, -a, -um	stultior, stultius	stultissimus, -a, -um
foolish	*rather foolish*	*very foolish*
	sort of foolish	*extremely foolish*
	pretty foolish	*totally foolish*
	too foolish	*amazingly foolish*
	more foolish	*most foolish*
Third Declension		
brevis, breve	brevior, brevius	brevissimus, -a, -um
short	*rather short*	*very short*
	etc.	etc.

Comparatives are third-declension adjectives, with **-ior** being masculine and feminine nominative singular and **-ius** being neuter. Even though they are third-declension adjectives, they are declined like third-declension nouns.

	Masculine	Feminine	Neuter
Singular			
Nominative	brevior	brevior	brevius
Genitive	breviōris	breviōris	breviōris
Dative	breviōrī	breviōrī	breviōrī
Accusative	breviōrem	breviōrem	brevius
Ablative	breviōre	breviōre	breviōre
Plural			
Nominative	breviōrēs	breviōrēs	breviōra
Genitive	breviōrum	breviōrum	breviōrum
Dative	breviōribus	breviōribus	breviōribus
Accusative	breviōrēs	breviōrēs	breviōra
Ablative	breviōribus	breviōribus	breviōribus

This is the declensional pattern for all comparative adjectives, including the irregulars, which we will get to soon. As you no doubt noticed, all superlative adjectives are regular first/second declension, so they don't need their own chart here.

COMPARISON OF ADJECTIVES ENDING IN -er

Adjectives ending in **-er**, regardless of the declension to which their positive degree forms belong, have peculiar superlatives.

Positive	Comparative	Superlative
līber, lībera, līberum	līberior, līberius	līberrimus, -a, -um
pulcher, pulchra, pulchrum	pulchrior, pulchrius	pulcherrimus, -a, -um
ācer, ācris, ācre	ācrior, ācrius	ācerrimus, -a, -um

Clearly, the greatest departure from the norm is in the superlative. Rather than adding **-issimus**, the **-r** of the stem is doubled and only **-imus** is attached. Another thing to note is what happens when an adjective's stem changes. For an adjective with no stem change, the endings are applied directly. For adjectives that do have stem changes, such as **pulcher** and **ācer**, the change appears in the comparative but not in the superlative forms.

A few adjectives that end in **-ilis** follow a similar pattern. Here are the most common of these.

facilis, facile easy
difficilis, difficile difficult
similis, simile like, similar
dissimilis, dissimile unlike, not similar

These adjectives double the **-l** of the stem in the superlative, like **-er** adjectives double the **-r**; for example, the superlative of **facilis** is **facillimus**.

COMPARISON OF IRREGULAR ADJECTIVES

With respect to comparative forms, the English *good* doesn't become *gooder* or *goodest*. Its Latin counterpart, **bonus**, doesn't either. There aren't many Latin adjectives that fall into this category (i.e., that have irregular comparative forms). They all need to be learned by heart. You already know what the positive forms mean. Luckily, almost all of them have English derivatives.

Positive	Comparative	Superlative
bonus, -a, -um	melior, melius	optimus, -a, -um
magnus, -a, -um	maior, maius	maximus, -a, -um
malus, -a, -um	peior, peius	pessimus, -a, -um
parvus, -a, -um	minor, minus	minimus, -a, -um
multus, -a, -um	plūs	plūrimus, -a, -um
multī, -ae, -a	plūrēs, plūra	plūrimī, -ae, -a

The comparative of **multus** has an idiosyncracy—in the singular, **plūs** is a neuter noun. Rather than agree with whatever it is referring to, it takes a genitive, and so *more wine* is **plūs vīnī**, literally, *more of wine,* like we say *a piece of pie.* This use of the genitive is called ***partitive genitive,*** because it shows a part *of* something. This construction is also used with **nihil** (*nothing*), as in **nihil vīnī**, literally, *nothing of wine,* i.e., *no wine.*

In the plural, **plūs** behaves like a normal comparative and agrees with its noun in gender, case, and number. It also bears a slightly different meaning, which is more in line with the other ideas behind the comparative degree.

plūs nāvium	more (of the) ships
plūrēs nāvēs	rather many ships, several ships

Written Practice 13-1

Using the vocabulary that follows, translate the following phrases into Latin in the cases specified.

Vocabulary

albus, -a, -um white
altus, -a, -um tall
bonus, -a, -um good
carmen, carminis *n.* song
celer, celeris, celere fast
commodus, -a, -um convenient
fortis, forte strong
gravis, grave heavy
hōra, -ae *f.* time
malus, -a, -um bad
mons, montis *m.* mountain
multus, -a, -um much
nāvis, nāvis *f.* ship

ōmen, ōminis *n.* omen
ovis, ovis *f.* sheep
parvus, -a, -um small
pōtiō, pōtiōnis *f.* a drink
puella, -ae *f.* girl
saxum, -ī *n.* rock

1. fairly good omens (*nom.*) _____
2. really bad songs (*dat.*) _____
3. white sheep (*gen.pl.*) _____
4. very strong drinks (*abl.*) _____
5. an extremely tall mountain (*abl.*) _____
6. more money (*acc.*) _____
7. the fastest ships (*acc.*) _____
8. a heavy rock (*dat.*) _____
9. a rather small girl (*gen.*) _____
10. a more convenient time (*nom.*) _____

Comparison of Adverbs

Before discussing the comparative forms of adverbs, we should review the simple formation of adverbs from adjectives, which you learned in Chapter 7.

As you recall, the rule to convert most English adjectives into adverbs is simply to add the suffix *-ly,* so *quick* becomes *quickly.* In Latin, it is almost as easy. First/second-declension adjectives add **-ē** to the stem (e.g.. **lentus** (*slow*) becomes **lentē** (*slowly*)). Third-declension adjectives add **-iter** (e.g., **celer** (*quick*) becomes **celeriter** (*quickly*)); those whose nominative and genitive forms end in **-ns, -ntis,** respectively, only add **-er** (e.g., **potens, potentis** (*powerful*) becomes **potenter** (*powerfully*)).

The rules for comparison of adverbs are extremely straightforward. In fact, if you have learned the material so far in this chapter, you already know them!

Just as with adjectives, formation of the comparative and superlative degrees of adverbs is the same, regardless of declension. We just reviewed the positive degree of adverbs. The comparative degree form is identical to the neuter nominative singular of the adjective. As for the superlative degree, since all superlative adjectives are first/second declension, and first/second-declension adjectives add **-ē** to the stem to form their adverbs, so too do all superlative adverbs.

lentus, -a, -um slow

lentē	*slowly*
lentius	*rather slowly, more slowly*
lentissimē	*very slowly, most slowly*

celer, celeris, celere quick

celeriter	*quickly*
celerius	*rather quickly, more quickly*
celerrimē	*very quickly, most quickly*

The basic meaning of a comparative adverb is the same as its adjective counterpart. Positive is regular, comparative is the next degree, and superlative is the meaning *in extremis*. (This Latin phrase comes from **extrēmus**, which is a superlative form related to the preposition **extrā**).

COMPARISON OF IRREGULAR ADVERBS

Some adjectives have irregular comparative forms. Adverbs do too, although you will be heartened to know that for the most part the rules above still apply. The forms in the chart below that do not follow the rules are in boldface.

	Positive	**Comparative**	**Superlative**
bonus, -a, -um *good*	**bene**	melius	optimē
malus, -a, -um *bad*	**male**	peius	pessimē
magnus, -a, -um *large, great*	**magnopere**	**magis**	maximē
parvus, -a, -um *small, little*	**paulum**	minus	minimē
multus, -a, -um *much*	**multum**	plūs	**plūrimum**
facilis, -e *easy*	**facile**	facilius	facillimē
difficilis, -e *difficult*	**difficile**	difficilius	difficillimē

A few adverbs in Latin have comparative forms, but are not made from adjectives. Here are the most common.

diū *for a long time*	diūtius	diūtissimē
saepe *often*	saepius	saepissimē

Written Practice 13-2

Translate the following adverbs into English.

1. libenter   _____
2. laetius   _____
3. clārius   _____
4. brevissimē   _____
5. pulcherrimē   _____
6. fēlīcissimē   _____
7. amīcē   _____
8. optimē   _____
9. dulcius   _____
10. facilius   _____

Ablative of Comparison

Ordinarily, the comparative and superlative forms of adjectives and adverbs merely show different levels of intensity, such as **bonus** (*good*), **melior** (*pretty good*), and **optimus** (*very good*). The only instance where **melior** is *better* and **optimus** *best* is where an actual comparison is being made.

Hic liber **melior** est.   *This book is **pretty good**.*

but

Hic liber **melior** illō librō est.   *This book is **better** than that book.*

In the second sentence, one book is being compared to another book. Notice how **illō librō** (*that book*) is in ablative case and is not introduced by any preposition. This is the ***ablative of comparison***. English uses the word *than* to express the idea, but in Latin, a simple ablative does the trick.

Comparison in Latin can also be expressed by using the word **quam** (roughly equivalent to *than*).

Hic liber **melior** quam ille liber est.   *This book is **better** than that book.*

When using this construction, the things being compared are in the same case. In this example, both are nominative, because the subject of **est** is **hic liber**.

The ablative of comparison applies only to comparative forms. The superlative employs a different construction, since it compares something to a group of things, not just one other.

Hic liber **optimus** est.   *This book is **very good**.*

Hic liber **optimus** omnium (librōrum) est.   *This book is **the best** of all (books).*

Ablative of Degree of Difference

As its name suggests, this ablative use specifies the amount of difference between two things. It is a quantity word, like **multō** (*by much*) or **paulō** (*by little*), and doesn't use a preposition.

Hic liber **multō** melior quam ille est.   LITERALLY: *This book is better **by much** than that one.*
BETTER: *This book is **much** better than that one.*

The Adverb *quam* with Adjectives and Adverbs

This little word can appear with all degrees of adjectives and adverbs. With each, it has a different meaning.

Positive	**Quam** celeriter currit ille canis!	*How fast that dog runs!*
Comparative	Ille canis currit celerius **quam** canis Gāiī.	*That dog runs faster than Gaius' dog.*
Superlative	Ille canis currit **quam** celerrimē.	*That dog runs as fast as any dog can run.*

The use of **quam** with the positive and comparative degrees is rather straight-forward; its use with the superlative requires comment. True to its nature, the superlative here expresses an extreme, even ultimate, degree. When you encounter **quam** with a superlative, it's easiest to read the construction with the idea **quam** _____ = *as* _____ *as possible,* then understand and adapt that idea to whatever specific context you find it in.

The Irregular Verb *mālō, malle, māluī*

You have been indirectly acquainted with this irregular verb since Chapter 10. It has been held off until this chapter, because it is a contraction of the comparative **magis** (*more*) and **volō** (*to be willing, want*), much like **nōlō** is a contraction of **nōn** and **volō**.

The English verb *prefer* is from Latin **prae** (*ahead, in front*) and **ferō** (*to carry, bring*). The Latin version literally means *to want more,* and since the idea of *more* comes into play, so too do **quam** and the ablative of comparison. A Roman would think *I want X more than Y,* while we would say *I prefer X over Y.*

Pōcula vitrea aēneīs mālō quia nōn olent.

Pōcula vitrea quam aēnea mālō quia nōn olent.

> LITERALLY: *I want glass cups more than bronze ones, because they don't smell bad.*
> BETTER: *I prefer glass cups to bronze ones, because they don't smell bad.*

The forms of **mālō**, being a contraction of **magis** + **volō**, shouldn't come as much of a surprise. Except in present tense, they are identical to the forms of **nōlō** (only with **māl-** in place of **nōl-**). The imperfect and future endings are the same.

mālō, malle, māluī to prefer

mālō	mālumus
māvīs	māvultis
māvult	mālunt

Numerals

In everyday speech, we refer to numbers quite frequently, but you don't run across them very often in Latin literature. The most common numbers that you will see are in the chart below.

There are two types of numerals, ***cardinal*** and ***ordinal***. Cardinal numerals are the ones you count with, such as *one, two, three.* The other type is called ordinals, because they are used to show order: *first, second, third,* etc.

You probably learned about Roman numerals in grade school. Here is a quick review to jog your memory in case you have forgotten. There are a few values that are represented by letters: **I** (1), **V** (5), **X** (10), **L** (50), **C** (100), **D** (500), and **M** (1000). When numerals are repeated and/or ones of lesser value follow, they are added together, for example, **X** (10), **XX** (20), **XXI** (21). However, when a numeral of lesser value precedes one of greater value, the lesser one is subtracted from the other, so **XXI** (21), but **XIX** (19).

Arabic	Roman	Cardinal	Ordinal
1	I	ūnus, -a, -um	prīmus, -a, -um
2	II	duo, duae, duo	secundus, -a, -um
3	III	trēs, tria	tertius, -a, -um
4	IV	quattuor	quartus, -a, -um
5	V	quinque	quintus, -a, -um
6	VI	sex	sextus, -a, -um
7	VII	septem	septimus, -a, -um
8	VIII	octō	octāvus, -a, -um
9	IX	novem	nōnus, -a, -um
10	X	decem	decimus, -a, -um
11	XI	undecim	undecimus, -a, -um
12	XII	duodecim	duodecimus, -a, -um
20	XX	vīgintī	vīcēsimus, -a, -um
100	C	centum	centēsimus, -a, -um
1000	M	mille	millēsimus, -a, -um

All but four cardinal numerals are indeclinable, meaning that their forms never change, no matter what the gender, case, or number is of the word they are modifying.

The numeral **ūnus** has an irregular declensional pattern, but not so unusual that you won't recognize it. It is basically a first/second-declension adjective with a genitive in **-īus** and a dative in **-ī**, just like the demonstrative adjectives. There is no plural, just as there is no singular for **duo** (*two*).

ūnus, -a, -um one

	Masculine	Feminine	Neuter
Nominative	ūnus	ūna	ūnum
Genitive	ūnīus	ūnīus	ūnīus
Dative	ūnī	ūnī	ūnī
Accusative	ūnum	ūnam	ūnum
Ablative	ūnō	ūnā	ūnō

In Latin's mother language, Proto-Indo-European, there were three grammatical numbers: the singular for one, the dual for two, and the plural for three or more. Over time, the plural took over the job of the dual and all the dual forms gradually disappeared, with two exceptions—**duo** (*two*) and **ambō** (*both*). Even though these forms are new to you, you will have no problem learning to recognize them.

duo, duae, duo two

	Masculine	Feminine	Neuter
Nominative	duo	duae	duo
Genitive	duōrum	duārum	duōrum
Dative	duōbus	duābus	duōbus
Accusative	duōs	duās	duo
Ablative	duōbus	duābus	duōbus

There is very little to say about **trēs** (*three*), other than that it declines like a third-declension adjective.

trēs, tria three

	Masculine	Feminine	Neuter
Nominative	trēs	trēs	tria
Genitive	trium	trium	trium
Dative	tribus	tribus	tribus
Accusative	trēs	trēs	tria
Ablative	tribus	tribus	tribus

The number **mille** (*thousand*) is unusual, because in the singular, like most other numerals, it is an indeclinable adjective, but in the plural, it becomes an **i**-stem neuter noun.

mille, mīlia thousand

	Singular	Plural
Nominative	mille	mīlia
Genitive	mille	mīlium
Dative	mille	mīlibus
Accusative	mille	mīlia
Ablative	mille	mīlibus

As you recall, substantives are adjectives used as nouns. Because all numerals are adjectives, they can be used as nouns as well, as in the phrase *five of the citizens*. Although you might expect them to be accompanied by a partitive genitive in Latin, you usually find them with the preposition **ē** and an ablative instead. Thus, rather than **quinque cīvium**, you find **quinque ē cīvibus**.

Adjectives of Special Declension

In the discussion of **ūnus** above, you were reminded of how it and demonstrative adjectives have that peculiar **-īus** ending for the genitive singular and **-ī** for the dative, while most of the other forms are normal first and second declension. There is an additional, small group of adjectives that follow this special pattern. Here are the most common.

alius, alia, aliud another, different [alias]
alter, altera, alterum the other (*of two*) [alternative]
nullus, -a, -um no, none, not any [null]
sōlus, -a, -um alone, only [sole]
tōtus, -a, -um whole, entire [total]
ullus, -a, -um any

N.B. The adjectives **alius** and **alter** take on a special meaning when doubled.

aliī ... aliī some ... others
alter ... alter the one ... the other

Written Practice 13-3

Translate the following passage into English.

Cum nuntius Graecus cum rēge Priamō collocūtus erat sermōnemque graviōrem fīnīverant, ad castra sua regressus est. Postquam omnia Graecīs narrāverat, maximē gāvīsī sunt, inter prīmōs Ulixēs, quia rex Trōiae consilium dolōsum, quod ab eō ipsō creātum erat, libentius accēpisse vīsus est. Priamus enim, ut bene sciēbat Ulixēs, pācem bellō māluit, praecipuē post mortem Hectoris, fīliī cārī suī, manū Achillis. Ambō populī exitum secundum reī dēsīderābant. Plūrimae nāvēs ergō in plūrimās partēs et statim et libentissimē fractae sunt, ut māteriam habērent, quā illum equum ingentem vacuumque aedificāre possent.

Itaque equus ā mīlitibus Graecīs celerrimē aedificātus est, deinde centum ex fortissimīs optimīsque Graecōrum convocātī sunt. Cum omnēs congressī erant, consilium hīs ab Ulixe explicātum est:

"Vōs cunctī nōn sōlum fortissimī, sed etiam optimī estis, et paucissima vōs verēminī. Haud dubitō. Quīdam modo vestrum tamen ēligī poteritis, nam hic equus magnus est, at nōn maximus, atque mīlia mīlitum equō continērī nōn possunt. Ēligentur igitur vīgintī modo ex vōbīs. Aliī in equum hāc nocte ingredientur, ab aliīs equus ad portās urbis trahētur et ibi relinquētur. Intereā, nāvēs nostrae abīsse vidēbuntur, sed, ut scīmus nōs sōlī, haud longē discesserint, ē conspectū tantum Trōiānōrum. Cum equus ā Trōiānīs intrā portās tractus erit, illā nocte, dum gaudēbunt, nōs vīgintī, quī in equō nōs cēlābimus, descendēmus. Illō tempore, nāvēs nostrae iam regressae erunt. Portās urbis furtim aperīre cōnābimur, ut sociī nostrī in urbem intrent. Sīc urbs Trōia cadet."

Post haec verba rēgis Ithacae, quīdam, ācerrimī omnium Graecōrum, ēlectī sunt, in equum ascendērunt, deinde omnēs occāsum sōlis exspectābant.

Vocabulary

accēpisse to have received/welcomed

Achillēs, Achillis *m.* Achilles

conspectus, -ūs *m.* view, sight

cum *conj.* when (N.B. *Be careful not to confuse this conjunction* **cum** *with the preposition* **cum**, *which takes an ablative and means* with. *They are used entirely differently.*)

dolōsus, -a, -um deceitful

Hector, Hectoris *m.* Hector (*prince of Troy*)

inter prīmōs most of all, especially (*literally,* among the first)

Ithaca, -ae *f.* Ithaca

occāsus, -ūs *m.* setting, going down

Priamus, -ī *m.* Priam (*king of Troy*)

quā … possent with which they could …

-que and (*When joining two words, this enclitic conjunction is attached to the end of the second word; when joining two clauses, it is attached to the end of the first word of the second clause.*)

sermō, sermōnis *m.* conversation

sōl, sōlis *m.* sun

tantum *adv.* only

Ulixēs, Ulixis *m.* Ulysses (*king of Ithaca*)

ut bene sciēbat Ulixēs as Ulysses well knew

ut māteriam habērent so that they could have lumber

ut scīmus nōs sōlī as only we know

ut sociī nostrī in urbem intrent so that our allies can enter the city

vacuus, -a, -um empty, hollow

Key Vocabulary

Vocabulary to learn for this chapter includes the irregular comparative forms of adjectives and adverbs, the cardinal and ordinal numerals presented above, and the special adjectives listed in that section. The following words should also be learned.

Adjectives

ambō, ambae, ambō both [ambidextrous]

cunctus, -a, -um all

fēlix, fēlīcis lucky, happy [felicitation]

lentus, -a, -um slow

libens, libentis glad, happy, willing [*ad lib*] (*The phrase* ad lib *is actually an abbreviation of* **ad libitum** (*to one's pleasure*).)

secundus, -a, -um favorable (*In addition to meaning* second, *this adjective can mean* following *or* favorable. *It is related to the verb* **sequor** (*to follow*). *The* favorable *idea may come from its nautical use, where a following wind (i.e., a wind at one's back) is a favorable one.*)

Adverbs

haud not

igitur therefore

intereā meanwhile
longē far
modo just, only
praecipuē especially
sīc like this, in this way, thus

Conjunction

at but

Nouns

exitus, -ūs *m.* outcome; act of going out [exit]
mons, montis *m.* mountain
mors, mortis *f.* death [mortuary]
pars, partis *f.* part; direction [part]
pax, pācis *f.* peace [pacify]
socius, sociī *m.* ally [social]

Preposition

intrā (+ *acc.*) inside, within

Verbs

abeō, abīre, abiī, abitum to go away
ascendō, -ere, ascendī, ascensum to climb up/into [ascend]
colloquor, colloquī, collocūtus sum to talk together, converse [colloquial]
congredior, congredī, congressus sum to gather [congress]
contineō, -ēre, continuī, contentum to hold (in), contain [contents]
convocō (1) to call together
dēsīderō (1) to desire, want, long for
dubitō (1) to doubt, hesitate [dubious]
ēligō, -ere, ēlēgī, ēlectum to pick out, choose [elect]
explicō (1) to explain [explicate]
fīniō, -īre, fīnīvī, fīnītum to finish, end [finish]
frangō, -ere, frēgī, fractum to break [fracture]
trahō, -ere, traxī, tractum to pull, drag [tractor]

QUIZ

Choose the form of the adjective that agrees with each of the following nouns. There may be more than one correct answer for some nouns.

1. monte
    (a) pulcher
    (b) pulchriōre
    (c) pulcherrimī
    (d) pulchrius

2. partium
    (a) facillimārum
    (b) facilem
    (c) faciliōrem
    (d) facillimum

3. pācī
    (a) fēlix
    (b) fēlīciōrī
    (c) fēlīcissimō
    (d) fēlīciōre

4. amīcīs
    (a) trēs
    (b) trium
    (c) tribus
    (d) tertiī

5. socius
    (a) fortiōrēs
    (b) fortis
    (c) fortēs
    (d) feh

6. itinera
   - (a) meliōrēs
   - (b) meliōra
   - (c) melior
   - (d) meliōribus

7. hominem
   - (a) sōlōrum
   - (b) sōlem
   - (c) sōlum
   - (d) sōlius

8. exitūs
   - (a) maius
   - (b) maiōribus
   - (c) maior
   - (d) maiōris

9. nāvēs
   - (a) celeriōrēs
   - (b) celerī
   - (c) celeriōrī
   - (d) celerrimae

10. fīliae
    - (a) ūna
    - (b) ūnā
    - (c) ūnī
    - (d) ūnam

CHAPTER 14

Giving Commands and Asking Questions

In this chapter, you will learn about:

Vocative Case

Imperative Mood

Asking Questions

Dative with Intransitive Verbs

Dative with Compound Verbs

Vocabulary Building

Suffixes

Key Vocabulary

Vocative Case

Since giving orders and asking questions confront someone directly, it is often useful to get that person's attention first. This is the job of the vocative case. It is the case used when addressing someone directly.

Formation of the vocative case—which, by the way, is the last case for you to learn—couldn't be simpler. It is identical to the nominative, with only two exceptions: For second-declension masculine nouns and adjectives whose nominative singular ends in **-us**, the **-us** changes to **-e**, and for ones ending in **-ius** or **-eus**, the ending changes to **-ī**.

Nominative	Marc**us**	Publ**ius**	**meus** f**īlius**
Vocative	Marc**e**	Publ**ī**	m**ī** f**īlī**

Imperative Mood

The grammatical term *mood* refers to the way the speaker treats an action. Don't worry if that explanation doesn't make much sense at the moment. For now, all you need to know is that the *imperative mood* treats an action as a command.

Formation of the imperative is quite simple. When giving an order to one person, simply drop the **-re** from the end of the infinitive of a verb. English makes no distinction in speaking to one or more people, but Latin does. When giving an order to more than one person, drop the **-re** of the infinitive and add **-te**. In the plural, third-conjugation and third-conjugation **-iō** verbs weaken the **-e-** before **-te** to **-i-**.

	First	Second	Third	Third -*iō*	Fourth
Infinitive	port**āre**	man**ēre**	trah**ere**	cap**ere**	sent**īre**
Singular Imperative	port**ā**	man**ē**	trah**e**	cap**e**	sent**ī**
Plural Imperative	port**āte**	man**ēte**	trah**ite**	cap**ite**	sent**īte**

There are four verbs that don't conform to this rule. They are so common in everyday speech that you can easily understand why. One-syllable commands are easier to bark.

Infinitive	dīcere	dūcere	facere	ferre
Singular Imperative	dīc	dūc	fac	fer
Plural Imperative	dīcite	dūcite	facite	ferte

To issue a negative command, e.g., *Don't go home!,* the adverb **nōn** is not used, contrary to what you might expect. Instead, you find the word **nōlī** (or **nōlīte** in the plural) and the infinitive of the verb. Since this rule is true for all verbs, a single example will suffice. *Don't go home!* would be **Nōlī domum īre!**, or if you are addressing more than one person, **Nōlīte domum īre!**

Asking Questions

From a linguistic standpoint, asking a question is not as simple as it might seem, in either Latin or English. Some questions request information, such as *Where are my keys?* In this question, the adverb *where* acts as a fill-in-the-blank placeholder for the answer, much like a variable does in algebra: *My keys are on the table.* Other questions want a simple *yes* or *no* answer, such as *Did you get the job?* Notice the English subject-verb flip-flop to express the idea. Still other questions prompt either a *yes* or a *no* answer, such as *You got the job, didn't you?* or *You didn't get the job, did you?* To ask such a question in English, we make a statement, then tack on the equivalent of a *yes?* or *no?* at the end. As you will see, Latin takes a different approach. Finally, questions can inquire about a subject, direct object, possession, etc., for example, *Whose keys are these?* Let's examine Latin's approach to each of these types of questions.

ASKING YES/NO QUESTIONS

When seeking a simple *yes* or *no* answer to a question, the enclitic **-ne** is used. (Enclitics are particles that have meaning but cannot stand alone as words.) The **-ne** is attached to the first word of a sentence, which is usually the verb.

Veniēsne mēcum hodiē?   *Will you come with me today?*

Unlike the enclitic **-que** (*and*), there is no way to translate this **-ne** as a separate word. It simply suggests that the question is looking for a *yes* or *no* answer. Also of note is that there are no words in Latin that correspond to the English words *yes* and *no.* Instead, the verb is sometimes repeated, as in **Veniam** (*I will come*) or **Nōn veniam** (*I won't come*). Otherwise, various adverbs are used, like **minimē** (*in the least,* i.e., *no*), **vērō** (*truly*), and **ita** or **sīc**, which both mean *just like what you said.*

ASKING ANTICIPATORY QUESTIONS

You can phrase a yes/no question that anticipates—or even baits someone into giving—either a *yes* or *no* answer. Consider the following examples.

Veniēsne mēcum hodiē?	*Will you come with me today?*
Nōnne mēcum hodiē veniēs?	*You'll come with me today, won't you?*
Num mēcum hodiē veniēs?	*You won't come with me today, will you?*

The first question is ambivalent: Yes or no. The second question, with **nōnne**, anticipates a *yes* answer. The third question, with **num**, is more pessimistic and expects a *no* answer. The cues are in the words **nōnne** and **num**.

If you have a hard time recalling which word introduces which type of question, it might be helpful to remember that **nōnne** is actually just **nōn** with the enclitic **-ne**. If you look at it that way, you can translate the question with **nōnne** as *You'll come with me today, no?*

ASKING FILL-IN-THE-BLANK QUESTIONS

Some questions require more than just a *yes* or *no* answer. They ask for specific information. Latin, like English, has a range of question words that create a blank indicating exactly what type of information is requested.

Reason	**Cūr** rediit?	***Why** did he return?*
Method/manner	**Quōmodo** hoc factum est?	***How** did this happen?*
Location	**Ubi** eum vīdistī?	***Where** did you see him?*
Time	**Quandō** eum vīdistī?	***When** did you see him?*
Source	**Unde** vēnērunt?	***Where** did they come **from**?*
Destination	**Quō** vādis?	***Where** are you going **to**?*
Quantity	**Quot** sunt?	***How many** are there?*
Description	**Quālis** homō est?	***What kind of** person is he?*
Size	**Quantus** fuit canis?	***How large** was the dog?*

N.B. The question words **quālis, -e** and **quantus, -a, -um** are adjectives.

ASKING QUESTIONS WITH INTERROGATIVE PRONOUNS

When the information being sought is the identity of a person or thing, interrogative pronouns are used. Because they are pronouns, they come in all cases and genders. In the singular, masculine and feminine forms are the same. In the plural, there are separate feminine forms, and all the plural forms are identical to those of the relative pronoun **quī, quae, quod**, which you already know.

Actually, there are only two new forms for you to learn: **quis** (*who*), which is the masculine and feminine nominative singular, and **quid** (*what*), which is the neuter nominative (and accusative) singular. Notice how the interrogative pronoun declines in English as well.

Nominative	**Quis** eī crēdet?	***Who*** *will believe him?*
Genitive	**Cuius** servī estis?	***Whose*** *slaves are you?*
Dative	**Cui** dōna dedērunt?	***To whom*** *did they give the gifts?*
Accusative	**Quem** in Forō vīdistī?	***Whom*** *did you see in the Forum?*
Ablative	Ā **quō** gestum est?	***By whom*** *was it accomplished?*

N.B. After the words **sī**, **nisi**, **num**, and **nē**, **quis** means *someone* or *anyone*. The usual word for *someone* or *anyone* is **aliquis**, which is merely **quis** with **ali-** as a prefix.

Sī **quis** mē petet, domī erō.   *If **anyone** is looking for me, I'll be at home.*

The **num** and **nē** in this list are not the same ones presented in this chapter. You will learn these in Chapter 15.

ASKING QUESTIONS WITH INTERROGATIVE ADJECTIVES

Very little needs to be said about interrogative adjectives. Being interrogative, they are involved in asking questions, and as adjectives, they must agree in gender, case, and number with the noun they modify. Their forms are identical to those of relative pronouns. A few examples will suffice.

Quem librum māluistī?   ***Which book*** *did you prefer?*

Quae perīcula passus est?   ***What dangers*** *did he suffer?*

Dē **quibus rēbus** colloquēbantur?   *About **what matters** were they speaking?*

Written Practice 14-1

Translate the following questions into English.

1. Ōditne ille servus dominum suum?

   _____

2. Quid in hortō faciunt puerī?

   _____

3. Quālēs flōrēs mihi dabit?

   _____

4. Nōnne longum est iter ad illud oppidum?

   _____

5. Cūr diūtius mēcum nōn morāberis?

   _____

6. Ubi erat ignis dē quō loquēbātur?

   _____

7. Quōmodo Rōmae sine pecūniā habitābō?

   _____

8. Quandō hoc Caesarī nuntiātum erat?

   _____

9. Quem in speculō vidēs nisi tē ipsum?

   _____

10. Quō in locō haec invēnērunt?

    _____

Dative with Intransitive Verbs

As you recall from Chapter 3, transitive verbs require a direct object. Intransitive verbs cannot take a direct object, because they show a state of being or locomotion; they do not act directly upon anything. This is an important point to review, because there are verbs that are intransitive in Latin but transitive in English. Thus, you might not find an accusative direct object where you would expect one. Instead, you see a word in the dative representing the person or thing to which the verb refers.

Publiō nōn confīdō.   *I don't trust **Publius**.*

In the English version, *Publius* is the direct object of *trust.* To the Roman mind, however, the verb **confīdō** really means *to have trust,* and so the example sentence would actually mean *In reference to Publius, I don't have trust.*

Another example is the verb **noceō** (*to harm*). Its real meaning is *to do harm,* so the Latin for *He harmed you* would be ***Tibi* nocuit**, not ***Tē nocuit***.

The most common of these verbs are in the Key Vocabulary at the end of this chapter. In order to remember the special status of these verbs, it would be best if you learned both the actual meaning and the way English expresses the idea.

Dative with Compound Verbs

Certain prefixes, when attached to verbs, sometimes cause them to take dative objects. There is no hard and fast rule for this. It is a gray area, so you will need to rely on your sense of the context (and the language) when you encounter a dative where you might have expected an accusative. Here are the prefixes to watch for.

ad-	*to, toward, near*
ante-	*in front of, before*
con-	(when **con-** means **cum**, not as an intensifier)
in-	(when **in-** means *in*, not *not*)
inter-	*between, among*
ob-	*in opposition, up against, facing*
post-	*after, behind*
prae-	*forward, in front of*
prō-	*for, on behalf of, in front of*
sub-	*under, at the base of, up (from under)*
super-	*over, on top of*

When one of these prefixes is attached to an intransitive verb that ordinarily would have no object, such as **currō** (*to run*), and the prefix changes the verb's meaning so that the English equivalent is transitive, you will probably find a dative object in Latin. For example, when the prefix **ob-** (*in opposition, up against, facing*)

attaches to **currō**, you get **occurrō** (*to run up against,* i.e., *to meet*). Although *meet* is a transitive verb in English, **occurrō** nearly always takes a dative.

In Forō Marcō occurrī.   *I met (ran into) Marcus in the Forum.*

Prefixes attached to transitive verbs often present a slightly different scenario. Remember how prepositions and prefixes are, linguistically speaking, close kin? Here, the transitive verb remains transitive with an accusative object, but the prefix also takes an object, though in the dative.

Caesar **Titum** *legiōnī prae*posuit.   *Caesar **put Titus** in charge of the legion.*

Written Practice 14-2

Translate the following sentences into English.

1. Placuitne tibi illa cēna?

   _____

2. Ignosce mihi sī heri errābam.

   _____

3. Mihi venīre tēcum in Siciliam numquam persuādēre poteris.

   _____

   _____

4. Exercituī tōtī ā Senātū praefectus erat Gnaeus.

   _____

5. Servī meī mihi nōn pārent, etsī eōs crudeliter verberō.

   _____

6. Caesar omnibus Gallīs, quī sē trādiderint, parcet.

   _____

7. Crēdite mihi. Nōn errō.

   _____

8. Nōlēbant eīs nocēre, itaque āmissae sunt.

   _____

9. Quamquam fīliī suī nōlēbant, pater eīs imperāvit atque pāruērunt.

_____

_____

10. Diēbus sine labōribus maximē studeō!

_____

Vocabulary Building

The focus of this section is the formation of verbs from nouns and adjectives, and from other verbs themselves.

Latin has an amazingly small core vocabulary. Mastery of the basic words, plus knowledge of prefixes, can multiply your vocabulary tremendously. Another aid is an understanding of the interrelationship of words with respect to parts of speech. English also demonstrates this feature. For example, _tree_ is a noun, but a dog can also _tree_ a cat. For a Latin example, **amīcus** (_friendly_) is an adjective, but used substantively (i.e., as a noun), it is _a friend_. You also know the related verb **amō** (_to like, love_).

Denominative verbs are those created from nouns or adjectives. Most of them are first conjugation, with regular principal parts, and are usually transitive.

aedificium	_building_	aedificō	_to build_
algidus	_cold_	algeō	_to be cold_
fīnis	_end_	fīniō	_to finish_
pugna	_a fight_	pugnō	_to fight_

Frequentative verbs show a repeated or sustained action. They are all first conjugation, formed on the supine stem (i.e., from the fourth principal part) of their base verbs, and end in **-tō** or **-itō**.

| iaciō, iacere, iēcī, **iact**um | _to throw_ |
| **iact**ō, -āre, -āvī, -ātum | _to buffet (keep tossing back and forth)_ |

Sometimes the meanings are not quite so obvious. **Habeō** (_to have, hold_) gives us **habitō** (_to dwell, inhabit (keep holding onto a place)_). **Venditō** (from **vendō** (_to sell_)) means _to try to sell_.

Inceptive verbs refer to action in its beginning stages. These verbs attach **-scō** to the present stem of their base verbs and are all third conjugation. They rarely occur

in perfect system tenses, since the perfect system tenses show something completed, not in progress. They can also be formed from adjectives and nouns, as the following examples demonstrate.

alō	*to nourish*	alescō	*to grow (up)*
senex	*old*	senescō	*to age*
vesper	*evening*	advesperascit	*it's turning dusk*

Written Practice 14-3

Using the vocabulary you have learned and the Latin-English Glossary at the end of this book, guess what the following verb forms mean. Translate each form into English and identify the word it is based on.

1. dormītābat _____ _____
2. iuvenescimus _____ _____
3. repulsāminī _____ _____
4. dōnant _____ _____
5. īrascēbāmur _____ _____
6. quiescēs _____ _____
7. vocābat _____ _____
8. ardescunt _____ _____
9. vīvescēbās _____ _____
10. volitābunt _____ _____

Suffixes

You learned about prefixes in Chapter 10. In this chapter, you have learned how bases can appear in various parts of speech. Latin plays a sort of mix-and-match game with its limited core vocabulary via *suffixes*. Suffixes are units of meaning that are attached to the ends of bases. Sometimes they create new adjectives, sometimes new nouns.

Of the many suffixes, the following ones are the most common—ergo, the most important ones to learn. They are grouped by the sense they convey.

Ability   This suffix is simply **-bilis, -bile**, which is a third-declension adjective. Like most suffixes, it can be attached to verb, noun, and adjective stems alike. The Latin adjective **incrēdibilis** is a good example. It means exactly what you think it does. Take apart the English derivative *incredible,* and you find *in-* ("not"), *-cred-* ("believe"), and *-ible* ("able").

This raises an important point. Spelling in Latin is simple. Each letter represents one and only one sound: See it, say it. English is not so precise. The letter *a* has at least nine different ways it might be pronounced! In Latin, it's only ever "ah." If you have poor spelling skills, then knowledge of Latin will be a boon to you. For instance, say the word *incredible* out loud and listen to yourself. Odds are the syllables *-ible* didn't sound like "eyeball." You can remember that *incredible* is spelled *-ible,* because **crēdō** is third conjugation, and third-conjugation verbs often weaken **-e-** to **-i-** when an ending is attached. Likewise, the English *laudable* ("worthy of praise") has an *a,* because **laudō** (*to praise*) is first conjugation.

Act or Result of Doing Something   The most important suffix in this group is the one from which we get "shun" words in English—words like *petition* and *repulsion.* These are third-declension nouns in Latin and come from supine stems plus the suffix **-iō, -iōnis**.

petō, petere, petīvī, *petīt***um** to look for	**petitiō, petiti***ōnis* f. petition (*the act or result of searching*)
repellō, repellere, reppulī, *repuls***um** to drive back	**repulsiō, repulsi***ōnis* f. repulsion (*the act or result of driving back*)

Performer   The Latin suffix **-or, -ōris** shows a person or thing that does something; it is linguistically related to English *-er,* as in *performer* (i.e., one who performs). It is third declension and is applied to the supine stem.

ōrō, ōrāre, ōrāvī, *ōrāt***um** to plead	**ōrāt***or*, **ōrāt***ōris* m. pleader, speaker
vincō, vincere, vīcī, *vict***um** to conquer	**vict***or*, **vict***ōris* m. conqueror, winner

N.B. The suffix **-or, -ōris** is masculine. The feminine version is **-trix, -trīcis**.

Fullness   The suffixes **-bundus** and **-ōsus** make first/second-declension adjectives showing fullness of something.

cantō (1) to sing	**cantā***bundus, -a, -um* full of song
cōpia, cōpiae f. supply	**cōpi***ōsus, -a, -um* wealthy

Origin or Pertinence   There are three common suffixes that show where something comes from or what it pertains to. The two first/second-declension suffixes are **-ānus** and **-icus**. Occasionally, there are slight spelling changes to bases in order to make the new words easier to pronounce.

Trōia, Trōiae *f.* Troy	**Trōi*ānus*, -a, -um** Trojan (*from, or pertaining to, Troy*)
cīvis, cīvis *c.* citizen	**cīv*icus*, -a, -um** civic (*of, or pertaining to, the citizenry*)
populus, populī *m.* the people	**pūbl*icus*, -a, -um** public (*of, or pertaining to, the people*)

The third suffix with this meaning is **-ālis, -āle**, which is third declension. If the base ends in **-l-**, you usually find **-āris, -āre** instead.

vīta, vītae *f.* life	**vīt*ālis*, vīt*āle*** vital (*of, or pertaining to, life*)
sōl, sōlis *m.* sun	**sōl*āris*, sōl*āre*** solar (*of, or pertaining to, the sun*)

Condition or Quality   There are several suffixes that can create nouns conveying condition or quality. Two of the most important ones are **-tās, -tātis** and **-tūdō, -tūdinis**. The English suffixes that derive from these are *-ty* and *-tude*, respectively.

līber, lībera, līberum free	**līber*tās*, līber*tātis*** *f.* liberty (*the condition or quality of being free*)
Latīnus, -a, -um Latin	**Latīni*tās*, Latīni*tātis*** *f.* Latinity (*the condition or quality of one's Latin—yes, that actually is a word!*)
longus, -a, -um long	**longi*tūdō*, longi*tūdinis*** *f.* length (*the condition or quality of being long*)

Location   The suffix **-ārium, -āriī** (or sometimes **-ōrium, -ōriī**) creates nouns that show a place for something. The suffix comes into English either directly from Latin or with the ending *-ary* or *-ory* (e.g., *sanctuary* from Latin **sanctuārium**).

terra, terrae *f.* earth, land	**terr*ārium*, terr*āriī*** *n.* terrarium (*a tank for dirt and plants and such*)
natō (1) to swim	**nat*ātōrium*, nat*ātōriī*** *n.* natatorium (*a room or building that has a swimming pool*)

Written Practice 14-4

For each of the following definitions, give a common English word that comes from a Latin root and uses one of the suffixes above.

1. a place for books   _____
2. something from the city   _____
3. able to stand   _____
4. the act or result of moving   _____
5. a person who gives gifts   _____
6. the act or result of giving gifts   _____
7. pertaining to the moon   _____
8. a container for water   _____
9. pertaining to dogs   _____
10. the condition of being naked   _____

Key Vocabulary

In addition to the question words and suffixes presented in this chapter, you should learn the following vocabulary.

Conjunction
nisi if not, unless, except

Nouns
ignis, ignis *m.* fire [ignite]
labor, labōris *m.* work, effort; suffering [labor]
speculum, -ī *n.* mirror

Verbs
crēdō, -ere, crēdidī, crēditum (+ *dative*) to believe, have trust [credit]
ignoscō, -ere, ignōvī, ignōtum (+ *dative*) to forgive, grant pardon
imperō (1) (+ *dative*) to command, give an order [imperative]
noceō, -ēre, nocuī, nocitum (+ *dative*) to hurt, do harm [innocent]

ōdī, ōdisse, ōsum to hate [odious] (*This verb is defective. It only has perfect system forms, but unlike* **coepī,** *the other defective verb you have learned, its sense is present, despite its perfect form.*)

parcō, -ere, pepercī, parsum (+ *dative*) to spare, forgive, be lenient

pāreō, -ēre, pāruī, pāritum (+ *dative*) to obey, be obedient

persuādeō, -ēre, persuāsī, persuāsum (+ *dative*) to persuade, make convincing [persuade]

placeō, -ēre, placuī, placitum (+ *dative*) to please, be pleasing [placebo] (*This verb can also be used impersonally.*)

praeficiō, -ere, praefēcī, praefectum to put (someone, *accusative*) in charge (of something, *dative*) [prefect]

praesum, praeesse, praefuī (+ *dative*) to be in charge (of)

studeō, -ēre, studuī (+ *dative*) to be eager, be busy with [student]

QUIZ

Choose the most appropriate answer for each of the following questions.

1. Quālis vir erat Tiberius?

    (a) Duo.

    (b) Gravis.

    (c) Rōmae.

    (d) Quia Gnaeus aberat.

2. Esne puer bonus?

    (a) Ita.

    (b) Quinque.

    (c) Secundā hōrā.

    (d) Athēnīs.

3. Cūr mēcum colloquī vīs?

    (a) Domī.

    (b) Secundā hōrā.

    (c) Multī.

    (d) In perīculō es.

4. Cui nōn confīdis?

    (a) Titō.

    (b) Duo.

    (c) Secundā hōrā.

    (d) Domī.

5. Quōmodo tē accēpērunt?

    (a) Magnō gaudiō.

    (b) Secundā hōrā.

    (c) Minimē.

    (d) Vērō.

6. Nōnne Homērus poēta fuit?

   (a) Sīc.

   (b) Minimē.

   (c) Secundā hōrā.

   (d) In perīculō es.

7. Unde vēnit?

   (a) Domī.

   (b) Pompēiīs.

   (c) Secundā hōrā.

   (d) Ita.

8. Quot canēs habet?

   (a) Trēs.

   (b) Secundā hōrā.

   (c) Minimē.

   (d) Prīmus.

9. Num tibi placuit?

   (a) Vērō.

   (b) Parvus.

   (c) Minimē.

   (d) In theatrō.

10. Quandō regressī sunt?

   (a) Rōmā.

   (b) Pecūniā.

   (c) Secundā hōrā.

   (d) Ūnā.

CHAPTER 15

Subjunctive Mood

In this chapter, you will learn about:

Grammatical Mood

In linguistics, the term ***mood*** refers to the way a speaker views, or at least treats, an action. Consider the following examples of mood in English.

> ***Be*** *here by noon.*
>
> ***You are*** *here by noon.*
>
> *I suggest* ***you be*** *here by noon.*

In the first example, the speaker treats the action as a command. This is called ***imperative mood,*** which you studied in Chapter 14.

In the second example, the speaker treats the action as a fact. This is called ***indicative mood,*** which, apart from last chapter's new verb forms, is all you have been introduced to so far. The example says, *Yes, in fact you* ***are*** *here.*

The third example falls into the domain of the ***subjunctive mood***. In saying that *you* ***be*** *here,* I'm not declaring, as the speaker, that you are in fact here, nor am I commanding you. It's only an idea, or wish, on my part.

In Modern English, the subjunctive mood is losing ground to the indicative. For example, the subjunctive *if* ***I were*** *you* is now often stated as the indicative, *if* ***I was*** *you.* But I'm not you. That's just an idea. *I was* asserts that at some point in the past, you and I were in fact the same person. *I were* is subjunctive.

Languages change over time. With few exceptions, English has consolidated case endings. The difference between *who* and *whom* shouldn't be any more difficult to recognize than the difference between *he* and *him,* but now *whom* is rarely heard. Likewise, English abandoned proper verb forms in favor of helping verbs, so loss of mood is no surprise.

In sum, in Latin's (and English's) mother language, Proto-Indo-European, there were four moods.

Indicative mood	treats action as *fact*
Imperative mood	treats action as *command*
Subjunctive mood	treats action as *idea*
Optative mood	treats action as *wish*

As had happened to the original Latin ablative, locative, and instrumental cases, which linguistically collapsed into the ablative, the forms of the ancient subjunctive and optative merged into the subjunctive. The Latin subjunctive mood now carries notions both of idea and desire, which, if you think about it, are very alike.

The subjunctive mood is extremely easy to form and recognize. Better yet, there are only four tenses. The most common tenses are the imperfect and the pluperfect, with the present and perfect tenses being less common. There are no future or future perfect tense forms. Why? The future is by nature hypothetical, i.e., merely an idea or wish, not a fact.

The Imperfect Subjunctive

Rather than give you a formula, let's see if you can determine the pattern for the imperfect subjunctive yourself. You need only a few models, since the subjunctive is formed the same way for all verbs, irregulars included. Here are four model conjugations.

Active   **Passive**

amō, amāre, amāvī, amātum to like, love

amārem	amārēmus	amārer	amārēmur
amārēs	amārētis	amārēris	amārēminī
amāret	amārent	amārētur	amārentur

capiō, capere, cēpī, captum to take, catch

caperem	caperēmus	caperer	caperēmur
caperēs	caperētis	caperēris	caperēminī
caperet	caperent	caperētur	caperentur

sum, esse, fuī, futūrus to be, exist

essem	essēmus
essēs	essētis
esset	essent

volō, velle, voluī to be willing, want

vellem	vellēmus
vellēs	vellētis
vellet	vellent

Did you figure out how the imperfect subjunctive is formed? It's simply the present active infinitive with the same personal endings you've known for a long time now.

Deponent verbs present a challenge in the subjunctive, since they have no present active infinitive to attach endings to. The solution is to use what the present active infinitive would be if the deponent verb had one.

First conjugation	cōnor, cōnārī	**conāre**r, *etc.*
Second conjugation	vereor, verērī	**verēre**r, *etc.*
Third conjugation	sequor, sequī	**sequere**r, *etc.*
Third conjugation **-iō**	morior, morī	**morere**r, *etc.*
Fourth conjugation	orior, orīrī	**orīre**r, *etc.*

The Pluperfect Subjunctive

The pluperfect subjunctive is a perfect system tense. As in indicative mood, the active voice in subjunctive mood uses the perfect active stem. Instead of **-era-** as a tense indicator, the pluperfect subjunctive active uses **-isse-**. Since perfect system tenses are formed the same way for all verbs, one example will be enough.

dūcō, dūcere, duxī, ductum to take, lead

duxissem	duxissēmus
duxissēs	duxissētis
duxisset	duxissent

As you recall, in indicative mood the passive voice for pluperfect tense is formed by combining the perfect participle with the imperfect of **sum**, e.g., **actus eram**. This also holds true for the pluperfect subjunctive passive, but instead of the imperfect indicative of **sum**, you use the imperfect subjunctive.

agō, agere, ēgī, actum to do; drive, lead

actus, -a, -um essem	actī, -ae, -a essēmus
actus, -a, -um essēs	actī, -ae, -a essētis
actus, -a, -um esset	actī, -ae, -a essent

N.B. Sometimes, you find **forem, forēs**, etc. instead of **essem, essēs**, etc. These forms are interchangeable.

Written Practice 15-1

Conjugate the following verbs in subjunctive mood in the tenses and voices specified.

1. **sentiō, sentīre, sensī, sensum** to feel, perceive

   Imperfect Active   **Imperfect Passive**

   _____ _____   _____ _____

   _____ _____   _____ _____

   _____ _____   _____ _____

2. **ferō, ferre, tulī, lātum** to carry, bring

   Imperfect Active   **Imperfect Passive**

   _____ _____   _____ _____

   _____ _____   _____ _____

   _____ _____   _____ _____

3. **habeō, habēre, habuī, habitum** to have, hold

   Imperfect Active   **Imperfect Passive**

   _____ _____   _____ _____

   _____ _____   _____ _____

   _____ _____   _____ _____

4. **hortor, hortārī, hortātus sum** to urge, encourage

   Imperfect Passive   **Pluperfect Passive**

   _____ _____   _____ _____

   _____ _____   _____ _____

   _____ _____   _____ _____

5. **iaciō, iacere, iēcī, iactum** to throw

   Imperfect Active   **Pluperfect Active**

   _____ _____   _____ _____

   _____ _____   _____ _____

   _____ _____   _____ _____

Dependent and Independent Clauses

Before plunging into uses of the subjunctive in Latin, we should discuss dependent and independent clauses. First of all, a *clause* is a group of words that contains a subject and a predicate. An *independent clause* is one that expresses a complete idea and can stand alone, e.g., *The naughty puppy is chewing a shoe.* A clause that expresses an idea but depends on a main, independent clause to make sense is called a *dependent clause*, e.g., *The naughty puppy is chewing a shoe **because he wants attention***. Dependent clauses are also sometimes called *subordinate clauses*, because they connect themselves to independent clauses by means of *subordinating conjunctions,* such as *because, when, if, although,* and *unless* in English. Even though there are independent uses of the subjunctive in Latin, most of the time you will find the subjunctive in subordinate clauses.

cum Clauses

One of the most common subordinating conjunctions in Latin is **cum**. This **cum** is not the same word you have already learned, i.e., the preposition **cum** (*with*). The **cum** we are talking about here is a conjunction meaning *when, since, because, although.* It was originally spelled **quom**, but over time its spelling evolved to look the same as its pronunciation. You will have no trouble distinguishing the two uses of **cum**, since the former is followed by a noun in the ablative, while the latter introduces a subordinate clause.

Cum clauses can express four different concepts. Context will tell you which idea is most appropriate. One type, the *temporal* **cum** *clause*, stresses when an event takes place. (The word *temporal* comes from Latin **tempus, temporis** (*time*).) This type of clause uses a verb in the indicative mood, not the subjunctive.

> **Cum** Brundisiī **habitābant**, tūtī erant.   ***When they were living*** *in Brundisium, they were safe.*

Another kind of **cum** clause is called *circumstantial*. As the name suggests, it shows the circumstances under which the main clause is true. Circumstantial **cum** clauses sound the same in English as temporal ones, so the shift in emphasis shown in Latin by mood change in the verb is lost in translation.

> **Cum** Brundisiī **habitārent**, tūtī erant.   ***When (As long as) they were living*** *in Brundisium, they were safe.*

In a third type, the *causal* **cum** *clause,* the conjunction translates as *because* or *since.* It takes a subjunctive.

Cum Brundisiī **habitārent**, tūtī erant.　　***Since they were living*** *in Brundisium, they were safe.*

Finally, there is the *concessive* **cum** *clause,* which also has its verb in the subjunctive. It concedes that, despite the circumstances of its content, the main clause is true; **cum** is translated *although.* When this is the sense intended, you will almost always find the adverb **tamen** (*nevertheless, anyway*) in the main clause.

Cum Brundisiī **habitārent**, tūtī　　***Although they were living*** *in* (tamen) erant.　　*Brundisium, they were safe (anyway).*

Another way to translate a concessive **cum** clause is by joining it to the main clause with the conjunction *but.*

They were living *in Brundisium,* ***but*** *they were safe (anyway).*

Written Practice 15-2

Translate the following sentences into English, basing your translation on the type of **cum** clause indicated in parentheses.

1. Cum hostēs trans flūmen morārentur, mīlitēs Rōmānī castra pōnere potuērunt. (causal)

   _____

   _____

2. Cum Lūcius Tarquinius rex scelestus esset, Sextus, fīlius suus, pēior tamen patre fuit. (concessive)

   _____

   _____

3. Cum Brūtus dux creātus esset, omnēs cīvēs gāvīsī sunt. (circumstantial)

   _____

   _____

4. Cum Tarquinius in Etrūriam effūgerat, Sextus celeriter interfectus est. (temporal)

_____

_____

5. Cum Tarquinius in Etrūriam effūgisset, Sextus celeriter interfectus est. (circumstantial)

_____

_____

6. Nōnne Caesar consul factus est, cum fīnem bellō contrā Gallōs confēcerat? (temporal)

_____

_____

7. Cum in Asiam iter facerēmus, hominibus multīs et mīrīs occurrimus. (circumstantial)

_____

_____

8. Cum illud incendium perīculōsissimum fuisset, nēmō effugere poterat. (causal)

_____

_____

9. Cum domī pernoctāre vellem, cum amīcīs meīs tamen morātus sum. (concessive)

_____

_____

10. Timuistīne cum larvam (_ghost_) frātris tuī vīdistī? (temporal)

_____

_____

Purpose Clauses

Another extremely common use of the subjunctive in Latin is to show purpose. In English, we usually show purpose with an infinitive, but Latin does so with a subordinate clause introduced by the conjunction **ut** (or **nē**) and a verb in the subjunctive.

Vēnērunt **ut** mē **auferrent**.　　　*They came (in order) to take me away.*

You can express this in English in another way that is more parallel to the Latin construction, but it is very awkward.

*They came **in order that they might take me away**.*

In order to show negative purpose, Latin has a special word, **nē**, that is used instead of **ut**. Translation of negative purpose clauses can be tricky. Here too, English has a rather archaic way of getting the idea across.

Mē abstulērunt **nē effugerem**.　　*They took me away **so that I wouldn't escape**.*
　　　　　　　　　　　　　　　　　　*OR They took me away **lest I escape**.*

N.B. Occasionally, you will see **ut** with the indicative. Instead of showing purpose, it means *when* in this case, much like **cum** does with the indicative.

Sometimes, instead of **ut**, the relative pronoun **quī** is used to introduce a purpose clause. This is called a ***relative clause of purpose***. A purpose clause with **ut** shows the purpose of the verb in the main clause, but one with **quī** refers to the purpose of the antecedent.

Hominēs vēnērunt **quī** mē **abstulērunt**.　　*People came **who took me away**.*
(INDICATIVE — FACT)

Hominēs vēnērunt **quī** mē **auferrent**.　　*People came, **who were supposed**
(SUBJUNCTIVE — IDEA)　　　　　　　　*to take me away**.*

There are a few other ways to show purpose in Latin. We will explore them in Chapter 16.

Written Practice 15-3

Translate the following sentences into English.

1. Proelium ā nostrīs ācriter pugnātum est ut hostēs vincerent.

   _____

   _____

2. Proelium ā nostrīs ācriter pugnātum est nē ā hostibus vincerentur.

   _____

   _____

3. Proelium ā nostrīs ācriter pugnātum est quī hostēs vincerent.

   _____

   _____

4. Servum in Forum mīsī ut cibum optimum emeret.

   _____

5. Servum in Forum mīsī quī cibum optimum emeret.

   _____

6. Ut domum regressus est, nihil nisi pānem habuit.

   _____

7. Vōs omnēs invitātī estis, ut apud mē quinque diēs morārēminī.

   _____

   _____

8. Nuntium mittere cōnātī sumus nē sollicita esset māter tua.

   _____

9. Habuistīne librum quem in itinere legerēs?

   _____

10. Ut haec tibi dīcerem, venīre nōn poteram.

    _____

The Present Subjunctive

The forms of the present subjunctive are really only variations on the present indicative. The key characteristic to watch for is seemingly misplaced vowels. The method for forming the present subjunctive is quite simple.

Step 1: Go to the first principal part of the verb.

Step 2: Change the **-ō** to the "wrong" vowel for the conjugation.

Step 3: Apply the usual active and passive personal endings.

For example, only first conjugation has **a** for its signature vowel, and so you would change the **-ō** to **e**. For the other conjugations, change the **-ō** to **a**. Look closely at the following charts, which illustrate this simple process.

Active		Passive	

amō, amāre, amāvī, amātum to like, love

amem	amēmus	amer	amēmur
amēs	amētis	amēris	amēminī
amet	ament	amētur	amentur

moneō, monēre, monuī, monitum to warn, advise

moneam	moneāmus	monear	moneāmur
moneās	moneātis	moneāris	moneāminī
moneat	moneant	moneātur	moneantur

agō, agere, ēgī, actum to do; drive, lead

agam	agāmus	agar	agāmur
agās	agātis	agāris	agāminī
agat	agant	agātur	agantur

capiō, capere, cēpī, captum to take, catch

capiam	capiāmus	capiar	capiāmur
capiās	capiātis	capiāris	capiāminī
capiat	capiant	capiātur	capiantur

audiō, audīre, audīvī, audītum to hear, listen

audiam	audiāmus	audiar	audiāmur
audiās	audiātis	audiāris	audiāminī
audiat	audiant	audiātur	audiantur

Of the irregular verbs, only **sum** and **volō** deviate from this pattern. Their mood indicator is **i**.

sum, esse, fuī, futūrus to be, exist

sim	sīmus
sīs	sītis
sit	sint

volō, velle, voluī to be willing, want

velim	velīmus
velīs	velītis
velit	velint

The compounds of these two verbs follow suit. Thus, we have **possim**, **nōlim**, **mālim**, and so on.

The Perfect Subjunctive

In active voice, the forms of the perfect subjunctive are nearly identical to the future perfect indicative. There is one significant exception: The first-person singular form ends in **-erim** rather than **-erō**. Since perfect system tenses are formed in the same way for all verbs, one example will demonstrate the pattern.

teneō, tenēre, tenuī, tentum to hold, have

tenuerim	tenuerīmus
tenuerīs	tenuerītis
tenuerit	tenuerint

The passive voice forms should come as no surprise, either. In indicative mood, the passive is formed with the perfect passive participle and the present *indicative* of **sum**. For the perfect *subjunctive* passive, use the present *subjunctive* of **sum** instead.

habeō, habēre, habuī, habitum to have, hold

habitus, -a, -um sim	habitī, -ae, -a sīmus
habitus, -a, -um sīs	habitī, -ae, -a sītis
habitus, -a, -um sit	habitī, -ae, -a sint

Written Practice 15-4

Change each of the following verb forms from indicative to subjunctive mood or vice versa, keeping the same tense and voice as the original form.

1. doceātis _____

2. sentit _____

3. eō _____

4. dīcātur _____

5. ingreditur _____

6. nōn vult _____

7. sunt _____

8. fit _____

9. ferāmur _____

10. scrībunt _____

Written Practice 15-5

Change each of the following verb forms from indicative to subjunctive mood or vice versa, keeping the same tense and voice as the original form.

1. timuit _____

2. locūtus sum _____

3. mōtī sīmus _____

4. relīquī _____

5. gessistis _____

Sequence of Tense

There is a special relationship between the tense of the verb in a main clause and the tense of the subjunctive verb in a subordinate clause. This relationship is called *sequence of tense*. In a nutshell, if the main verb is in a present or future tense, the subordinate verb will be in the present subjunctive if the action is taking place at the same time or after the action of the main verb. It will be in the perfect subjunctive if the action has already been completed. Similarly, if the main verb is in a past

tense, the imperfect subjunctive shows something occurring at the same time or after. The pluperfect subjunctive indicates something that had happened before the main verb. The following chart will make these relationships clear.

Tense of Main Verb	Tense of Subjunctive Verb	
	Same Time or After	Time Before
Present		
Future	Present	Perfect
Future perfect		
Imperfect		
Perfect	Imperfect	Pluperfect
Pluperfect		

You saw this principle in action earlier in this chapter in our discussion of **cum** and purpose clauses.

Vēnērunt **ut** mē **auferrent**.　　　*They came **to take** me **away**.*

The main verb, **vēnērunt**, is in perfect tense, so the subjunctive verb, **auferrent**, is in the imperfect subjunctive, because it refers to an action that would happen *after* the main verb. We can recast this sentence into the other sequence.

Veniunt **ut** mē **auferant**.　　　*They are coming **to take** me **away**.* (ha-ha)

This time, the main verb is in the present, so the subjunctive verb is also in the present.

Result Clauses

The subjunctive is used in subordinate clauses that relate the result of the action of the main verb. *There was so much smoke **that they couldn't find the door*** shows a *result clause* in English. Not being able to find the exit was the *result* of so much smoke. Here is the Latin translation of this example.

Tantus fūmus erat **ut iānuam invenīre nōn possent**.

There are a few elements in this example that need comment. Like purpose clauses, the result clause is introduced by the subordinating conjunction **ut**. Unlike purpose clauses, which substitute **nē** for **ut** when the clause is negative, in result clauses you see **ut … nōn** instead. Lastly, the appearance of the "so" word **tantus** is a strong sign of the grammatical construction to come: Result clauses are almost always heralded by a "so" word. Here is a list of the most common "so" words to watch for.

ita in such a way
sīc in such a way
tālis, -e of such a kind
tam so, to such a degree
tantus, -a, -um so big, so great
tot so many

Result clauses can also follow certain verbs and expressions, such as **effēcit ut …** (*he made it that …*), **accidit ut …** (*it happened that …*), and **necesse erat ut …** (*it was necessary that …*).

Accidit ut nēmō effūgisset.   *It happened that no one had escaped.*

Written Practice 15-6

Translate the following sentences into English.

1. Accidit ut tū domī nōn adessēs cum pervenīrēmus.

   _____

2. Vīs ignis efficiet ut nēmō supersit.

   _____

3. Tam celeriter cucurrit ut certāmen facillimē vinceret.

   _____

4. Necesse erit ut vōs omnēs dē hāc rē taceātis.

   _____

5. Flōrēs, quōs mihi dederat, tālēs erant ut vix crēderem.

   _____

6. Ille mīles heri ita pugnāvit ut omnis hostis eum verērētur.

   _____

7. Alpēs (*The Alps*) tam altī sunt ut in summā parte aliquid nivis (*snow*) semper maneat.

_____

_____

8. Tot aedificia Rōmae fuērunt ut omnia ūnō diē vīsitāre nōn possēmus.

_____

_____

9. Flūmen tam parvum ibi fluit (*flows*) ut sine difficultāte transeātis.

_____

_____

10. Effēcit ut ibi nōn relinquerer.

Conditions

If you have ever done any computer programming, then you know what a condition is. A condition is an if/then proposition, the preceding sentence being a good example of one. If X is true, then Y is too. In Latin, there is a word for *if* (**sī**), but not one for *then*.

Latin identifies six different types of conditional sentences; three are factual (i.e., indicative), and three are hypothetical (i.e., subjunctive). The three in each group correspond to the three time frames of present, past, and future. As usual, Latin grammar has a special term for each of these six constructions.

Simple Fact Present

Present indicative + present indicative

Sī hoc putat, sapit.   *If he thinks this, he is wise.*

Simple Fact Past

Past indicative + past indicative

Sī hoc putābat, sapiēbat.   *If he thought this, he was wise.*

Future "More Vivid"

Future indicative + future indicative

Sī hoc putābit, sapiet.   *If he thinks this, he will be wise.*

All of these types use the indicative, because they treat the actions as facts. The future is, of course, not a fact, but the indicative is assertive and treats it as if it were—hence the term "more vivid." As you rightly suspect, where there is a "more vivid" construction, there is also a "less vivid" one. The following three conditions employ the subjunctive. They treat the actions as ideas with no conviction that they are true.

Future "Less Vivid"

Present subjunctive + present subjunctive

Sī hoc putet, sapiat.   *If he (might) think this, he would be wise.*

Present Contrary-to-Fact

Imperfect subjunctive + imperfect subjunctive

Sī hoc putāret, sapīret.   *If he thought this, he would be wise.*

Past Contrary-to-Fact

Pluperfect subjunctive + pluperfect subjunctive

Sī hoc putāvisset, sapīvisset.   *If he had thought this, he would have been wise.*

It was noted earlier in this chapter that the subjunctive still exists in a few places in Modern English; the present contrary-to-fact condition is one of them. An example is the sentence *If he were here, he'd be glad.* But he isn't here, so *were* is used rather than *was*. *Were* is the past subjunctive of the verb *to be* in English, which is why it is appropriate for a present contrary-to-fact condition.

Written Practice 15-7

Tell which type of condition each of these sentences uses, then translate the sentence into English.

1. Sī canem meum inveniet, eum cūrābit. _____

_____

2. Sī canem meum invenīret, eum cūrāret. _____

_____

3. Sī canem meum invēnit, eum cūrāvit. _____

_____

4. Sī herī advēnissēs, saltem nōs adiūvissēs. _____

_____

5. Sī id quod facere cōnor scīs, cūr mēcum nōn es? _____

_____

6. Sī Rōmam regrediātur, sine dubiō pessimē accipiātur.

_____

_____

7. Sī dē istā rē mihi narrēs, tūtus sīs. _____

_____

8. Dōnum tibi datum esset, sī scīvissēmus. _____

_____

9. Sī mihi crēdis, mē sequī nōn dubitās. _____

_____

10 Sī mihi crēderēs, mē sequī nōn dubitārēs. _____

_____

Independent Uses of the Subjunctive

The subjunctive can be used as a main verb, without depending on another clause to make sense. These uses all treat actions as ideas or wishes.

The **deliberative subjunctive** is used in questions that imply doubt. The negative has **nōn** rather than **nē**.

Quid tibi dīcam?	*What should I tell you?*
Nōn tibi dīcerem?	*Shouldn't I have told you?*

The **potential subjunctive** expresses a hypothetical possibility. It also uses **nōn** in the negative.

Eum stultum esse putēs.	*You'd think he was stupid.*
Mihi loquī nōn audeat.	*He wouldn't dare speak to me.*

The *optative subjunctive* declares a wish. It is often preceded by the word **utinam**. The negative particle is **nē**.

(Utinam) frāter meus adsit!	*I wish my brother were here!*
(Utinam) nē frāter tuus adsit!	*I wish your brother weren't here!*

The *hortatory subjunctive* gets its name from the deponent verb **hortor** (*to urge*). It uses **nē** in the negative.

Domum regrediāmur.	*Let's go back home.*
Nē ingrediātur.	*Don't let him enter.*

The Subjunctive After Verbs of Fearing

Latin uses a very counterintuitive construction after verbs that denote fear—**nē** introduces something affirmative, and **ut** (or **nē nōn**) something negative.

Timeō **nē** veniant.	*I'm afraid **that they are** coming.*
Timeō **ut** veniant.	*I'm afraid **that they are not** coming.*

The reason for this apparently contradictory construction is that there are actually two ideas being expressed. First is the fear: **timeō** (*I am afraid*). Second is a wish brought on by the fear: **nē veniant** (*Don't let them come!*).

Written Practice 15-8

Translate the following passage into English.

Itaque, cum Graecī equum tantum construxerant ut vīgintī hominēs continēre posset, in nāvēs reliquās—eās quae nōn dēlētae erant ut equus aedificārētur—ingressī sunt. Tum haud procul ē conspectū Trōiānōrum nāvigāvērunt. Cum equum ad portās urbis trahere in animō habuissent, in lītore tamen relictus est. Equī enim deō Neptūnō sacrī sunt, itaque dōnum deō vidērētur, ut iter fēlix atque tūtum ad Graeciam habērent. Quam ob rem, homō quīdam, nōmine Sinōn, relictus est, quī insidiās parāret. Crēderent Trōiānī fābulae eius?

Cum ā Trōiānīs acceptus esset, eīs dixit, "Istōs Graecōs relīquī ego nam scelestī sunt. In Graeciam iam regrediuntur, et dōnum ingens, formā equī, Neptūnō con-

struxērunt, ut tūtē trans mare iter facerent. Mōs apud nōs efficit ut nōs ambō pereāmus īrā deī nisi hoc dōnum accipiātis et intrā mūrōs trahātis."

Trōiānī gāvīsī sunt cum Graecī tandem abiissent, at, cum metuerent nē īra deī ullius eīs nōceret, contiō convocāta est nē malum fātum accideret. Aliī clāmābant, "Statim intrā mūrōs trahātur equus! Utinam fīnem istī bellō videāmus!" Aliī, autem, dubitābant, et cum dubitārent, Lāocoōn, vātēs Neptūnī, arcessītus est nē errārent. Cum advēnit, dixit, "Quod perīculum hīc lateat? Etsī dōna ferunt, Graecīs nōn confīdō. Nisi eum combūrētis, vōs graviter paenitēbit."

Quamquam verba vātis ab omnibus audīta erant et Lāocoontī crēdidērunt, tam iūcundī erant ut monitīs eius nōn pārērent, et continuō fūnēs parāre coepērunt ut equum reciperent.

Vocabulary

arcessō, -ere, arcessīvī, arcessītum to summon
conspectus, -ūs *m.* view, sight
contiō, contiōnis *f.* meeting
fūnis, fūnis *m.* rope
Lāocoōn, Lāocoontis *m.* Laocoon
quam ob rem for this reason
reliquus, -a, -um left behind, remaining
Sinōn, Sinōnis *m.* Sinon
vātēs, vātis *c.* priest, prophet; poet

Written Practice 15-9   Synopsis

Here are a few synopses so that you can review old forms and practice your new ones!

1. **metuō, metuere, metuī, metūtum** *3pl., masculine*

Indicative Mood

	Active	Passive
Present	_____	_____
Imperfect	_____	_____
Future	_____	_____
Perfect	_____	_____
Pluperfect	_____	_____
Future Perfect	_____	_____

Subjunctive Mood

	Active	Passive
Present	_____	_____
Imperfect	_____	_____
Perfect	_____	_____
Pluperfect	_____	_____

2. **videō, vidēre, vīdī, vīsum** *1sg., feminine*

Indicative Mood

	Active	Passive
Present	_____	_____
Imperfect	_____	_____
Future	_____	_____
Perfect	_____	_____
Pluperfect	_____	_____
Future Perfect	_____	_____

Subjunctive Mood

	Active	Passive
Present	_____	_____
Imperfect	_____	_____
Perfect	_____	_____
Pluperfect	_____	_____

3. **ferō, ferre, tulī, lātum** *3sg., neuter*

Indicative Mood

	Active	Passive
Present	_____	_____
Imperfect	_____	_____
Future	_____	_____
Perfect	_____	_____
Pluperfect	_____	_____
Future Perfect	_____	_____

Subjunctive Mood

	Active	Passive
Present	_____	_____
Imperfect	_____	_____
Perfect	_____	_____
Pluperfect	_____	_____

4. **dōnō, dōnāre, dōnāvī, dōnātum** *1pl., masculine*

Indicative Mood

	Active	Passive
Present	_____	_____
Imperfect	_____	_____
Future	_____	_____
Perfect	_____	_____
Pluperfect	_____	_____
Future Perfect	_____	_____

Subjunctive Mood

	Active	Passive
Present	_____	_____
Imperfect	_____	_____
Perfect	_____	_____
Pluperfect	_____	_____

Key Vocabulary

Adjectives

iūcundus, -a, -um content, happy [jocund]
mīrus, -a, -um amazing, wonderful [admirable]
sacer, sacra, sacrum sacred, holy [sacred]
scelestus, -a, -um wicked, evil
sollicitus, -a, -um upset, anxious, worried [sollicitous]
tālis, -e such, of such a kind
tantus, -a, -um so big, so great
tot so many
tūtus, -a, -um safe [tutor]

Adverbs

continuō immediately, without missing a beat
ita like this, in this way, thus

procul at a distance, far
saltem at least
tam so, to such a degree
utinam Oh would that …, if only …, I wish that …

Conjunctions

autem however; moreover
cum (*with indicative*) when; (*with subjunctive*) when; since, because; although
etsī even if
nē not, lest
ut (*with indicative*) when; (*with subjunctive*) in order that; with the result that; as, because

Nouns

certāmen, certāminis *n.* race, contest, struggle
cibus, -ī *m.* food
dōnum, -ī *n.* gift [donation]
fābula, -ae *f.* story [fable]
fātum, -ī *n.* fate, destiny; misfortune [fate]
flūmen, flūminis *n.* river [flume]
forma, -ae *f.* shape, image [form]
incendium, -ī *n.* fire, *especially* a fire [incendiary]
insidiae, -ārum *f.pl.* trap, trick, ambush [insidious]
lītus, lītoris *n.* beach, shore [littoral]
mōs, mōris *m.* custom, characteristic; (*plural*) character, morals [moral]
pānis, pānis *m.* bread
vīs, vis *f.* force; (*plural*) strength [violence]
    This is one of the very few irregular nouns in Latin.

	Singular	Plural
Nominative	vīs	vīrēs
Genitive	vis	vīrium
Dative	vī	vīribus
Accusative	vim	vīrēs
Ablative	vī	vīribus

*Notice that there is a stem change, but only in the plural. This stem change to **vīr-** may lead you to confuse it with the noun **vir** (man). Two things will help you keep them straight. First, the **ī** in **vīr-** is long, not short as in **vir**. Second, **vīrēs** is third declension, whereas **vir** is second. There is no overlap in endings.*

Preposition

contrā (+ *acc.*) against, facing, opposite

Verbs

adiuvō, -āre, adiūvī, adiūtum to help [adjutant]
combūrō, -ere, combussī, combustum to burn up [combustion]
construō, -ere, construxī, constructum to build, set up [construct]
dēleō, -ēre, dēlēvī, dēlētum to destroy [delete]
efficiō, -ere, effēcī, effectum to do, effect, bring it about that [effect]
emō, -ere, ēmī, emptum to buy [emporium]
interficiō, -ere, interfēcī, interfectum to kill
lateō, -ēre, latuī to lie hidden [latent]
metuo, -ere, metuī, metūtum to fear
pernoctō (1) to spend the night
superō (1) to overcome, conquer, win, overtake
supersum, superesse, superfuī, superfutūrus to survive; remain
taceō, -ēre, tacuī, tacitum to be quiet [tacit]

QUIZ

Choose the correct form for each verb, as indicated.

1. amō: *third-person singular, future perfect passive indicative*

    (a) amātus erat

    (b) amābātur

    (c) amātus erit

    (d) amārentur

2. dēleō: *second-person plural, imperative*

    (a) dēlēs

    (b) dēlēte

    (c) dēleās

    (d) dēleāris

3. interficiō: *present active infinitive*

    (a) infectus esse

    (b) interfectī

    (c) interficere

    (d) interfectūrus esse

4. metuō: *first-person plural, present subjunctive active*

    (a) metuimus

    (b) metuimur

    (c) metuāmus

    (d) metuerēmus

5. noceō: *second-person plural, imperfect subjunctive active*

    (a) noceātis

    (b) nocuistis

    (c) nocērētis

    (d) nocuissētis

6. nōlō: *third-person plural, present subjunctive active*

   (a) nōluissent

   (b) nōlint

   (c) nōluerint

   (d) nollent

7. adiuvō: *third-person singular, pluperfect subjunctive passive*

   (a) adiūtus esset

   (b) adiūtus sit

   (c) adiuvāret

   (d) adiūvisset

8. emō: *second-person singular, perfect subjunctive active*

   (a) ēmerīs

   (b) emis

   (c) emās

   (d) ēmerās

9. ferō: *present passive infinitive*

   (a) tulisse

   (b) lātus esse

   (c) ferrī

   (d) lātūrus esse

10. supersum: *third-person singular, present subjunctive active*

   (a) supersit

   (b) superesse

   (c) superesset

   (d) superfuisset

CHAPTER 16

Participles, Gerunds, and Indirect Discourse

In this chapter, you will learn about:

Participles

Participles are adjectives made from verbs. In English, there are two kinds of participles: present (e.g., *breaking*) and past (e.g., *broken*). Latin has these same two participles as, for example, **frangens** (*breaking*) and **fractus** (*broken*). Both are from the verb **frangō, frangere, frēgī, fractum**. Latin also has future participles, which have no parallel in English. For instance, the future active participle of our sample verb is **fractūrus**. It refers to something *about to break,* but which hasn't yet broken. We have no word to express that in English, so we use an entire phrase, such as *which is about to break,* or *which is going to break,* or *which intends to break.* Latin relies on the future participle to express all these ideas. Latin's fourth participle is the future passive (e.g., **frangendus**).

PARTICIPLE FORMS

Present participles in English are easily recognized by their characteristic ending *-ing,* such as *breaking.* Past participles, however, have unpredictable forms: The past participle of *break* is *broken,* but the one for *walk* is *walked,* not *walken,* and that of *put* is *put.* The one for *hang* is *hung* if the reference is to a picture on the wall, but *hanged* if referring to the execution of a person.

In a similar vein, three of Latin's four participles have characteristic markers that make them easy to recognize. The perfect (i.e., past) participle, however, does not. Here are charts for each conjugation.

	Active	Passive	Active	Passive
	First Conjugation		**Second Conjugation**	
Present	portans	—	monens	—
Perfect	—	portātus	—	monitus
Future	portātūrus	portandus	monitūrus	monendus
	Third Conjugation		**Third Conjugation -*iō***	
Present	dūcens	—	capiens	—
Perfect	—	ductus	—	captus
Future	ductūrus	dūcendus	captūrus	capiendus
	Fourth Conjugation			
Present	audiens	—		
Perfect	—	audītus		
Future	audītūrus	audiendus		

Since participles are adjectives, they can appear in more ways than are presented in these charts. They also have gender, case, and number. In this sense, **captus** is no different from **bonus**.

The *present active participle* attaches **-ns, -ntis** to the present stem. It is a third-declension adjective like **ingens, ingentis**, but usually the ablative singular ends in **-e**, like a noun, instead of **-ī**, as you might expect in an adjective. A good way to recognize the present active participle is by its stem **-nt-**, as in *present*. This participle is one of the few active forms that deponent verbs have, e.g., **ingrediens, ingredientis** (*entering*). There is no present passive participle in Latin.

The *perfect passive participle* is a regular first/second-declension adjective built on the stem provided by a verb's fourth principal part. With deponent verbs, you use the third principal part, e.g., **ingredior, ingredī, *ingressus* sum**.

The *future active participle* simply adds **-ūrus, -ūra, -ūrum** to the stem of the perfect passive participle; thus, **captus** becomes **captūrus**. Use the second word of this paragraph as a mnemonic (memory trick).

The *future passive participle* is a first/second-declension adjective built on the present stem of a verb. The mnemonic for recognizing its form only works if you know that it is also called the **gerundive**. It is an oddball among the participles and will be discussed in depth later.

Before moving on to the uses of participles, a few more remarks regarding their formation should be made. First, deponent verbs have all four participles, including the active ones. Second, among the irregular verbs, **volō** and its compounds have only a present participle form. **Sum** has only a future active participle (**futūrus**), and **possum** has only **potens**. **Ferō** and **eō** have complete sets. The present participle of **eō** (**iens**) has a stem change to **euntis** in the genitive.

PARTICIPLE USES

There are a couple of things to keep in mind about the use of participles. They are adjectives, and as adjectives they agree in gender, case, and number with the nouns they modify. Their tense labels are purely grammatical jargon. The present participle is called *present* only because it is formed from the present stem—the one that serves the present system tenses. In reality, it and the other participles, whatever their official, grammatical names, have *relative* time values.

The present participle refers to something happening at the same time as the main verb, whatever the tense of the main verb. In the sentence *We heard the dog barking,* the *heard* and the *barking* were simultaneous. The main verb *heard* is past tense, but the present participle *barking* suggests a concurrent action. When the present participle is used as a noun, it usually refers to a person who does something. For example, **amans** often means *a lover*.

The relative time concept applies to perfect and future participles as well. A perfect participle shows something that happened *before* the main verb, while a future participle points to something that will occur *after* the main verb.

Avis per fenestram **fractam** volāvit.	*The bird flew through the **broken** window.* (The window was broken *before* the bird flew through it.)
Nōs **moritūrī** tē salūtāmus.	*We **who are about to die** salute you.* (We're not dead yet.)

The future passive participle, also called the *gerundive,* is more than just the passive version of the future active one. You will most often encounter it performing two other tasks—but more about that later.

Participial Phrases

You began working with perfect passive participles when you studied passive voice in Chapter 12. These participles are used with forms of the verb **sum** to make the perfect passive tenses. They and all the other participles are also used in *participial phrases*.

A *phrase* is a group of words that expresses an idea, but that isn't a whole clause or sentence. For example, *down the drain* is a prepositional phrase. There's an idea there, but it isn't a sentence; it's a preposition and a noun. A participial phrase is a noun and a participle, usually in that order.

Canis in hortō lātrans līberōs terruit.	***The dog barking in the garden*** *frightened the children.*

If you examine the grammar of this sentence closely, you'll see how the participial phrase functions as a grammatical unit. The phrase **canis in hortō lātrans** is nominative, ergo it is the subject. The accusative **līberōs** is the direct object. The verb is **terruit**. Classic Latin word order.

Notice how the head noun, **canis**, starts the phrase and how the participle **lātrans**, which agrees in gender, case, and number, ends it. Extra information that pertains to the noun and participle is in the middle. The head noun and the participle form a sandwich—they act as bookends of the grammatical unit.

It is very important that you see participial phrases as units, because Latin uses them extensively. Keep in mind that as adjectives, participles must agree with the nouns they modify, but as verbs, they can also have direct objects and other elements you might expect to find in a clause.

Latin is a very economical language, and participial phrases can pack a lot of information into very few words. When translating, it is usually best to extract and expand them into full-blown clauses. Here are a few ways to approach them.

Simple adjective	*The dog **barking** in the garden frightened the children.*
Relative clause	*The dog, **which** was barking in the garden, frightened the children.*
Temporal clause	***While** the dog was barking in the garden, he frightened the children.*
Causal clause	***Since/Because** the dog was barking in the garden, he frightened the children.*
Coordinate clause	*The dog was barking in the garden **and** he frightened the children.*
Concessive clause	***Although** the dog was barking in the garden, he frightened the children.*

A couple of these approaches require comment. First, with temporal clauses, don't forget the relative time value of participles. This example is with a present participle, which refers to the same time as the main verb. A perfect participle, which shows time before, would require *after* rather than *while,* and a future participle would require *before.*

Canis **lātrātūrus** līberōs terruit.   *The dog frightened the children **before** it started to bark.*

Second, as was true with concessive **cum** clauses, the concessive approach is usually signaled by the appearance of **tamen** in the main clause.

Ablatives Absolute

As you just learned, participial phrases are grammatical sandwiches consisting of a head noun and participle, with other pertinent information in between. The case of the head noun is very important, because it shows the role of the phrase in the sentence. Take, for example, the sentence **Canis in hortō lātrans līberōs terruit.** Here, **canis** is nominative, because it is the subject of **terruit. Lātrans** is nominative in order to agree with **canis.** On the other hand, in the sentence **Canem in hortō lātrantem nōn audīvī,** the head noun **canem** is the accusative direct object of **audīvī.**

The ***ablative absolute*** construction is a type of participial phrase in which the head noun has no grammatical role to play in the sentence. It provides information, but it stands apart. An ablative absolute consists of a head noun and a participle (or sometimes a noun with another noun or adjective); both are in the ablative and set off from the main sentence. As with normal participial phrases, extra material is placed in the middle. It can be translated like any participial phrase, with one exception: the relative clause approach.

Lūdō confectō, domum regressī sumus.

Simple adjective	*With the game having been finished, we returned home.*
Temporal clause	*After the game was finished, we returned home.*
Causal clause	*Because/Since the game was finished, we returned home.*
Coordinate clause	*The game was finished and we returned home.*
Concessive clause	*Although the game was finished, we returned home.*

Written Practice 16-1

Make participle charts for the following verbs.

Active   **Passive**

1. **pōnō, pōnere, posuī, positum**

   Present   _____   _____

   Perfect   _____   _____

   Future   _____   _____

2. **ferō, ferre, tulī, lātum**

   Present   _____   _____

   Perfect   _____   _____

   Future   _____   _____

3. **videō, vidēre, vīdī, vīsum**

   Present   _____   _____

   Perfect   _____   _____

   Future   _____   _____

	Active	Passive
4. **sentiō, sentīre, sensī, sensum**		
Present	_____	_____
Perfect	_____	_____
Future	_____	_____
5. **cōnor, cōnārī, cōnātus sum**		
Present	_____	_____
Perfect	_____	_____
Future	_____	_____

Written Practice 16-2

Underline the participial phrase in each of the following sentences, then translate the sentence into English, using the approaches indicated.

1. Equī currentēs ē proeliō effūgērunt.

   Simple adjective _____

   Relative clause _____

   Temporal clause _____

   Concessive clause _____

2. Hostēs in proeliō victī mox interfectī sunt.

   Causal clause _____

   Concessive clause _____

   Temporal clause _____

   Simple adjective _____

3. Hostibus in proeliō victīs, omnēs pācem volēbant.

   Causal clause _____

   Coordinate clause _____

   Temporal clause _____

   Simple adjective _____

4. Verbīs modo mihi ab amīcō dictīs vix crēdō.

Coordinate clause _____

Causal clause _____

Simple adjective _____

Relative clause _____

5. Marcum in Forum itūrum monuerāmus.

Causal clause _____

Relative clause _____

Temporal clause _____

Coordinate clause _____

Gerunds

A gerund is a verbal noun. In English, gerunds end in -*ing,* just like present participles, but their usage as a noun is quite distinct. In the expression *reading is fundamental, reading* is clearly the subject, and therefore a noun.

FORMS OF GERUNDS

Latin gerunds are formed by attaching **-nd-** to the present stem. They are second-declension neuter nouns that occur only in the singular and have no nominative. (Subjective infinitives fill that need.)

	First	Second	Third	Third -*iō*	Fourth
Nominative	—	—	—	—	—
Genitive	amandī	monendī	dūcendī	iaciendī	audiendī
Dative	amandō	monendō	dūcendō	iaciendō	audiendō
Accusative	amandum	monendum	dūcendum	iaciendum	audiendum
Ablative	amandō	monendō	dūcendō	iaciendō	audiendō

USES OF GERUNDS

Gerunds in Latin serve as nouns, just as they do in English. You can be fond *of skiing,* suitable *for framing,* hate *waiting,* or learn *by doing.* A couple of uses of the Latin gerund, however, need *exploring.*

The words **causā** and **grātiā** are often preceded by a gerund in the genitive case to show purpose. This is virtually interchangeable with the construction using **ut/nē** and the subjunctive. It is often translated *for the sake of,* rather than *in order that.* Compare the basic ideas of **colloquendī causā vēnī** (*I came for the sake of chatting*) with **vēnī ut colloquerēmur** (*I came in order that we might chat*).

The preposition **ad** with the gerund in the accusative also shows purpose: **Ad colloquendum vēnī** (*I came to chat*).

Gerundives

The gerundive can be thought of as an adjectival form of the gerund. Its forms are identical to those of the future passive participle. Gerundives are used in two basic ways; one is in conjunction with gerunds, while the other is wholly its own.

Since gerunds are verbal nouns, their verbal aspect allows for direct objects and the like. In these situations, the gerundive appears and an odd grammatical swap occurs. Let's use an English sentence as an illustration: *I got to New York by riding the train. By riding* is a gerund phrase. *The train* is the direct object of *riding.* Latin gerunds don't take direct objects. Instead, the gerundive swaps places with the direct object: I got there *by train riding,* not *riding the train.*

~~vēra dīcendō~~	*by telling true things*
vērīs dīcendīs	*by true things being told*

The other, perhaps more common, place to find the gerundive is in a construction called the ***passive periphrastic***. Here, the gerundive can denote a sense of urgency, necessity, or obligation. A few Latin gerundives have carried into English. For example, a *memorandum* is *a thing that must be remembered.* An *agenda* is a list of *things that must be done.*

The passive periphrastic construction involves the gerundive accompanied by a form of **sum**. Rather than an ablative of agent, which you would expect, there is a ***dative of agent***, which makes sense given the basic idea of the dative.

Hoc [tibi] faciendum est.	*This must be done. (And it's your problem, so what are you going to do about it?)*

Written Practice 16-3

Translate the following sentences into English.

1. Hominēs pecūniae potiendae nimis cupidī nōn nimis sapientēs sunt.

   _____

   _____

2. Fulvius Rōmam ad omnia videnda īre voluit.

   _____

3. Sī hoc bellum ā nōbīs conficiētur, hoc proelium mīlitibus ācriter pugnandum erit.

   _____

   _____

4. Errandō plūrima discere possumus.

   _____

5. Illī epistulae scrībendae operam dīligenter dedī ut sententiam meam intellegerēs.

   _____

   _____

Supines

The *supine* is another type of verbal noun, which you have seen as the fourth principal part of a verb. It is a fourth-declension neuter noun with only two forms: accusative and ablative singular, e.g., **captum** and **captū**. It is also restricted to only two uses.

The accusative of the supine is used with verbs of motion to show purpose. The following sentences demonstrate the four purpose constructions you have already learned.

	*They are going to go to the woods **to hunt deer**.*
Supine	In silvās **cervōs vēnātum** prōgressūrī sunt.
Gerundive with **causā/grātiā**	In silvās **cervōrum vēnandōrum causā** prōgressūrī sunt.

Gerundive with **ad**   In silvās **ad cervōs vēnandōs** prōgressūrī sunt.

Clause with **ut** and subjunctive   In silvās prōgressūrī sunt **ut cervōs vēnentur.**

The ablative of the supine is used only as an **ablative of respect**. This is a new ablative use for you. It does not require a preposition and shows in what respect something is true.

Illō diē cervī **vēnātū** nōn difficilēs   *That day, the deer were not difficult **to***
erant.   ***hunt*** (literally, *with respect to hunting*).

Indirect Discourse

The term **indirect discourse** refers to the various grammatical constructions used to report a direct quotation. The original quote may have taken the form of a question, a command, or a statement.

Direct question   *Where are my keys?*
Indirect question   *I don't know **where your keys are**.*

Direct command   *Find them!*
Indirect command   *I told you **to find them**.*

Direct statement   *Your keys are on the table.*
Indirect statement   *I think **that your keys are on the table**.*

Both English and Latin employ special constructions to relate these types of expressions. We will examine each of them in the following sections.

One thing that all forms of indirect discourse have in common is that they are introduced by verbs of *saying, thinking, knowing,* or *perceiving.*

*I **told** you that he is leaving.*

*I **suspect** that he is leaving.*

*I **understand** that he is leaving.*

*I **hear** that he is leaving.*

Following are the most common verbs that introduce indirect discourse. Some you have already learned, others are part of the Key Vocabulary at the end of this chapter.

arbitror to think
audiō to hear
cognoscō to learn; know
crēdō to believe
dēmonstrō to show
dīcō to say, tell
doceō to teach
imperō to order
intellegō to understand
narrō to tell
negō to deny
nesciō not to know
nuntiō to announce
ōrō to beg
ostendō to show
putō to think
respondeō to answer
sciō to know
scrībō to write
sentiō to feel
spērō to hope
videō to see

What varies among the kinds of indirect discourse is the construction that follows these types of verbs. This is true in both English and Latin, but differences in approach vary widely between the two languages, making it impossible to translate the constructions word for word.

Indirect Questions

The Latin grammatical structure most parallel to its English counterpart is indirect question. The structure is the same; the difference lies in the mood of the verb. English uses the indicative mood, while Latin prefers the subjunctive.

Sciō **cūr mē amet**.   *I know **why he likes me***.

The construction begins with a question word, followed by other information in the clause, and ends with a verb in the subjunctive.

Written Practice 16-4

Translate the following sentences into English.

1. Nuntius Caesarī rettulit ubi hostēs castra nova posuissent.

   _____

2. Intellegitis quōmodo Lūcius vōbīs insidiās faciat.

   _____

3. Nescīvērunt quae perīcula in montibus eīs latērent.

   _____

4. Vīdit unde vēnissent.

   _____

5. Sciēbāmus quis esset et cūr nōs peteret.

   _____

Indirect Commands

Indirect command is a rather harsh term to describe this construction. It doesn't necessarily report an imperative. The central idea revolves around reporting what someone is trying to get someone else to do; the verb **persuādeō** (*to persuade*) is a good example. An indirect command uses the same **ut/nē** (with the subjunctive) structure as purpose clauses, and if you think about it, the basic concepts behind these two constructions are very much the same: Each states an action in order that something else may happen. In the example below, the first **ut** clause is an indirect command and the second is a purpose clause.

Eī persuāsī **ut mēcum pranderet**   *I persuaded him **to have lunch with me**
ut colloquārēmur.   **so we could talk***.

Written Practice 16-5

Translate the following sentences into English.

1. Petīvērunt ab eīs ut auxilium ferrent.

_____

2. Vōs ōrāvimus nē hoc facerētis.

_____

3. Senātum monet nē bellum in illōs inferat.

_____

4. Titum hortātus sum ut paucōs diēs nōbīscum morārētur.

_____

5. Exercituī imperābat ut sē retinēret.

_____

Indirect Statements

The construction for indirect statement in Latin is radically different from that in English, and students very often have a hard time getting used to it.

In English, we express an indirect statement by simply hooking a main verb (of saying, thinking, knowing, or perceiving) to the original statement with the conjunction *that*. Sometimes we get grammatically sloppy, especially in colloquial English, and forgo the conjunction *that,* shortening *I knew that he was here* to *I knew he was here.*

Latin's tack is completely different; the statements are not linked, so there is no conjunction. Instead, Latin converts the original statement into a sort of direct object in the form of an infinitive phrase.

English	*I hope*	*that*	*you are sending him the letter.*
	MAIN CLAUSE	CONJUNCTION	CLAUSE
Latin	Spērō		tē eī epistulam mittere.
	MAIN CLAUSE		INFINITIVE PHRASE

Notice how **tē**, the subject of the indirect statement, is in the accusative? Here, **spērō** (*I hope)* is the main verb, then **tē ... mittere** is *what* I hope, i.e., the direct object. Look closely at the structure of the infinitive phrase, and you'll notice that it follows the usual subject-object-verb Latin word order, but the subject of the mini-clause is in the accusative. Subjects of infinitives are always in the accusative, even in English. For example, we say *He told **me** to come,* not *He told **I** to come.*

As you recall, reflexive pronouns and adjectives refer back to the subject of the main verb. Since Latin treats indirect statements as objects of a main verb rather than as separate clauses, if the subject of an indirect statement is the same as that of the main verb, a reflexive is used. This is an important point to keep in mind, because English can be rather ambiguous, and Latin is not.

Marcus dixit **sē** epistulam scrībere.	*Marcus said that he (Marcus) was writing a letter.*
Marcus dixit **eum** epistulam scrībere.	*Marcus said that he (someone else) was writing a letter.*
Marcus dixit canem **suum** lātrāre.	*Marcus said that his dog (Marcus') was barking.*
Marcus dixit canem **eius** lātrāre.	*Marcus said that his dog (someone else's) was barking.*

Before going deeper into indirect statement, you need to know about relative time value, but we can't explore that until you know about the other infinitives. It is by their various tenses that things become relative.

Perfect and Future Infinitives

Infinitives are vague verb forms that express an action, but don't ascribe a doer. Very early in your study of Latin, you learned that infinitives appear as the second principal part of a verb, then that they have voice—active and passive, e.g., **dīcere** (*to say*) and **dīcī** (*to be said*). They also have *tense*. So far, all the infinitives you have encountered have been *present* infinitives. There are also *perfect* and *future* ones.

Since you have already learned the active and passive forms for infinitives for all conjugations in Chapter 10, for the moment you need to focus only on these new ones.

	Active	Passive		Active	Passive
	First Conjugation			**Second Conjugation**	
Present	portāre	portārī		monēre	monērī
Perfect	portāvisse	portātus esse		monuisse	monitus esse
Future	portātūrus esse	portātum īrī		monitūrus esse	monitum īrī
	Third Conjugation			**Third Conjugation** *-iō*	
Present	dūcere	dūcī		capere	capī
Perfect	duxisse	ductus esse		cēpisse	captus esse
Future	ductūrus esse	ductum īrī		captūrus esse	captum īrī
	Fourth Conjugation				
Present	audīre	audīrī			
Perfect	audīvisse	audītus esse			
Future	audītūrus esse	audītum īrī			

Perfect tense infinitives in active voice use the perfect active stem plus **-isse**. For passive voice, they use the perfect passive participle plus **esse**, which makes sense because that is how the perfect passive tenses are made.

Future infinitive forms aren't difficult, either. The active infinitive is simply the future active participle with **esse**. It should be noted, however, that the **esse** part is left off sometimes (e.g., **ductūrus** instead of **ductūrus esse**), and that the future infinitive of **sum**, **futūrus esse**, is often abbreviated to **fore**. The future passive infinitive consists of the supine with **īrī**. It is quite rare, so you needn't worry about it.

Relative Time Value in Indirect Statements

Present, perfect, and future infinitives have the same relative time values that you learned earlier in this chapter concerning present, perfect, and future participles. Present infinitives refer to something happening *at the same time* as the main verb, whatever tense the main verb may be. Perfect infinitives show *time before* the main verb, and future infinitives *time after*. The Latin concept of relative time value is extremely important with indirect statement, since the English mode of expression is so different. In the following examples, pay close attention to the tense of the main verb and the tense of the infinitive.

Putō eum pecūniam capere.	*I think that he is taking the money.*
Putō eum pecūniam cēpisse.	*I think that he took the money.*
Putō eum pecūniam captūrum esse.	*I think that he will take the money.*
Putābam eum pecūniam capere.	*I thought that he was taking the money.*
Putābam eum pecūniam cēpisse.	*I thought that he had taken the money.*
Putābam eum pecūniam captūrum esse.	*I thought that he was about to take the money.*
Putābō eum pecūniam capere.	*I will think that he will be taking the money.*
Putābō eum pecūniam cēpisse.	*I will think that he took the money.*
Putābō eum pecūniam captūrum esse.	*I will think that he will be going to take the money.*

The most important thing to remember here is that the tenses of infinitives are relative, whatever their formal grammatical name. For example, present infinitives show the same time as that of the main verb—not present time—and so on. This can become awkward when translating. Look at the very last Latin sentence above. The main verb is future; the infinitive is also future, making it a sort of double future, where the reference is to something happening in the future after something else that will be happening in the future. We have no tidy way of expressing this in English.

Things become even more challenging when the main verb is in the pluperfect, (which is already a double past), and the infinitive is perfect. A triple past!? In such situations, the idea is clear in Latin, but for the translation you have to get creative or simply settle for as close as you can get. It is an excellent example of the true meaning behind the expression "lost in translation."

Written Practice 16-6

Translate the following sentences into English. Pay close attention to shifts in tense of both main verbs and infinitives.

1. Arbitrātus est fīliam suam apud vōs tūtam esse.

   _____

2. Scīvistisne iter in Germāniam sīc arduum fore?

   _____

3. Caesar senātōribus ostendet sē bellum iustum in Gallōs intulisse.

_____

_____

4. Caesar senātōribus ostenderat sē bellum iustum in Gallōs illātūrum esse.

_____

_____

5. Ā Lūciō nōbīs narrātum est illōs dē quādam rē nōn consultōs esse.

_____

_____

6. Saepe negābat Titus fratrem suum ullum facinus facere.

_____

7. Saepe negābat Titus fratrem suum ullum facinus fēcisse.

_____

8. Saepe negābat Titus fratrem suum ullum facinus factūrum.

_____

9. Cum mihi ubi morātus esset explicāret, mīrātus sum mē eum nōn melius cognōvisse.

_____

_____

10. Mūtātīs mūtandīs, tandem intellexērunt omnia, quae facienda essent, facta esse.

_____

_____

Written Practice 16-7

Translate the following passage into English.

Trōiae, Graecīs discessīs, complūrēs Trōiānī magnum equum ā Graecīs relictum mīrantēs in lītore constābant. Dictum est hunc equum dōnō Neptūnō constructum esse, nē naufragārent. Lāocoōn, vātēs Neptūnī, cum conspexit tantōs circum equum mīrantēs, statim in lītus eōs monitum festīnāvit. Dixit ille istō dōnō accipiendō nīl nisi clādem fierī. Complūrēs, autem, equī in urbem trahendī causā, rēs parābant. Dum parābant, subitō duo anguēs ingentēs ē marī appāruērunt. Serpentēs ā quibusdam deīs, quī Graecōs mālēbant, missī erant, quī Lāocoontem occīderent. Miserō ita appropinquāvērunt ut brevī tempore morerētur. Etiam ambō fīliī eius, quī aderant, occīsī sunt.

Lāocoonte necātō, Trōiānī sensērunt equum recipiendum esse. Equum igitur in urbem trahere cōnātī sunt, at tam altus erat equus ut per portās haud facile traherētur. Utinam vātī pārērent! Equō in mediā urbe stante et hostibus ēgressīs, populus gaudēre coepit. Nēmō rogāvit quō Graecī abiissent vel cūr discessissent. Nēmō mīrātus est mortem vātis. Monuerat, sed nōn imperāverat ut ille equus in lītore manēret. Sī periit, sīc volēbant deī. Itaque, sine cūrā, gāvīsī sunt. Fīnem bellō tandem habēbant.

Multō vīnō haustō ac omnibus, iam madidīs, per urbem dormientibus, urbs tranquilla facta est. Illī Graecī in equō sē cēlantēs furtim fūnibus descendērunt, et sociīs exspectantibus portās urbis ad eās aperiendās petīvērunt. Portīs apertīs, occāsiōne datā, irruit exercitus Graecus tōtus. In urbem vim et ignem ubīque tulērunt. Plūrimī cīvēs in lectīs suīs dormientēs interfectī sunt. Ubīque omnia conturbāta sunt. Quid eīs faciendum est? Quis superesset?

Virī Trōiānī arma sua petēbant, sed frustrā. Mulierēs Trōiānae cum līberīs suīs effugere cōnātae sunt, sed frustrā. Fertur omnēs captās ad ōram statim ductās esse. Graecī in Graeciam eās referre in animō habuērunt ut venderentur. Ūnus, autem, nomine Aenēās, cum patre vetere fīliōque effūgit. Cum intellexit Aenēās Trōiam cāsūram esse, comitēs sociōsque celeriter collēgit, quī nāvēs parārent. Aenēās enim in Hesperiam statim proficīscī voluit ut Trōia nova conderētur.

Ille poēta Rōmānus, Publius Vergilius Marō, carmen longum, nomine Aenēida, scrīpsit. Quae fābula itinera Aenēae narrat. Carmen ipsum incipit:

"Arma virumque canō, Trōiae quī prīmus ab orīs …"

Vocabulary

Aenēās, Aenēae *m.* Aeneas

Aenēis, Aenēidos *f.* the Aeneid (*The title of the work is actually a Greek word, and* **Aenēida** *is a Greek accusative.*)

anguis, anguis *m.* snake

clādēs, clādis *f.* destruction, slaughter

colligō, -ere, collēgī, collectum to gather, collect

comes, comitis *m.* buddy, companion

complūrēs = **plūrimī**

condō, -ere, condidī, conditum to found, build

conspiciō, -ere, conspexī, conspectum to see

constō, -āre, constitī to stand together

construō, -ere, construxī, constructum to build

conturbō (1) to throw into confusion

dōnō Neptūnō as a gift to Neptune
fertur it is said
fūnis, fūnis *m.* rope
hauriō, -īre, hausī, haustum to drain
Hesperia, -ae *f.* Hesperia
irruō, -ere, irruī to rush in
Lāocoōn, Lāocoontis *m.* Laocoon
madidus, -a, -um drunk
naufragō, -āre, naufragāvī to suffer shipwreck (*from* **nāvis** + **frangō**)
serpens, serpentis *m.* snake
tranquillus, -a, -um still, quiet
ubique everywhere
vātēs, vātis *m.* priest

Key Vocabulary

Here are some important words that you should memorize.

Adjectives

arduus, -a, -um rough, difficult, harsh [arduous]
cupidus, -a, -um desirous (of), eager (for) [Cupid]
iustus, -a, -um just, fair; lawful; suitable [just]
vērus, -a, -um true, real [verify]

Adverbs

dīligenter carefully [diligent]
frustrā in vain, to no avail [frustration]
nimis too, excessively
subitō suddenly

Conjunctions

dum while
vel or (*This word is not interchangeable with* **aut** (or). **Aut** *joins mutually exclusive things, as in* life **or** death. *You can't have both.* **Vel** *suggests open-ended possibilities. For example,* you can stay here **or** go home (but you also have other options). *This conjunction sometimes appears as the enclitic* **-ve**, *which works like* **-que** (e.g., **domī rūrīve** (*at home or in the country*)).

Nouns

arma, -ōrum *n.pl.* weapons, arms
carmen, carminis *n.* song, poem
facinus, facinoris *n.* crime, deed
lectus, -ī *m.* bed
lūdus, -ī *m.* game, play; school [elude]
mulier, mulieris *f.* woman
occāsiō, occāsiōnis *f.* opportunity [occasion]
opera, -ae *f.* work
    operam dare to pay attention
ōra, -ae *f.* shore
sententia, -ae *f.* opinion, thought, meaning [sentence]

Verbs

appāreō, -ēre, appāruī, appāritum to appear [appear]
appropinquō (1) to approach (*This verb can use* **ad** *with the accusative or a dative to show destination.*)
arbitror (1) to think [arbitrate]
canō, -ere, cecinī, cantum to sing
cognoscō, -ere, cognōvī, cognitum to learn; (*perfect*) know, be acquainted with [cognizant]
construō, -ere, construxī, constructum to build, set up [construct]
consulō, -ere, consuluī, consultum to consult [consult]
discō, -ere, didicī to learn [discipline]
errō (1) to wander; be wrong [error]
explicō (1) to explain [explicate]
festīnō (1) to hurry
incipiō, -ere, incēpī, inceptum to begin [incipient]
mūtō (1) to change [mutate]
necō (1) to kill [internecine]
negō (1) to deny, say no [negate]
nesciō, -īre, nescīvī, nescītum not to know
nuntiō (1) to announce [announce]
ōrō (1) to beg, ask, plead [oration]
ostendō, -ere, ostendī, ostentum to show [ostentatious]
potior, -īrī, potītus sum to obtain (*usually with a genitive object*)
putō (1) to think [compute]
referō, referre, rettulī, relātum to bring back; report
respondeō, -ēre, respondī, responsum to answer [respond]

sapiō, -ere, sapīvī to know, be wise; have taste [*homo sapiens*]

sentiō, -īre, sensī, sensum to feel, perceive, experience, realize [sense]

spērō (1) to hope, expect [desperate]

vendō, -ere, vendidī, venditum to sell [vend]

QUIZ

Choose the most appropriate translation for each of the following sentences.

1. Dīcit mē errātūrum esse.

    (a) He said that I was wrong.

    (b) He says that I had been wrong.

    (c) He says that I am wrong.

    (d) He says that I'll be wrong.

2. Dīcet mē errāvisse.

    (a) He says that I'll be wrong.

    (b) He says that I was wrong.

    (c) He'll say that I was wrong.

    (d) He'll say that I am wrong.

3. Dīcit mē errāre.

    (a) He says that I am wrong.

    (b) He says that I was wrong.

    (c) He said that I was wrong.

    (d) He had said that I was wrong.

4. Dīcet mē errāre.

    (a) He said that I was wrong.

    (b) He says that I was wrong.

    (c) He'll say that I had been wrong.

    (d) He'll say that I am wrong.

5. Dixit mē errāvisse.

    (a) He said that I had been wrong.

    (b) He said that I was wrong.

    (c) He had said that I had been wrong.

    (d) He was saying that I was wrong.

6. Dīcit mē errāvisse.

    (a) He says that I am wrong.

    (b) He says that I was wrong.

    (c) He says that I will be wrong.

    (d) He says that I didn't order that.

7. Dīcet mē errātūrum esse.

    (a) He'll say that I was wrong.

    (b) He'll say that I am wrong.

    (c) He'll say that I'd be wrong.

    (d) He would say that I might be wrong.

8. Dixit mē errāre.

    (a) He had said that I had been wrong.

    (b) He will have said that I was wrong.

    (c) He said that I was wrong.

    (d) He was saying that I'd be wrong.

9. Dixerat mē errāre.

    (a) He had said that I was wrong.

    (b) He will have said that I was wrong.

    (c) He has said that I was wrong.

    (d) He is saying that I am wrong.

10. Dixit mē errātūrum.

    (a) He had said that I had been wrong.

    (b) He said that I would be wrong.

    (c) He has said that I was wrong.

    (d) He is saying that I will be wrong.

Choose the form of the adjective that agrees with each of the following nouns.

1. puerō
   - (a) huic
   - (b) hic
   - (c) hoc
   - (d) hāc

2. nuntius
   - (a) ille
   - (b) illōrum
   - (c) illud
   - (d) illum

3. verba
   - (a) quīdam
   - (b) quaedam
   - (c) quondam
   - (d) quoddam

4. portā
   - (a) eandem
   - (b) eaedem
   - (c) eādem
   - (d) eāsdem

5. mīlitum
   - (a) ipsōrum
   - (b) ipsī
   - (c) ipse
   - (d) ipsum

6. annum
   - (a) hoc
   - (b) hic
   - (c) hōc
   - (d) hunc

7. mātre
   - (a) illud
   - (b) illī
   - (c) illā
   - (d) illa

8. maria
   - (a) ipsa
   - (b) ipsum
   - (c) ipsā
   - (d) ipse

9. monte
   - (a) altus
   - (b) altiōre
   - (c) altissimī
   - (d) altius

10. partī
   - (a) facillimārum
   - (b) facilem
   - (c) faciliōrem
   - (d) facillimae

11. pācem
   - (a) fēlix
   - (b) fēlīciōrī
   - (c) fēlīcissimō
   - (d) fēlīciōrem

12. socius
   - (a) ācrius
   - (b) ācer
   - (c) ācris
   - (d) ācre

13. itinera

    (a) pēiōrēs

    (b) pēiōra

    (c) pēior

    (d) pēius

14. hominem

    (a) sōlōrum

    (b) sōlem

    (c) sōlum

    (d) sōlius

15. nāvēs

    (a) maiōrēs

    (b) maiōrī

    (c) maiōris

    (d) maximī

Choose the most appropriate translation for each of the following verb phrases and forms.

16. creāta est

    (a) he was a creature

    (b) she was elected

    (c) he is being elected

    (d) it has been made

17. ēgrediuntur

    (a) they are being attacked

    (b) they are leaving

    (c) they will depart

    (d) they will be forced

18. nāta est

   (a) she had been born

   (b) they arose

   (c) she was born

   (d) she was giving birth

19. they will follow

   (a) secūtī sunt

   (b) sequuntur

   (c) sequentur

   (d) sequēbantur

20. I seem

   (a) vidēbor

   (b) videō

   (c) videor

   (d) videar

21. oriēbātur

   (a) he was rising

   (b) she will be chosen

   (c) it has risen

   (d) it will rise

22. mīror

   (a) I see myself

   (b) to be seen

   (c) I seem

   (d) I am amazed

23. audīrī

   (a) to hear

   (b) to be heard

   (c) you are heard

   (d) you will be heard

24. līberāminī

    (a) small children

    (b) you are free

    (c) you are being freed

    (d) you are setting free

25. ausī erant

    (a) they were dared

    (b) they dare

    (c) they dared

    (d) they had dared

Choose the most appropriate answer for each of the following questions.

26. Nōnne vir bonus erat Tiberius?

    (a) Sīc.

    (b) Minimē.

    (c) Secundā hōrā.

    (d) In perīculō est.

27. Tibine placuit?

    (a) Ita.

    (b) Quīnque.

    (c) Secundā hōrā.

    (d) Athēnīs.

28. Cūr mēcum proficiscī nōn vīs?

    (a) Domī.

    (b) Secundā hōrā.

    (c) Multī.

    (d) Hīc manēre mālō.

29. Cui crēdis?

   (a) Titum.

   (b) Duo.

   (c) Lūciō.

   (d) Domī.

30. Quōmodo accipientur?

   (a) Cum gaudiō.

   (b) Secundā hōrā.

   (c) Minimē.

   (d) Vērō.

31. Quālis Homērus poēta fuit?

   (a) Duo.

   (b) Magnus.

   (c) In Graeciā.

   (d) Scrībet.

32. Quō abiit?

   (a) Domum.

   (b) Pompēiīs.

   (c) Secundā hōrā.

   (d) Ita.

33. Quot canēs habet?

   (a) Trēs.

   (b) Duobus.

   (c) Minimē.

   (d) Prīmus.

34. Num tibi placuit?

   (a) Vērō.

   (b) Parvus.

   (c) Minimē.

   (d) In theatrō.

35. Quandō pervenient?

    (a) Rōmā.

    (b) Pecūniā.

    (c) Secundā hōrā.

    (d) Ūnā.

Choose the correct form for each verb, as indicated.

36. amō: *third-person plural, pluperfect indicative passive*

    (a) amātī erant

    (b) amābantur

    (c) amātī erint

    (d) amārentur

37. dēleō: *second-person singular, imperative*

    (a) dēlēs

    (b) dēlēte

    (c) dēleās

    (d) dēlē

38. interficiō: *present passive infinitive*

    (a) interficī

    (b) interfectī

    (c) interficere

    (d) interfectūrus esse

39. metuō: *first-person plural, present subjunctive active*

    (a) metuimus

    (b) metuimur

    (c) metuāmus

    (d) metuerēmus

40. noceō: *second-person plural, pluperfect subjunctive active*

   (a) noceātis

   (b) nocuistis

   (c) nocērētis

   (d) nocuissētis

41. nōlō: *third-person singular, present subjunctive active*

   (a) nōluisset

   (b) nōlit

   (c) nōluerit

   (d) nollet

42. adiuvō: *third-person singular, perfect subjunctive passive*

   (a) adiūtus esset

   (b) adiūtus sit

   (c) adiuvāret

   (d) adiūvisset

43. emō: *second-person plural, perfect subjunctive active*

   (a) ēmerītis

   (b) ēmistis

   (c) emātis

   (d) ēmerātis

44. ferō: *present active infinitive*

   (a) tulisse

   (b) ferre

   (c) ferrī

   (d) lātūrus esse

45. supersum: *first-person singular, present subjunctive active*

   (a) supersim

   (b) superesse

   (c) superessem

   (d) superfuissem

Choose the most appropriate translation for each of the following sentences.

46. Dīcit mē errātūrum.

    (a) He said that I was wrong.

    (b) He says that I had been wrong.

    (c) He says that I am wrong.

    (d) He says that I'll be wrong.

47. Dīcit mē errāvisse.

    (a) He says that I'll be wrong.

    (b) He says that I was wrong.

    (c) He'll say that I was wrong.

    (d) He'll say that I am wrong.

48. Dīcit mē errāre.

    (a) He says that I am wrong.

    (b) He says that I was wrong.

    (c) He said that I was wrong.

    (d) He had said that I was wrong.

49. Dixit mē errāre.

    (a) He said that I was wrong.

    (b) He says that I was wrong.

    (c) He'll say that I had been wrong.

    (d) He'll say that I am wrong.

50. Dixit mē errāvisse.

    (a) He said that I had been wrong.

    (b) He said that I was wrong.

    (c) He had said that I had been wrong.

    (d) He was saying that I was wrong.

FINAL EXAM

Choose the most appropriate answer to complete each statement.

1. Latin nouns are divided into groups called _____.

    (a) declensions

    (b) conjugations

    (c) accommodations

    (d) inflections

2. The Latin abbreviation meaning *for the sake of example* is _____.

    (a) et al.

    (b) N.B.

    (c) i.e.

    (d) e.g.

3. The term _____ refers to a change in word order to show grammatical function.

    (a) declension

    (b) conjugation

    (c) analysis

    (d) inflection

4. Optative is an example of grammatical _____.

    (a) mood

    (b) tense

    (c) voice

    (d) case

5. Locative is an example of grammatical _____.

    (a) mood

    (b) attitude

    (c) voice

    (d) case

Choose the best translation for each of the following verb phrases and forms.

6. he made
   - (a) facit
   - (b) fēcit
   - (c) faciēbat
   - (d) fēcistī

7. they used to have
   - (a) habēbant
   - (b) habuērunt
   - (c) habērent
   - (d) habuerant

8. you (*sg.*) kept looking for
   - (a) petis
   - (b) petēbās
   - (c) petīvistī
   - (d) petīvistis

9. I came
   - (a) veniō
   - (b) vēnī
   - (c) veniēbam
   - (d) vēnistī

10. I seem
   - (a) videor
   - (b) vīdī
   - (c) vidērem
   - (d) vīsus sum

11. he used to be
   - (a) sit
   - (b) fuit
   - (c) est
   - (d) erat

12. they have praised
    (a) laudārent
    (b) laudent
    (c) laudant
    (d) laudāvērunt

13. he is finding
    (a) invēnit
    (b) invenit
    (c) invenīret
    (d) veniēbat

14. they are saving
    (a) servāvērunt
    (b) servāvissent
    (c) servant
    (d) servent

15. fertur
    (a) she does
    (b) he will have been taken
    (c) it is carried
    (d) to be brought

16. ēgrediuntur
    (a) they are entering
    (b) they are leaving
    (c) they will depart
    (d) they are dying

17. nātae sunt
    (a) they had been born
    (b) they arose
    (c) she was born
    (d) they were born

18. they will follow
    - (a) secūtī sunt
    - (b) sequēbantur
    - (c) sequentur
    - (d) sequantur

19. sentīrī
    - (a) to feel
    - (b) to be felt
    - (c) you are felt
    - (d) you will be felt

20. gāvīsī sunt
    - (a) they were rejoicing
    - (b) they rejoice
    - (c) they rejoiced
    - (d) they had rejoiced

Choose the best translation for each of the following sentences.

21. Tibi hīc manēre oportet.
    - (a) He is bringing you here to stay.
    - (b) You ought to stay here.
    - (c) You had to stay here.
    - (d) You regret to have stayed here.

22. Nihil Titum piget.
    - (a) Titus is ashamed of nothing.
    - (b) Titus is not a hog.
    - (c) Nothing annoys Titus.
    - (d) Nothing bores Titus.

23. Tē hoc facere nōlunt.

    (a) They won't want you to do this.

    (b) They don't want you to do this.

    (c) This needed to be done by you.

    (d) They will forbid you to do this.

24. Huius librī mē taedet.

    (a) This book used to bore me.

    (b) This book used to annoy me.

    (c) I am tired of this book.

    (d) I felt ashamed of this book.

25. Rōmā ēgredī tibi necesse erat.

    (a) You have to leave Rome.

    (b) You had to go out of Rome.

    (c) You won't be able to leave Rome.

    (d) You will have to enter Rome.

Identify the case of each of the following noun phrases.

26. puellīs laetīs

    (a) nominative plural

    (b) genitive singular

    (c) accusative plural

    (d) ablative plural

27. mīlitēs omnēs

    (a) nominative singular

    (b) genitive plural

    (c) accusative plural

    (d) ablative plural

28. canī parvō

    (a) nominative plural

    (b) dative singular

    (c) genitive singular

    (d) ablative singular

29. aquā dulcī

    (a) nominative singular

    (b) genitive singular

    (c) accusative plural

    (d) ablative singular

30. oculōrum pulchrōrum

    (a) nominative plural

    (b) genitive plural

    (c) accusative singular

    (d) ablative plural

31. hominēs malōs

    (a) nominative plural

    (b) genitive singular

    (c) accusative plural

    (d) ablative plural

32. dominī gravis

    (a) nominative plural

    (b) genitive singular

    (c) accusative plural

    (d) ablative singular

33. silvārum ingentium

    (a) nominative singular

    (b) genitive plural

    (c) accusative singular

    (d) ablative plural

34. magna māter
    (a) nominative singular
    (b) genitive singular
    (c) accusative plural
    (d) ablative singular

35. virīs bonīs
    (a) nominative plural
    (b) genitive plural
    (c) accusative plural
    (d) ablative plural

Identify the case or part of speech of each of the following Latin words.

36. perīculum
    (a) nominative singular
    (b) ablative singular
    (c) accusative plural
    (d) adverb

37. imperia
    (a) dative plural
    (b) nominative plural
    (c) genitive singular
    (d) adverb

38. hodiē
    (a) ablative singular
    (b) nominative singular
    (c) fifth declension
    (d) adverb

39. numquam
    - (a) accusative singular
    - (b) genitive plural
    - (c) nominative singular
    - (d) adverb

40. corporum
    - (a) accusative singular
    - (b) genitive plural
    - (c) genitive singular
    - (d) adverb

41. corpore
    - (a) ablative singular
    - (b) fifth declension
    - (c) dative singular
    - (d) adverb

42. nīl
    - (a) nominative plural
    - (b) genitive singular
    - (c) accusative plural
    - (d) adverb

43. clārō
    - (a) ablative singular
    - (b) accusative singular
    - (c) accusative plural
    - (d) adverb

44. puella
    - (a) ablative singular
    - (b) nominative singular
    - (c) genitive plural
    - (d) adverb

45. brevēs

    (a) nominative singular

    (b) nominative plural

    (c) accusative singular

    (d) adverb

Identify the tense of each of the following verb forms.

46. intulimus

    (a) perfect

    (b) pluperfect

    (c) future perfect

    (d) present

47. monēberis

    (a) future

    (b) present

    (c) imperfect

    (d) future perfect

48. ambulāverint

    (a) pluperfect

    (b) imperfect

    (c) perfect passive

    (d) perfect

49. properābās

    (a) present

    (b) imperfect

    (c) pluperfect

    (d) future

50. laudāvērunt
    (a) future perfect
    (b) pluperfect
    (c) present
    (d) perfect

51. rogantur
    (a) future perfect
    (b) imperfect
    (c) future
    (d) present

52. cadent
    (a) perfect
    (b) pluperfect
    (c) future
    (d) present

53. fugiant
    (a) future
    (b) pluperfect
    (c) present
    (d) imperfect

54. vincēs
    (a) future
    (b) present
    (c) future perfect
    (d) pluperfect

55. habēbitis
    (a) future
    (b) present
    (c) imperfect
    (d) pluperfect

Choose the best translation for each of the following words and phrases.

56. domum
    (a) in the house
    (b) at home
    (c) from home
    (d) homeward bound

57. Rōmae
    (a) from Rome
    (b) to Rome
    (c) around Rome
    (d) in Rome

58. rūs
    (a) toward the country
    (b) from the country
    (c) in the country
    (d) by means of the country

59. in oppidum
    (a) to the town
    (b) near the town
    (c) from the town
    (d) on the town

60. Athēnās
    (a) from Athens
    (b) in Athens
    (c) at Athens
    (d) to Athens

Choose the form of the adjective that agrees with each of the following nouns.

61. puer
    (a) huic
    (b) hic
    (c) hoc
    (d) hāc

62. templum
    (a) ille
    (b) illōrum
    (c) illud
    (d) illum

63. verbum
    (a) quīdam
    (b) quaedam
    (c) quondam
    (d) quoddam

64. portae
    (a) eandem
    (b) eaedem
    (c) eādem
    (d) eāsdem

65. mīlitem
    (a) ipsōrum
    (b) ipsī
    (c) ipse
    (d) ipsum

66. annum
    (a) hoc
    (b) hic
    (c) hōc
    (d) hunc

67. māter
    (a) illud
    (b) illī
    (c) illā
    (d) illa

68. mare
    (a) ipsa
    (b) ipsum
    (c) ipsā
    (d) ipse

69. monte
    (a) altus
    (b) altiōre
    (c) altissimī
    (d) altius

70. partium
    (a) facillimārum
    (b) facilem
    (c) faciliōrem
    (d) facillimō

71. pax
    (a) fēlix
    (b) fēlīciōrī
    (c) fēlīcissimō
    (d) fēlīciōrem

72. socius
    (a) ācrius
    (b) ācer
    (c) ācris
    (d) ācre

73. iter

    (a) pēiōrum

    (b) pēiōra

    (c) pēior

    (d) pēius

74. hominum

    (a) sōlōrum

    (b) sōlem

    (c) sōlum

    (d) sōlius

75. nāvēs

    (a) maiōrēs

    (b) maiōrī

    (c) maiōris

    (d) maximī

Choose the most appropriate answer for each of the following questions.

76. Num vir bonus erat Tiberius?

    (a) Sīc.

    (b) Minimē.

    (c) Secundā hōrā.

    (d) In perīculō est.

77. Tibine placet?

    (a) Ita.

    (b) Quinque.

    (c) Secundā hōrā.

    (d) Athēnīs.

78. Cūr domī manēre vīs?

    (a) Fēlīciter.

    (b) Secundā hōrā.

    (c) Multī.

    (d) Hīc manēre mālō.

79. Cui crēderem?

    (a) Titum.

    (b) Duo.

    (c) Lūciō.

    (d) Rūrī.

80. Quōmodo iter fēcit?

    (a) Nāve.

    (b) Secundā hōrā.

    (c) Minimē.

    (d) Vērō.

81. Quālis fīlius est?

    (a) Trēs.

    (b) Iuvenis.

    (c) Humī.

    (d) Habet.

82. Quō abiit?

    (a) Domō.

    (b) Pompēiōs.

    (c) Secundā hōrā.

    (d) Minimē.

83. Quot amīcōs habēs?

    (a) Sex.

    (b) Duobus.

    (c) Minimē.

    (d) Prīmus.

84. Nōnne tibi placuit?

    (a) Vērō.

    (b) Castra.

    (c) Minimē.

    (d) In theatrō.

85. Quandō fīet?

    (a) Rōmā.

    (b) Servī.

    (c) Secundā hōrā.

    (d) Nēmō.

Choose the correct form for each verb, as indicated.

86. portō: *first-person plural, pluperfect indicative passive*

    (a) portātī sīmus

    (b) portāmur

    (c) portātī erāmus

    (d) portābāmur

87. teneō: *second-person plural, imperative*

    (a) tenēre

    (b) tenēte

    (c) teneās

    (d) tenē

88. interficiō: *present infinitive active*

    (a) interficī

    (b) interfectī

    (c) interficere

    (d) interfectūrus esse

89. metuō: *first-person plural, present subjunctive active*

   (a) metuimus

   (b) metuimur

   (c) metuāmus

   (d) metuerēmus

90. noceō: *second-person plural, pluperfect subjunctive active*

   (a) noceātis

   (b) nocuistis

   (c) nocērētis

   (d) nocuissētis

91. nōlō: *second-person singular, present subjunctive active*

   (a) nōluissēs

   (b) nōlīs

   (c) nōlueris

   (d) nollēs

92. adiuvō: *third-person plural, perfect indicative passive*

   (a) adiūtī esse

   (b) adiūtī sunt

   (c) adiuvārent

   (d) adiūvissent

93. emō: *first-person plural, perfect subjunctive active*

   (a) ēmerīmus

   (b) ēmimus

   (c) emāmus

   (d) ēmerāmus

94. ferō: *present infinitive passive*

   (a) tulisse

   (b) ferre

   (c) ferrī

   (d) lātūrus esse

95. absum: *first-person singular, present subjunctive active*

    (a) absim

    (b) abesse

    (c) abessem

    (d) āfuissem

Choose the most appropriate translation for each of the following sentences.

96. Dīcit sē errāvisse.

    (a) He says that he is wrong.

    (b) He says that he was wrong.

    (c) He says that he will be wrong.

    (d) He says that he didn't order that.

97. Dīcet sē errātūrum esse.

    (a) He'll say that he was wrong.

    (b) He'll say that he will be wrong.

    (c) He'll say that he'd have been wrong.

    (d) He would say that he could be wrong.

98. Dixit sē errāre.

    (a) He had said that he had been wrong.

    (b) He will have said that he was wrong.

    (c) He said that he was wrong.

    (d) He was saying that he'd be wrong.

99. Dixerat sē errāre.

    (a) He had said that he was wrong.

    (b) He will have said that he was wrong.

    (c) He has said that he was wrong.

    (d) He is saying that he is wrong.

100. Dixit sē errātūrum.

    (a) He had said that he had been wrong.

    (b) He said that he would be wrong.

    (c) He has said that he was wrong.

    (d) He is saying that he will be wrong.

ANSWER KEY

CHAPTER 1

QUIZ

1. a		6. d	
2. b		7. c	
3. b		8. a	
4. c		9. d	
5. a		10. b	

CHAPTER 2

Written Practice 2-1

1. petīvī, I looked for / did look for / have looked for
   petīvistī, you looked for / did look for / have looked for
   petīvit, he/she/it looked for / did look for / has looked for
   petīvimus, we looked for / did look for / have looked for
   petīvistis, you looked for / did look for / have looked for
   petīvērunt, they looked for / did look for / have looked for
2. cecidī, I fell / did fall / have fallen
   cecidistī, you fell / did fall / have fallen
   cecidit, he/she/it fell / did fall / has fallen
   cecidimus, we fell / did fall / have fallen
   cecidistis, you fell / did fall / have fallen
   cecidērunt, they fell / did fall / have fallen
3. vīdī, I saw / did see / have seen
   vīdistī, you saw / did see / have seen
   vīdit, he/she/it saw / did see / has seen
   vīdimus, we saw / did see / have seen
   vīdistis, you saw / did see / have seen
   vīdērunt, they saw / did see / have seen

  4. fuī, I was / have been
     fuistī, you were / have been
     fuit, he/she/it was / has been
     fuimus, we were / have been
     fuistis, you were / have been
     fuērunt, they were / have been

  5. dixī, I said / did say / have said
     dixistī, you said / did say / have said
     dixit, he/she/it said / did say / has said
     diximus, we said / did say / have said
     dixistis, you said / did say / have said
     dixērunt, they said / did say / have said

Written Practice 2-2

1. fēcistis
2. habuērunt
3. audīvī
4. petīvimus
5. dedērunt
6. cecidistī
7. duxī
8. audīvērunt
9. dixit
10. vēnit

Written Practice 2-3

1. he said
2. you (*pl.*) did
3. I saw
4. we had
5. he gave
6. he came
7. I heard
8. they looked for
9. you (*pl.*) led
10. you (*sg.*) fell

Written Practice 2-4

1. portābam, I was carrying
  portābās, you were carrying
  portābat, he/she/it was carrying
  portābāmus, we were carrying
  portābātis, you were carrying
  portābant, they were carrying

2. cadēbam, I was falling
  cadēbās, you were falling
  cadēbat, he/she/it was falling
  cadēbāmus, we were falling
  cadēbātis, you were falling
  cadēbant, they were falling

3. movēbam, I was moving
  movēbās, you were moving
  movēbat, he/she/it was moving
  movēbāmus, we were moving
  movēbātis, you were moving
  movēbant, they were moving

4. sentiēbam, I was feeling
   sentiēbās, you were feeling
   sentiēbat, he/she/it was feeling
   sentiēbāmus, we were feeling
   sentiēbātis, you were feeling
   sentiēbant, they were feeling

Written Practice 2-5

1. habēbātis
2. audiēbant
3. veniēbam
4. putābāmus
5. dabant
6. vidēbās
7. cadēbam
8. dūcēbant
9. dīcēbat
10. petēbat

Written Practice 2-6

1. he used to make
2. we used to have
3. I used to see
4. we used to come
5. they used to look for
6. you (*pl.*) used to come
7. you (*sg.*) used to fall
8. they used to lead
9. she used to give
10. you (*sg.*) used to do

QUIZ

1. a
2. d
3. a
4. d
5. b
6. b
7. a
8. b
9. b
10. b

CHAPTER 3

Written Practice 3-1

1. second
2. fifth
3. third
4. third
5. first
6. fourth
7. third
8. second
9. third
10. first

Written Practice 3-2

1. transitive
2. transitive
3. transitive
4. transitive
5. transitive
6. intransitive
7. transitive
8. transitive
9. transitive
10. intransitive

Written Practice 3-3

1. Germānum, Germānōs
2. comitem, comitēs
3. mentem, mentēs
4. formam, formās
5. ventum, ventōs
6. agrum, agrōs
7. arborem, arborēs
8. fāmam, fāmās
9. mīlitem, mīlitēs
10. linguam, linguās

Written Practice 3-4

1. first, dea
2. third, X
3. second, hortus
4. first, mensa
5. third, X
6. second, morbus
7. first, agricola
8. third, X
9. second, lupus
10. third, X
11. second, geminus
12. first, insula
13. third, X
14. second, avus
15. third, X

Written Practice 3-5

Answers may vary.

1. They were falling. They kept falling.
2. We were welcoming the people. We used to welcome the people.
3. They saw the fathers. They have seen the fathers.
4. He used to love (his) mother. He began to love (his) mother.
5. I used to hear voices. I kept hearing voices.
6. He drove the horses. He has driven the horses.
7. You (*sg.*) read the book. You (*sg.*) have read the book.
8. You (*pl.*) read the books. You (*pl.*) have read the books.
9. We were holding the soldier. We kept holding the soldier.
10. He stood. He has stood.
11. You (*sg.*) were running away. You (*sg.*) kept running away.
12. They caught the enemy. They have caught the enemy.
13. I wrote a book. I have written a book.
14. We looked for the boys. We did look for the boys.
15. They were leading the man. They began to lead the man.

Written Practice 3-6

1. dolor, pain, grief [dolorous]
2. flamma, flame [flammable]
3. sermō, conversation, speech [sermon]
4. litterae, letters (of the alphabet) [letter]
5. cīvēs, citizens [civic]
6. campī, fields [campus]
7. invidia, envy [invidious]
8. pudor, shame [impudent]
9. lapidēs, stones [lapidary]
10. rāmus, branch [ramification]

Written Practice 3-7

Answers may vary.

1. The boy was looking for the dog. The boy kept looking for the dog.
2. The mother was holding the boy. The mother used to hold the boy.
3. The enemy captured us. The enemy did capture us.
4. You heard the voice. You have heard the voice.
5. I gathered flowers. I did gather flowers.
6. The men were driving the horses. The men began to drive the horses.
7. You used to have a master. You had a master.
8. You read the book. You have read the book.
9. The boys used to love (their) mother. The boys loved (their) mother.
10. The dogs led the soldiers. The dogs have led the soldiers. OR The soldiers led the dogs. The soldiers have led the dogs. (*Context is the only way to know for sure on this one!*)

QUIZ

1. transitive
2. intransitive
3. intransitive
4. transitive
5. transitive
6. transitive
7. transitive
8. transitive
9. intransitive
10. transitive

CHAPTER 4

Written Practice 4-1

1. optō   optāmus
   optās   optātis
   optat   optant
2. postulō   postulāmus
   postulās   postulātis
   postulat   postulant
3. clāmō   clāmāmus
   clāmās   clāmātis
   clāmat   clāmant
4. stō   stāmus
   stās   stātis
   stat   stant

Written Practice 4-2

1. I enter, I am entering, I do enter
2. you (*pl.*) choose, you (*pl.*) are choosing, you (*pl.*) do choose
3. they shout, they are shouting, they do shout
4. we block, we are blocking, we do block
5. he applauds, he is applauding, he does applaud

Written Practice 4-3

1. amāmus	4. rogō
2. laudat	5. vocant
3. stat	

Written Practice 4-4

1. maneō   manēmus
     manēs   manētis
     manet   manent
2. videō   vidēmus
     vidēs   vidētis
     videt   vident
3. teneō   tenēmus
     tenēs   tenētis
     tenet   tenent
4. moveō   movēmus
     movēs   movētis
     movet   movent
5. dēbeō   dēbēmus
     dēbēs   dēbētis
     dēbet   dēbent

Written Practice 4-5

1. we feel pain, we are feeling pain, we do feel pain
2. you (*sg.*) stay, you (*sg.*) are staying, you (*sg.*) do stay
3. he/she/it persuades, he/she/it is persuading, he/she/it does persuade
4. I bite, I am biting, I do bite
5. they stick, they are sticking, they do stick

Written Practice 4-6

1. habent	4. movet
2. vidēmus	5. teneō
3. docēs	

Written Practice 4-7

1. mittō   mittimus
     mittis   mittitis
     mittit   mittunt
2. intellegō   intellegimus
     intellegis   intellegitis
     intellegit   intellegunt
3. claudō   claudimus
     claudis   clauditis
     claudit   claudunt
4. tollō   tollimus
     tollis   tollitis
     tollit   tollunt

5. surgō   surgimus
     surgis   surgitis
     surgit   surgunt

Written Practice 4-8

1. I play, I am playing, I do play
2. you (*pl.*) bend, you (*pl.*) are bending, you (*pl.*) do bend
3. they stretch, they are stretching, they do stretch
4. we allow, we are allowing, we do allow
5. he/she/it covers, he/she/it is covering, he/she/it does cover

Written Practice 4-9

1. relinquit
2. dīcō
3. scrībitis
4. vincunt
5. pōnimus

Written Practice 4-10

1. faciō   facimus
     facis   facitis
     facit   faciunt
2. capiō   capimus
     capis   capitis
     capit   capiunt
3. fugiō   fugimus
     fugis   fugitis
     fugit   fugiunt

Written Practice 4-11

1. they fall short, they are falling short, they do fall short
2. I throw forward, I am throwing forward, I do throw forward
3. you (*sg.*) grab, you (*sg.*) are grabbing, you (*sg.*) do grab
4. he/she/it desires, he/she/it is desiring, he/she/it does desire
5. you (*pl.*) lure, you (*pl.*) are luring, you (*pl.*) do lure

Written Practice 4-12

1. fugimus
2. accipit
3. faciunt
4. capis
5. capiō

Written Practice 4-13

1. sentiō   sentīmus
     sentīs   sentītis
     sentit   sentiunt
2. veniō   venīmus
     venīs   venītis
     venit   veniunt
3. serviō   servīmus
     servīs   servītis
     servit   serviunt

Written Practice 4-14

1. I feel, I am feeling, I do feel
2. they arrive, they are arriving, they do arrive
3. you (*pl.*) throw, you (*pl.*) are throwing, you (*pl.*) do throw
4. they toss under, they are tossing under, they do toss under
5. we are slaves, we're very much slaves right now, we really are slaves

Written Practice 4-15

1. capimus
2. accipit
3. audiunt
4. invenīs
5. dormit

Written Practice 4-16

1. he/she/it was OR there was
2. you (*sg.*) are
3. they were OR there were
4. you (*sg.*) have been
5. I am

Written Practice 4-17

1. fuistis
2. erant
3. esse
4. erat
5. erant

QUIZ

1. a
2. a
3. b
4. b
5. d
6. c
7. c
8. b
9. d
10. b

CHAPTER 5

Written Practice 5-1

1. oculōrum, second
2. aquae, first
3. mulierum, third
4. principiī, second
5. iuvenis, third
6. sermōnum, third
7. animārum, first
8. vēlōcitātis, third
9. hircōrum, second
10. fāmae, first

Written Practice 5-2
1. the courage of the soldiers
2. the master's slaves
3. a father's son
4. the voices of the girls
5. a mother's concerns
6. the master of no one
7. the men's horses
8. enemies of Rome
9. the boy's book
10. a person's spirit

Written Practice 5-3
1. amīcus puerōrum
2. servī dominī
3. animus mīlitum
4. canis puellae
5. oculī equōrum

Written Practice 5-4
1. your (*sg.*) master
2. our slave
3. my cares
4. your (*pl.*) voices
5. your (*sg.*) water

Written Practice 5-5
1. librī tuī
2. cūrārum nostrārum
3. dominī meī
4. hostis vestrī
5. fīliārum meārum

Written Practice 5-6
1. fundō
2. gladiō
3. grātiīs
4. rūpī
5. equitibus
6. ūvīs
7. nectarī
8. vallō
9. falcibus
10. lacrimae

Written Practice 5-7
1. Slaves are giving water to the soldiers.
2. The mother was showing the boys the horses.
3. The book was mine.
4. Publius used to be our friend.
5. The father entrusted his daughter to his friend Septimius.

QUIZ

1. c	6. d
2. d	7. d
3. a	8. c
4. d	9. a
5. b	10. c

PART ONE TEST

1. a	18. d	35. d
2. b	19. c	36. d
3. a	20. a	37. d
4. d	21. b	38. b
5. b	22. a	39. c
6. c	23. a	40. b
7. a	24. a	41. c
8. a	25. a	42. d
9. d	26. b	43. b
10. b	27. a	44. d
11. c	28. a	45. c
12. a	29. b	46. b
13. c	30. a	47. d
14. a	31. d	48. c
15. a	32. c	49. b
16. a	33. b	50. b
17. a	34. d	

CHAPTER 6

Written Practice 6-1

ruber	rubra	*rubrum*
rubrī	rubrae	*rubrī*
rubrō	rubrae	*rubrō*
rubrum	rubram	*rubrum*
rubrō	*rubrā*	*rubrō*
rubrī	rubrae	*rubra*
rubrōrum	rubrārum	*rubrōrum*
rubrīs	rubrīs	*rubrīs*
rubrōs	rubrās	*rubra*
rubrīs	*rubrīs*	*rubrīs*

Written Practice 6-2

1. homō Rōmānus, a Roman person
2. puellae laetae, of a happy girl
3. canem amīcum, a friendly dog (accusative)
4. canis amīcus, a friendly dog (nominative)
5. fīliī meī, my son's

Written Practice 6-3

1. canēs bonī
2. equus pulcher
3. aqua bona
4. silva parva
5. māter vestra
6. vox tua
7. puellae laetae
8. oculus malus
9. mīlitēs amīcī
10. librī nostrī

Written Practice 6-4

1. There were many small forests.
2. The happy boys used to have loud voices.
3. No one is capturing the Roman men.
4. Your father welcomed me.
5. The courage of our soldiers was great.

Written Practice 6-5

1. Mātrēs bonae puerōs parvōs cūrant.
2. Liber erat bonus.
3. Amīcōs tuōs amō.
4. Mīlitēs nostrī multōs hostēs vīcērunt.
5. Multōs equōs habēbāmus.

Written Practice 6-6

omnis	omnis	*omne*
omnis	omnis	*omnis*
omnī	omnī	*omnī*
omnem	omnem	*omne*
omnī	*omnī*	*omnī*
omnēs	omnēs	*omnia*
omnium	omnium	*omnium*
omnibus	omnibus	*omnibus*
omnēs	omnēs	*omnia*
omnibus	*omnibus*	*omnibus*

Written Practice 6-7

1. cūram difficilem, a difficult concern
2. omnēs mīlitēs, all the soldiers
3. canis ingentis, of a huge dog
4. hostis ācer, a fierce enemy
5. virī nōbilis, of a noble man

Written Practice 6-8

1. librī brevēs
2. equī celerēs
3. aqua dulcis
4. omnis silva
5. cūra gravis

Written Practice 6-9

1. A brave person is afraid of no one.
2. My sister used to have a serious mind.
3. We saw fierce dogs.
4. Everyone welcomes us.
5. Your (*sg.*) horse is fast.

QUIZ

1. b
2. c
3. c
4. d
5. d
6. a
7. b
8. c
9. b
10. d

CHAPTER 7

Written Practice 7-1

1. cōpiōsē, abundantly
2. maestē, sadly
3. tristiter, sadly
4. fortiter, bravely
5. saevē, savagely
6. ingenter, hugely
7. alacriter, in a lively manner
8. amīcē, like a friend
9. negōtiōsē, busily
10. dīligenter, carefully

Written Practice 7-2

1.

arvum lātum	arva lāta
arvī lātī	arvōrum lātōrum
arvō lātō	arvīs lātīs
arvum lātum	arva lāta
arvō lātō	arvīs lātīs

2. collum gracile   colla gracilia
    collī gracilis   collōrum gracilium
    collō gracilī   collīs gracilibus
    collum gracile   colla gracilia
    collō gracilī   collīs gracilibus
3. tempus breve   tempora brevia
    temporis brevis   temporum brevium
    temporī brevī   temporibus brevibus
    tempus breve   tempora brevia
    tempore brevī   temporibus brevibus

Written Practice 7-3

1. ventō
2. perīculō
3. flammīs
4. iūre
5. arvīs
6. mōre
7. cīvibus
8. crētā
9. creātiōne
10. ūvīs

Written Practice 7-4

1. dē multīs perīculīs
2. cum omnibus amīcīs meīs
3. inter hominēs miserōs
4. ex aquā frīgidā
5. sine vōbīs
6. ab undīs ingentibus
7. prō amīcitiā tuā
8. sub monte altō
9. ad lītus Italiae
10. prae mīlitibus fortibus

Written Practice 7-5

1. Iam in Āfricā diū manēbant., ablative of place where, Now they were staying in Africa for a long time.
2. Heri ē castrīs celeriter fūgērunt., ablative of place from which, Yesterday, they fled quickly out of the camp.
3. Hodiē in pompā multōs hominēs clārōs facile vīdimus., ablative of place where, Today, we easily saw many famous people in the parade.
4. Nōn erat Tullō magnum imperium., dative of possession, Tullus didn't have great power.
5. Dente lupus, cornū taurus petit., ablative of means, A wolf attacks with his tooth, a bull with his horn.
6. Nihil nisi multa corpora ibi in mediō locō post bellum invēnistis., ablative of place where, You (pl.) found nothing except many bodies there in the middle of the place after the war.
7. Nunc servus puerōs magnā cum cūrā spectat., ablative of manner, Now the slave is watching the boys/children with great concern.

8. Hominēs in <u>urbe</u> novā saepe tristēs sunt., ablative of place where, People in a new city are often sad.
9. Dominus bonus servōs <u>virgā</u> numquam verberat., ablative of means, A good master never beats his slaves with a switch.

QUIZ

1. c	6. a
2. c	7. b
3. a	8. d
4. d	9. b
5. a	10. d

CHAPTER 8

Written Practice 8-1

1. portābō, I will carry
   portābis, you will carry
   portābit, he/she/it will carry
   portābimus, we will carry
   portābitis, you will carry
   portābunt, they will carry
2. docēbō, I will teach
   docēbis, you will teach
   docēbit, he/she/it will teach
   docēbimus, we will teach
   docēbitis, you will teach
   docēbunt, they will teach

Written Practice 8-2

1. rogābis, you (*sg.*) will ask
2. laudābimus, we will praise
3. tenēbitis, you (*pl.*) will hold
4. dōnābō, I will give
5. vocābunt, they will call
6. valēbit, he will be well
7. monēbis, you (*sg.*) will warn
8. rīdēbimus, we will laugh
9. stābō, I will stand
10. servābit, he will save

Written Practice 8-3

1. caedam, I will cut
   caedēs, you will cut
   caedet, he/she/it will cut
   caedēmus, we will cut
   caedētis, you will cut
   caedent, they will cut

2. īciam, I will strike
       īciēs, you will strike
       īciet, he/she/it will strike
       īciēmus, we will strike
       īciētis, you will strike
       īcient, they will strike
   3. perveniam, I will arrive
       perveniēs, you will arrive
       perveniet, he/she/it will arrive
       perveniēmus, we will arrive
       perveniētis, you will arrive
       pervenient, they will arrive

Written Practice 8-4

1. cadēs, you (*sg.*) will fall
2. fugiēmus, we will run away
3. capiam, I will take
4. legent, they will read
5. venient, they will come
6. mittēs, you (*sg.*) will send
7. inveniēmus, we will find
8. agam, I will do
9. dīcet, he will say
10. relinquēs, you (*sg.*) will abandon

Written Practice 8-5

1. he is afraid
2. we were teaching
3. they will seize
4. they are giving back
5. we will give
6. you (*sg.*) are writing
7. I will do
8. you (*pl.*) asked
9. you (*pl.*) are seeing
10. I am looking for

Written Practice 8-6

    fueram, I had been
    fuerās, you had been
    fuerat, he/she/it had been
    fuerāmus, we had been
    fuerātis, you had been
    fuerant, they had been

Written Practice 8-7

crēdiderō, I will have believed
crēdideris, you will have believed
crēdiderit, he/she/it will have believed
crēdiderimus, we will have believed
crēdideritis, you will have believed
crēdiderint, they will have believed

Written Practice 8-8

1. Tomorrow, our soldiers will have arrived in Germany.
2. There had been great dangers there.
3. We had warned you about the fierce enemy.
4. After I come to the Forum, my friends will greet me.
5. Yesterday, they had killed many unfortunate people.
6. The soldiers will have walked sadly into camp with the baggage.
7. The slaves will be happy after their master gives them freedom.
8. The mugger had grabbed the man's money before he ran into the crowd.
9. You will soon see your mother.
10. The son will have stayed with his father for the entire day.

QUIZ

1. a
2. b
3. a
4. b
5. a
6. c
7. d
8. c
9. a
10. b

CHAPTER 9

Written Practice 9-1

1. ad Aegyptum, in Aegyptō, ab Aegyptō
2. Corinthum, Corinthī, Corinthō
3. Delphōs, Delphīs, Delphīs
4. Fīdēnās, Fīdēnīs, Fīdēnīs
5. ad Graeciam, in Graeciā, ā Graeciā
6. ad insulam, in insulā, ab insulā
7. Mediolānum, Mediolānī, Mediolānō
8. ad oppidum, in oppidō, ab oppidō
9. ad patriam, in patriā, ā patriā
10. Perusiam, Perusiae, Perusiā
11. ad Siciliam, in Siciliā, ā Siciliā
12. Tībur, Tīburī, Tībure
13. ad urbem, in urbe, ab urbe
14. Veiōs, Veiīs, Veiīs
15. ad vīcum, in vīcō, ā vīcō

Written Practice 9-2

1. not an **i**-stem

fulgur	fulgura
fulguris	fulgurum
fulgurī	fulguribus
fulgur	fulgura
fulgure	fulguribus

2. parisyllabic

classis	classēs
classis	classium
classī	classibus
classem	classēs OR classīs
classe	classibus

3. monosyllabic

ars	artēs
artis	artium
artī	artibus
artem	artēs OR artīs
arte	artibus

4. neuter in **-ar**

calcar	calcāria
calcāris	calcārium
calcārī	calcāribus
calcar	calcāria
calcārī	calcāribus

Written Practice 9-3

1.

aciēs	aciēs
aciēī	aciērum
aciēī	aciēbus
aciem	aciēs
aciē	aciēbus

2.

morsus	morsūs
morsūs	morsuum
morsuī	morsibus
morsum	morsūs
morsū	morsibus

Written Practice 9-4

Many years ago, there was a long and difficult war between the Greeks and the Trojans. The cause of the war was Helen, the wife of Menelaus. Helen was the daughter of Leda, a beautiful young woman, and Jupiter, king of all the gods. Menelaus had a brother named Agamemnon. Agamemnon lived in Mycenae, which was a wealthy and ancient city in Greece, and he was king there. One night, Helen had left Mycenae and Menelaus and had sailed across the sea to Troy with Paris, a young man whose father was king of Troy. In the morning, Menelaus could not find his wife. Where was she? Where had she gone off to?

Troy was not a small town, but an old and large city near the sea in Asia. Menelaus approached his brother and asked for help from him. He immediately called other powerful kings and together they sailed with many ships from Greece to Troy. All the citizens of Troy were very afraid and they closed the gates of the city and did not welcome the Greeks.

Written Practice 9-5

1. iaciō
   iaciēbam
   iaciam
   iēcī
   iēceram
   iēcerō
2. dīcis
   dīcēbās
   dīcēs
   dixistī
   dixerās
   dixeris
3. estis
   erātis
   eritis
   fuistis
   fuerātis
   fueritis
4. tenent
   tenēbant
   tenēbunt
   tenuērunt
   tenuerant
   tenuerint
5. sentīmus
   sentiēbāmus
   sentiēmus
   sensimus
   senserāmus
   senserimus

6. habitat
   habitābat
   habitābit
   habitāvit
   habitāverat
   habitāverit

QUIZ

1. b	6. b
2. c	7. b
3. a	8. a
4. b	9. b
5. c	10. c

CHAPTER 10

Written Practice 10-1

1. potuerant
2. potuerint
3. poterātis OR potuistis
4. poteris
5. poterant
6. possumus
7. potuerās
8. possum
9. possunt
10. poterit

Written Practice 10-2

1. They are able to do everything.
2. Titus began to understand this.
3. I don't know how to swim, because I am afraid of the water.
4. They weren't able to bring me help.
5. We gladly wish to drink either this wine or that (one).
6. You ought to learn to read Latin literature.
7. They used to know how to write Greek letters.
8. Tomorrow, you will be able to arrive home.
9. Quintus, Marcus' son, doesn't know how to be good.
10. I began to drink too much (of the) wine, and so now I am obviously drunk.

Written Practice 10-3

1. voluī	6. voluerāmus
2. volētis	7. nōluerint
3. nōn vult	8. nōn vultis
4. volēbant	9. nōlēbam
5. nōn vīs	10. volet

Written Practice 10-4

1. complementary, On that day Caesar wanted to send the soldiers into battle.
2. complementary, Marcus is not willing to get together with us in the Forum.
3. **texere** objective, **docēre** complementary, Servilia wanted to teach Octavia how to weave.
4. — (*There is no infinitive in this sentence!*), I forced everyone into the house.
5. **intellegere** objective, **cōgere** complementary, I began to make Lucius understand this.
6. complementary, The stupid man wanted to drive the oxen through the forest.
7. — (*No infinitive in this one either!*), At that time, Plinius was living with his uncle in Misenum.
8. objective, I will not allow you to stay in this city.
9. objective, He will forbid slaves to go out of the house without an order.
10. objective, Gnaeus has already ordered you never to be here.

Written Practice 10-5

1. He is not ashamed of his own deeds.
2. It's not okay for you to go back now.
3. Sometimes, it's hard to love him.
4. What did you like at the dinner?
5. I don't regret anything.
6. Lucius is really annoyed by Titus' arrival.
7. It wasn't right for us to leave Publius at the party.
8. That guy bores me.
9. Caesar had to read this letter immediately.
10. You should stay the night at my house.

Written Practice 10-6

1. īmus
2. iī
3. ībunt
4. ierās
5. ībātis
6. ierit
7. eō
8. ierant
9. ībitis
10. iit

Written Practice 10-7

1. tulit
2. ferēs
3. tulerant
4. fertis
5. ferēbāmus
6. tulerō
7. fers
8. ferunt
9. ferēmus
10. ferre

Written Practice 10-8

1. to be above, survive
2. to come around
3. it isn't allowed
4. to stand between
5. to bring back/again
6. to call together
7. to finish

8. to put against
9. to close back up
10. not able to be called back

QUIZ

1. d	6. b
2. c	7. b
3. c	8. a
4. a	9. b
5. a	10. b

PART TWO TEST

1. d	18. a	35. a
2. b	19. b	36. b
3. b	20. a	37. a
4. d	21. a	38. a
5. b	22. a	39. d
6. c	23. c	40. d
7. b	24. d	41. c
8. b	25. d	42. b
9. a	26. d	43. a
10. d	27. d	44. c
11. a	28. c	45. a
12. b	29. b	46. a
13. d	30. c	47. b
14. d	31. d	48. d
15. b	32. b	49. c
16. a	33. d	50. d
17. c	34. b	

CHAPTER 11

Written Practice 11-1

1. haec vīna, nominative OR accusative
2. hīs epistulīs, ablative
3. hic deus, nominative
4. huius noctis, genitive
5. huic rēgī, dative OR hōc rēge, ablative
6. hoc tempus, nominative OR accusative
7. hīs virginibus, dative
8. hī puerī, nominative
9. hanc rem, accusative
10. hōrum librōrum, genitive

Written Practice 11-2

1. illius equī, genitive
2. illud mare, nominative OR accusative
3. illārum matrum, genitive
4. illīs locīs, dative
5. illa rēs, nominative
6. illīs mīlitibus, ablative
7. illī virginī, dative OR illā virgine, ablative
8. illum cīvem, accusative
9. illōrum templōrum, genitive
10. illae puellae, nominative

Written Practice 11-3

1. That night, the shouting of the crowd frightened them.
2. He kept it for himself.
3. He had already sold his (own) house.
4. Their borders are not safe.
5. Their (own) borders are not safe.
6. Caesar ordered his (own) men to attack those creeps' battleline.
7. They were taking all his friends on this journey with them.
8. When the messenger arrives, they will know everything.
9. Both this woman and that woman have never agreed.
10. Nevertheless, I taught you about this yesterday.

Written Practice 11-4

1. that, nominative plural
2. whose, genitive singular
3. that, accusative singular
4. (in) which, ablative singular
5. (to) which, dative singular
   that, nominative singular
6. that, accusative plural
7. whom, accusative plural
8. whose, genitive singular
9. (with) what, ablative singular
10. (to) whom, dative singular

Written Practice 11-5

When the Greeks had arrived, they pitched camp near the sea outside the walls of the city of Troy. They used to go around the walls of the city every day, but every day each gate that they found always stood closed and the Trojans were unwilling to open them. And so they waged this war, which we call the Trojan War, for 10 years. There were many (and) fierce battles, in which many brave men bravely fought and died for their country. After those 10 years, however, neither the Greeks nor the Trojans had won, and both these men and those men were very tired and miserable. Everyone wanted to end that nasty war.

Ulysses, however, whom some considered a clever man, but others an evil one, finally adopted a certain new plan, which was both clever and evil. He wanted, you see, to build a wooden horse, huge and hollow, in which a few soldiers were able to hide themselves in secret, then as a gift—actually, as a trick—for the citizens of Troy, to bring this horse to the gates of the city and leave it there.

The Greeks sent a messenger to Priam, the king of the Trojans, to whom he said: "O king, I have come to you and want you to hear a few words of mine, if I may. We are not able to conquer you, nor will we ever be able to. We know this well. And so we want to go back home either soon or as soon as possible. Our men are now building a huge statue as a gift for you. When we (will) have completed this, we will get on board our ships, and you will find this gift outside your walls in a certain place where we will have left it for you." After he had said these deceitful words, he went away, returned to his camp, and reported to his men all that he had said.

QUIZ

1. a
2. d
3. c
4. b
5. d
6. d
7. d
8. c
9. c
10. a

CHAPTER 12

Written Practice 12-1

1. you (*pl.*) are hiding, cēlāminī, you (*pl.*) are being hidden
2. they were being built, aedificābant, they were building
3. we are giving, damur, we are given
4. you (*sg.*) are being taught, docēs, you (*sg.*) are teaching
5. it is held, habet, it holds
6. she will praise, laudābitur, she will be praised
7. I move, moveor, I am being moved
8. they could, —, — (*Possum* is intransitive, and so it has no passive forms.)
9. you (*sg.*) will be held, tenēbis, you (*sg.*) will hold
10. I will love, amābor, I will be loved

Written Practice 12-2

1. you (*sg.*) heard, audītus es, you (*sg.*) were heard
2. it had put, positum erat, it had been put
3. I was abandoned, relīquī, I abandoned
4. they will have been killed, occīderint, they will have killed
5. you (*pl.*) caught, captī estis, you (*pl.*) were caught
6. they had been made, fēcerant, they had made
7. we forced, coactī sumus, we were forced
8. it opened, apertum est, it was opened
9. she was welcomed, accēpit, she welcomed
10. I seized, rapta sum, I was seized

Written Practice 12-3

1. pōnere, to put, pōnī, to be put
2. dīcere, to say, dīcī, to be said
3. portāre, to carry, portārī, to be carried
4. aperīre, to open, aperīrī, to be opened
5. iacere, to throw, iacī, to be thrown
6. appellāre, to call, appellārī, to be called
7. habēre, to have, habērī, to be had
8. sentīre, to feel, sentīrī, to be felt
9. nolle, to be unwilling, —, —
10. invenīre, to find, invenīrī, to be found

Written Practice 12-4

1. Soon, the boys will be called back home by their mother, who is always worried, and they will be sad, because they will not want to go back.
2. Those prisoners, who were still staying in the prison, wanted to be freed.
3. These men, however, will be punished tomorrow.
4. After many years, the Germans, who had been fiercely attacked by Tiberius, were able to be conquered.
5. Finally, the lions, which we were all waiting for, were brought into the arena.
6. His poor daughters will have been killed before he comes back from Athens.
7. That night, I myself was not awakened by the noise, which could be heard by everyone.
8. We are still very afraid of all those dangers, which we began to escape.
9. The excellent dinner, which you have been awaiting for a long time now, will soon be brought into the dining room for us by the slaves.
10. Lucius Tarquinius Superbus was never elected king by the Roman people; instead, he seized the kingdom from his father, and so the scoundrel was liked by no one.

Written Practice 12-5

1. they were testing
2. I was afraid
3. you (*sg.*) will have overtaken
4. you (*pl.*) are trying
5. it had seemed
6. he will go out
7. ausī sunt
8. fīēmus
9. morāta est
10. mortua est
11. sequēbāris
12. gaudeō

Written Practice 12-6   Synopsis

1. legimus   legimur
   legēbāmus   legēbāmur
   legēmus   legēmur
   lēgimus   lectī sumus
   lēgerāmus   lectī erāmus
   lēgerimus   lectī erimus

2. vidēs   vidēris
   vidēbās   vidēbāris
   vidēbis   vidēberis
   vīdistī   vīsa es
   vīderās   vīsa erās
   vīderis   vīsa eris

3. —   nascuntur
   —   nascēbantur
   —   nascentur
   —   nātī sunt
   —   nātī erant
   —   nātī erunt

4. fert   fertur
   ferēbat   ferēbātur
   feret   ferētur
   tulit   lātum est
   tulerat   lātum erat
   tulerit   lātum erit

5. audētis   —
   audēbātis   —
   audēbitis   —
   —   ausae estis
   —   ausae erātis
   —   ausae eritis

QUIZ

1. b   6. d
2. b   7. d
3. a   8. b
4. d   9. d
5. a   10. c

CHAPTER 13

Written Practice 13-1
1. meliora ōmina
2. pessimīs carminibus
3. albārum ovium
4. fortissimīs pōtiōnibus
5. altissimō monte
6. plūs pecūniae
7. celerrimās nāvēs
8. gravī saxō
9. minōris puellae
10. commodior hōra

Written Practice 13-2
1. gladly
2. rather/more happily
3. rather/more clearly
4. very/most briefly
5. very/most beautifully
6. very/most luckily
7. in a friendly manner
8. excellently
9. rather/more sweetly
10. rather/more easily

Written Practice 13-3

When the Greek messenger had spoken with King Priam and they had ended their rather serious conversation, he returned to his camp. After he had told everything to the Greeks, they rejoiced very greatly, especially Ulysses, because the king of Troy seemed to have accepted quite gladly the deceitful plan, which had been created by him himself. Priam, you see, as Ulysses well knew, preferred peace to war, especially after the death of Hector, his dear son, by the hand of Achilles. Both peoples wanted a successful outcome to the situation. Therefore, very many of the ships were both immediately and very gladly broken into very many parts, so that they could have lumber with which they could build that huge and hollow horse.

And so the horse was very quickly built by the Greek soldiers, then a hundred of the bravest and best of the Greeks were called together. When everyone had gathered, the plan was explained to these men by Ulysses:

"All of you are not only very brave, but also excellent men, and you fear very few things. I don't doubt (this). Only certain ones of you, however, will be able to be chosen, because this horse is large, but not very large, and so thousands of soldiers cannot be held by the horse. Therefore, only 20 of you will be chosen. Some will enter the horse this night, and by others the horse will be dragged to the gates of the city and will be left there. Meanwhile, our ships will seem to have gone away, but, as only we know, they will not have gone far, only out of the sight of the Trojans. When the horse has (will

have) been dragged within the gates by the Trojans, that night, while they will be rejoicing, we 20, who will be hiding (ourselves) in the horse, will climb down. At that time, our ships will have already returned. We will try to open the gates of the city in secret, so that our allies can enter the city. In this way, the city of Troy will fall."

After these words of the king of Ithaca, certain men, the fiercest of all the Greeks, were chosen, they climbed into the horse, then everyone waited for the setting of the sun.

QUIZ

1. b
2. a
3. b
4. c
5. b
6. b
7. c
8. d
9. a OR d
10. c

CHAPTER 14

Written Practice 14-1

1. Does that slave hate his master?
2. What are the boys doing in the garden?
3. What sort of flowers will he give me?
4. The route to that town is long, isn't it?
5. Why won't you stay with me longer?
6. Where was the fire about which he was talking?
7. How will I live in Rome without money?
8. When had this been announced to Caesar?
9. Whom do you see in the mirror if not you yourself?
10. In what place did they find these things?

Written Practice 14-2

1. Did that dinner please you?
2. Forgive me if I was wrong yesterday.
3. You will never be able to persuade me to come with you to Sicily.
4. Gnaeus had been put in charge of the whole army by the Senate.
5. My slaves don't obey me, even if I beat them cruelly.
6. Caesar will forgive all the Gauls who (will) have surrendered themselves.
7. Believe me. I'm not wrong.
8. They didn't want to hurt them, so they were sent away.
9. Although his sons were unwilling, the father ordered them and so they obeyed.
10. I am extremely eager for days without work!

Written Practice 14-3

1. he kept nodding off, dormiō
2. we are regaining our youth, iuvenis
3. you (*pl.*) are being driven back, repellō
4. they are giving as a gift, dōnum
5. we were getting angry, īra
6. you (*sg.*) will (begin to) rest, quiēs
7. he was calling, vox
8. they are starting to burn, ardeō
9. you (*sg.*) were coming to life, vīvō
10. they will flutter about, volō

Written Practice 14-4

1. library		6. donation
2. urban		7. lunar
3. stable		8. aquarium
4. motion		9. canine
5. donor		10. nudity

QUIZ

1. b		6. a
2. a		7. b
3. d		8. a
4. a		9. c
5. a		10. c

CHAPTER 15

Written Practice 15-1

1. sentīrem   sentīrēmus   sentīrer   sentīrēmur
   sentīrēs   sentīrētis   sentīrēris   sentīrēminī
   sentīret   sentīrent   sentīrētur   sentīrentur
2. ferrem   ferrēmus   ferrer   ferrēmur
   ferrēs   ferrētis   ferrēris   ferrēminī
   ferret   ferrent   ferrētur   ferrentur
3. habērem   habērēmus   habērer   habērēmur
   habērēs   habērētis   habērēris   habērēminī
   habēret   habērent   habērētur   habērentur
4. hortārer   hortārēmur   hortātus essem   hortātī essēmus
   hortārēris   hortārēminī   hortātus essēs   hortātī essētis
   hortārētur   hortārentur   hortātus esset   hortātī essent
5. iacerem   iacerēmus   iēcissem   iēcissēmus
   iacerēs   iacerētis   iēcissēs   iēcissētis
   iaceret   iacerent   iēcisset   iēcissent

Written Practice 15-2

1. Since the enemy were wasting time across the river, the Roman soldiers were able to pitch camp.
2. Lucius Tarquinius was an evil king, but Sextus, his son, was worse than his father.
3. When Brutus had been chosen leader, all the citizens rejoiced.
4. When Tarquinius had fled to Etruria, Sextus was quickly killed.
5. When Tarquinius had fled to Etruria, Sextus was quickly killed.
6. Caesar was made consul when he had made an end to the war against the Gauls, wasn't he?
7. When we were travelling to Asia, we met many amazing people.
8. Because that fire had been very dangerous, no one was able to escape.
9. Even though I wanted to spend the night at home, I stayed with my friends anyway.
10. Were you afraid when you saw the ghost of your brother?

Written Practice 15-3

1. The battle was fiercely fought by our men in order to defeat the enemy.
2. The battle was fiercely fought by our men so they wouldn't be defeated by the enemy.
3. The battle was fiercely fought by our men, who were supposed to defeat the enemy.
4. I sent a slave to the Forum to buy excellent food.
5. I sent a slave to the Forum, who was supposed to buy excellent food.
6. When he returned home, he had nothing except bread.
7. You were all invited to stay at my house for five days.
8. We tried to send a message so your mother wouldn't be worried.
9. Did you have a book that you could read on the trip?
10. I wasn't able to come to tell you these things.

Written Practice 15-4

1. docētis
2. sentiat
3. eam
4. dīcitur
5. ingrediātur
6. nōlit
7. sint
8. fīat
9. ferimur
10. scrībant

Written Practice 15-5

1. timuerit
2. locūtus sim
3. mōtī sumus
4. relīquerim
5. gesserītis

Written Practice 15-6

1. It happened that you weren't at home when we arrived.
2. The force of the fire will make it that no one will survive.
3. He ran so quickly that he won the race very easily.
4. It will be necessary that you all keep quiet about this matter.
5. The flowers that he had given me were such that I could scarcely believe it.
6. Yesterday, that soldier fought in such a way that every enemy (soldier) feared him.
7. The Alps are so tall that on the top part there is always some snow.
8. There were so many buildings in Rome that we couldn't visit all of them in one day.
9. A river so small flows there that you can go across it without difficulty.
10. He made it so that I was not left there.

Written Practice 15-7

1. future more vivid, If he finds my dog, he will take care of him.
2. present contrary-to-fact, If he found my dog, he would take care of him.
3. simple fact past, If he found my dog, he took care of him.
4. past contrary-to-fact, If you had come yesterday, at least you would/could have helped us.
5. simple fact present, If you know what (that which) I am trying to do, why aren't you with me?
6. future less vivid, If he returns to Rome, without doubt he'd be very poorly received.
7. future less vivid, If you tell me about that nasty situation, you would be safe.
8. past contrary-to-fact, A gift would have been given to you if we had known.
9. simple fact present, If you believe me, you don't hesitate to follow me.
10. present contrary-to-fact, If you believed me, you wouldn't hesitate to follow me.

Written Practice 15-8

And so, when the Greeks had built a horse so big that it could hold 20 men, they got onto the remaining ships—the ones that had not been destroyed for the horse to be built. Then they sailed not far out of the sight of the Trojans. They had had in mind (intended) to pull the horse to the gates of the city, but it was left on the beach. Horses, you see, are sacred to the god Neptune, and so it would seem like a gift to the god, so that they would have a lucky and safe journey to Greece. For this reason, a certain man, Sinon by name, was left behind, who was supposed to prepare the trap. Would the Trojans believe his story?

When he had been welcomed by the Trojans, he said to them, "I abandoned those nasty Greeks because they are evil. They are going back to Greece now, and they have built a huge gift to Neptune in the shape of a horse, so they could make the journey across the sea safely. The custom among us makes it that we both might die by the anger of the god unless you take this gift and bring it inside the walls."

The Trojans rejoiced because the Greeks had finally gone away, but since they were afraid that the anger of any god might harm them, a meeting was called so no bad fate would befall (them). Some were shouting, "Let the horse be dragged inside the walls immediately! We want to see an end to this terrible war!" Others, however, were hesitant, and since they were doubtful, Laocoon, a priest of Neptune, was summoned so they wouldn't be making a mistake. When he arrived, he said, "What danger could possibly be lying hidden here? Even if they are bearing gifts, I don't trust Greeks. If you don't burn it, you will sorely regret it."

Although the words of the priest had been heard by everyone and they believed Laocoon, they were so happy that they did not obey his warnings, and at once they began to get ropes ready to take the horse.

Written Practice 15-9   Synopsis

1. **Indicative Mood**

metuunt	metuuntur
metuēbant	metuēbantur
metuent	metuentur
metuērunt	metūtī sunt
metuerant	metūtī erant
metuerint	metūtī erunt

   Subjunctive Mood

metuant	metuantur
metuerent	metuerentur
metuerint	metūtī sint
metuissent	metūtī essent

2. **Indicative Mood**

videō	videor
vidēbam	vidēbar
vidēbō	vidēbor
vīdī	vīsa sum
vīderam	vīsa eram
vīderō	vīsa erō

   Subjunctive Mood

videam	videar
vidērem	vidērer
vīderim	vīsa sim
vīdissem	vīsa essem

3. **Indicative Mood**

fert	fertur
ferēbat	ferēbātur
feret	ferētur
tulit	lātum est
tulerat	lātum erat
tulerit	lātum erit

   Subjunctive Mood

ferat	ferātur
ferret	ferrētur
tulerit	lātum sit
tulisset	lātum esset

4. **Indicative Mood**

dōnāmus	dōnāmur
dōnābāmus	dōnābāmur
dōnābimus	dōnābimur
dōnāvimus	dōnātī sumus
dōnāverāmus	dōnātī erāmus
dōnāverimus	dōnātī erimus

Subjunctive Mood

dōnēmus	dōnēmur
dōnārēmus	dōnārēmur
dōnāverīmus	dōnātī sīmus
dōnāvissēmus	dōnātī essēmus

QUIZ

1.	c	6.	b
2.	b	7.	a
3.	c	8.	a
4.	c	9.	c
5.	c	10.	a

CHAPTER 16

Written Practice 16-1

1.	pōnens	—
	—	positus
	positūrus	pōnendus
2.	ferens	—
	—	lātus
	lātūrus	ferendus
3.	videns	—
	—	vīsus
	vīsūrus	videndus
4.	sentiens	—
	—	sensus
	sensūrus	sentiendus
5.	cōnans	—
	—	cōnātus
	cōnātūrus	cōnandus

Written Practice 16-2

1. Equī currentēs ē proeliō effūgērunt.
   Simple adjective: The running horses escaped from the battle.
   Relative clause: The horses, which were running, escaped from the battle.
   Temporal clause: While the horses were running, they escaped from the battle.
   Concessive clause: Although the horses were running, they escaped from the battle.

2. <u>Hostēs in proeliō victī</u> mox interfectī sunt.
   Causal clause: Since/Because the enemy were conquered in battle, they were soon killed.
   Concessive clause: Although the enemy were conquered in battle, they were soon killed.
   Temporal clause: After the enemy were conquered in battle, they were soon killed.
   Simple adjective: The enemy conquered in battle were soon killed.
3. <u>Hostibus in proeliō victīs</u>, omnēs pācem volēbant.
   Causal clause: Because/Since the enemy had been conquered in battle, everyone wanted peace.
   Coordinate clause: The enemy had been conquered in battle and everyone wanted peace.
   Temporal clause: After the enemy had been conquered in battle, everyone wanted peace.
   Simple adjective: With the enemy having been conquered in battle, everyone wanted peace.
4. <u>Verbīs modo mihi ab amīcō dīctīs</u> vix crēdō.
   Coordinate clause: The words were just spoken to me by a friend and I scarcely believe them.
   Causal clause: Since/Because the words were just spoken to me by a friend, I scarcely believe them.
   Simple adjective: I scarcely believe the words just spoken to me by a friend.
   Relative clause: I scarcely believe the words, which were just spoken to me by a friend.
5. <u>Marcum in Forum itūrum</u> monuerāmus.
   Causal clause: We had warned Marcus, since/because he was about to go to the Forum.
   Relative clause: We had warned Marcus, who was about to go to the Forum.
   Temporal clause: We had warned Marcus when he was about to go to the Forum.
   Coordinate clause: Marcus was about to go to the Forum and we had warned him.

Written Practice 16-3

1. People too desirous of obtaining money are not too wise.
2. Fulvius wanted to go to Rome to see everything.
3. If this war will be finished by us, this battle will have to be fought fiercely by the soldiers.
4. We can learn very many things by making mistakes.
5. I carefully paid attention to writing that letter so you would understand my meaning.

Written Practice 16-4

1. The messenger reported to Caesar where the enemy had pitched their new camp.
2. You understand how Lucius is setting/making a trap for you.
3. They didn't know what dangers lay hidden for them in the mountains.
4. He saw where they had come from.
5. We knew who he was and why he was looking for us.

Written Practice 16-5
1. They asked (of) them to bring help.
2. We begged you not to do this.
3. He is advising the Senate not to bring war against those people.
4. I urged Titus to stay with us for a few days.
5. He kept ordering the army to hold itself back.

Written Practice 16-6
1. He thought that his daughter was safe at your house.
2. Did you know that the journey to Germany would be rough like this?
3. Caesar will show the senators that he waged a just war against the Gauls.
4. Caesar had shown the senators that he would wage a just war against the Gauls.
5. It was told to us by Lucius that they had not been consulted regarding a certain matter.
6. Titus often denied that his brother was committing any crime.
7. Titus often denied that his brother had committed any crime.
8. Titus often denied that his brother would commit any crime.
9. When he explained to me where he had been staying, I was amazed that I hadn't known him better.
10. After the things that needed to be changed had been changed, they finally understood that everything that had to be done had been done.

Written Practice 16-7
At Troy, after the Greeks had left, very many Trojans stood together on the beach marvelling at the great horse that had been left behind by the Greeks. It was said that this horse had been built as a gift to Neptune so they wouldn't suffer shipwreck. Laocoon, a priest of Neptune, when he saw so many people around the horse marvelling, immediately hurried to the beach to warn them. He said that by accepting that gift there would be nothing except slaughter. Very many, however, for the sake of pulling the horse into the city, were getting things ready. While they were preparing, suddenly two huge snakes appeared out of the sea. The snakes, which were to kill Laocoon, had been sent by certain gods, who preferred the Greeks. They approached the poor man in such a way that in a short time he died. Both his sons, who were with him, were also killed.

After Laocoon was killed, the Trojans felt that the horse had to be accepted. Therefore, they tried to drag the horse into the city, but the horse was so tall that it wasn't easily pulled through the gates. If only they had obeyed the priest! With the horse standing in the middle of the city and since the enemy had left, the people began to rejoice. No one asked where the Greeks had gone off to or why they had departed. No one wondered about the death of the priest. He had advised, but he had not ordered that that horse stay on the beach. If he died, that's what the gods wanted. And so they partied without a care. Finally, they had an end to the war.

Once much wine had been drained and everyone, now plastered, throughout the city was sleeping, the city became quiet. Those Greeks, who were hiding (themselves) in the horse, stealthily came down by means of ropes, and they looked for the gates of the city in order to open them for their waiting allies. After the gates were opened, since an opportunity was granted, the whole Greek army rushed in. Into the city they brought violence and fire everywhere. Very many citizens were killed sleeping in their beds.

Everywhere everything was thrown into confusion. What did they have to do? Who would survive?

The Trojan men went after their weapons, but to no avail. Trojan women with their children tried to escape, but to no avail. It is said that all the captured women were immediately taken to the shore. The Greeks intended (had in mind) to bring them back to Greece so they could be sold. One man, however, named Aeneas, escaped with his old father and son. When Aeneas realized (understood) that Troy was about to fall, he quickly gathered his friends and allies to prepare ships. Aeneas, you see, wanted to set out for Hesperia so that a new Troy could be founded.

The famous Roman poet, Publius Vergilius Maro, wrote a long poem named the Aeneid. This story tells about the travels of Aeneas. The poem itself begins:

"I sing of arms and the man, who first from the shores of Troy …"

QUIZ

1. d	6. b
2. c	7. c
3. a	8. c
4. d	9. a
5. a	10. b

PART THREE TEST

1. a	18. c	35. c
2. a	19. c	36. a
3. b	20. c	37. d
4. c	21. a	38. a
5. a	22. d	39. c
6. d	23. b	40. d
7. c	24. c	41. b
8. a	25. d	42. b
9. b	26. a	43. a
10. d	27. a	44. b
11. d	28. d	45. a
12. b	29. c	46. d
13. b	30. a	47. b
14. c	31. b	48. a
15. a	32. a	49. a
16. b	33. a	50. a
17. b	34. c	

FINAL EXAM

1. a	35. d	69. b
2. d	36. a	70. a
3. c	37. b	71. a
4. a	38. d	72. b
5. d	39. d	73. d
6. b	40. b	74. a
7. a	41. a	75. a
8. b	42. b	76. b
9. b	43. a	77. a
10. a	44. b	78. d
11. d	45. b	79. c
12. d	46. a	80. a
13. b	47. a	81. b
14. c	48. d	82. b
15. c	49. b	83. a
16. b	50. d	84. a
17. d	51. d	85. c
18. c	52. c	86. c
19. b	53. c	87. b
20. c	54. a	88. c
21. b	55. a	89. c
22. c	56. d	90. d
23. b	57. d	91. b
24. c	58. a	92. b
25. b	59. a	93. a
26. d	60. d	94. c
27. c	61. b	95. a
28. b	62. c	96. b
29. d	63. d	97. b
30. b	64. b	98. c
31. c	65. d	99. a
32. b	66. d	100. b
33. b	67. d	
34. a	68. b	

LATIN-ENGLISH GLOSSARY

ā (ab) *prep.* + *abl.* from, away from; by
abeō, abīre, abiī, abitum to go away
abhinc *adv.* ago
absum, abesse, āfuī, āfutūrus to be away
ac *see* **atque**
accēdō, -ere, accessī, accessum to approach,
    go near
accidō, -ere, accidī to happen, befall; fall down,
    ask for help
accipiō, -ere, accēpī, acceptum to welcome,
    receive; take
ācer, ācris, ācre sharp, keen, fierce
aciēs, -ēī *f.* edge; battleline
ācriter *adv.* fiercely
ad *prep.* + *acc.* to, toward, near, at
addō, -ere, addidī, additum to add
adeō *adv.* still, so far, up to this point;
    so much, so
adeō, adīre, adiī, aditum to go to, approach
adhūc *adv.* still, up to this point in time, even
adiuvō, -āre, adiūvī, adiūtum to help
adōrō, -āre, -āvī, -ātum to adore
adsum, adesse, adfuī, adfutūrus to be present,
    be nearby
adveniō, -īre, advēnī, adventum to arrive, come
adventus, -ūs *m.* arrival
aedēs, aedium *f.pl.* house
aedificium, -ī *n.* building
aedificō, -āre, -āvī, -ātum to build
aeger, aegra, aegrum sick, ill, poor
Aegyptus, -ī *f.* Egypt

aēneus, -a, -um of bronze
aequus, -a, -um level, flat, even; fair
aes, aeris *n.* copper, bronze; money
aetās, aetātis *f.* age, lifetime
aeternus, -a, -um eternal
aevum, -ī *n.* age, lifetime, a period of time
afferō, afferre, attulī, allātum to bring,
    bring to
Āfrica, -ae *f.* Africa
ager, agrī *m.* field, land
aggredior, -ī, aggressus sum to attack, step
    forward
agmen, agminis *n.* marching column, train
agō, -ere, ēgī, actum to do; drive, lead; be busy
agricola, -ae *m.* farmer
agricultūra, -ae *f.* agriculture
āiō *defective* to say, say yes (*opposite of* **negō**)
āla, -ae *f.* wing
alacer, alacris, alacre lively
albus, -a, -um white, dull white
alescō, -ere to grow (up)
algeō, -ēre, alsī to be cold
algidus, -a, -um cold
aliēnus, -a, -um someone else's; foreign
aliquandō *adv.* sometimes, at some time
aliquis, aliquis, aliquid *pron.* someone,
    something, anyone, anything
alius, -a, -um another, different
    aliī ... aliī some ... others
alō, -ere, aluī, alitum to nourish
altē *adv.* soundly

alter, altera, alterum the other (of two)
   alter ... alter the one ... the other
altus, -a, -um tall, high, deep (*an extreme vertical distance*)
ambō, ambae, ambō both
ambulō, -āre, -āvī, -ātum to walk
amīca, -ae *f.* (female) friend
amīcitia, -ae *f.* friendship
amīcus, -ī *m.* (male) friend
amīcus, -a, -um friendly
āmittō, -ere, āmīsī, āmissum to send away, let go, lose
amnis, amnis *m.* stream, river
amō, -āre, -āvī, -ātum to like, love
amor, amōris *m.* love
an *conj.* or, whether
anima, -ae *f.* soul, breath; breeze
animal, animālis *n.* animal
animus, -ī *m.* soul, mind; spirit, courage
annus, -ī *m.* year
ante *prep + acc.* before, in front of
antequam *conj.* before
antīquus, -a, -um old, old-fashioned, ancient
aperiō, -īre, aperuī, apertum to open, uncover
Apollō, Apollinis *m.* Apollo
appāreō, -ēre, -uī, -itum to appear
appellō, -āre, -āvī, -ātum to call (*often by name*)
appropinquō, -āre, -āvī, -ātum + *dat.* to approach
aptus, -a, -um suitable, fit, fitted to/for
apud *prep. + acc.* among, in the presence of, near, at the home of
aqua, -ae *f.* water
arbitror, -ārī, -ātus sum to think
arbor, arboris *f.* tree
ardeō, -ēre, arsī to burn, be on fire
arduus, -a, -um rough, difficult, harsh
arēna, -ae *f.* arena
argentum, -ī *n.* silver; money
arma, -ōrum *n.pl.* weapons, arms
armō, -āre, -āvī, -ātum to equip with weapons
ars, artis *f.* art, skill, method
arvum, -ī *n.* land, arable land, a plowed field
ascendō, -ere, ascendī, ascensum to climb up/into
at *conj.* but, moreover
Athēnae, -ārum *f.pl.* Athens
atque (ac) *conj.* and, and so, and even
auctor, auctōris *m.* originator, founder, author

audax, audācis bold, daring, rash
audeō, -ēre, ausus sum to dare
audiō, -īre, audīvī, audītum to hear, listen
auferō, auferre, abstulī, ablātum to carry away
augeō, -ēre, auxī, auctum to increase, enlarge
aura, -ae *f.* air
aureus, -a, -um golden, made of gold
auris, auris *f.* ear
aurum, -ī *n.* gold; money
aut *conj.* or (*a choice between mutually exclusive things*)
   aut ... aut either ... or
autem *conj.* however; moreover
auxilium, -ī *n.* help
avis, avis *f.* bird
avunculus, -ī *m.* uncle (*mother's brother*)
avus, -ī *m.* grandfather

baculum, -ī *n.* stick
beātus, -a, -um blessed, happy
bellum, -ī *n.* war
bene *adv.* well
benedīcō, -ere, benedixī, benedictum to speak well of, bless
bibō, -ere, bibī to drink
bonus, -a, -um good
bōs, bovis *c.* ox, cow
brevis, -e short

cadō, -ere, cecidī, cāsum to fall
caecus, -a, -um blind
caedēs, caedis *f.* slaughter; gore
caedō, -ere, cecīdī, caesum to cut
caelum, -ī *n.* sky, heaven
caeruleus, -a, -um blue, greenish-blue, grayish-green
Caesar, Caesaris *m.* Caesar (*Roman general, dictator, and author*)
calcar, calcāris *n.* spur
campus, -ī *m.* field
candidus, -a, -um white, bright white
canis, canis *c.* dog
canō, -ere, cecinī, cantum to sing, play (an instrument)
cantō, -āre, -āvī, -ātum to sing, play (an instrument)
cantus, -ūs *m.* a song; music session
capiō, -ere, cēpī, captum to take, catch; adopt
captīvus, -ī *m.* prisoner

caput, capitis *n.* head
carcer, carceris *m.* prison
careō, -ēre, -uī, -itum + *abl.* to lack, be without
carmen, carminis *n.* song, poem
Carthāgō, Carthāginis *f.* Carthage
cārus, -a, -um dear, expensive
casa, -ae *f.* hut
castra, -ōrum *n.pl.* camp (*military*)
castus, -a, -um clean, chaste, pure
cāsus, -ūs *m.* a fall, accident, disaster
causa, -ae *f.* cause, reason; lawsuit
  causā + *gen.* for the sake of
caveō, -ēre, cāvī, cautum to beware, be on guard
cēdō, -ere, cessī, cessum to go, withdraw, yield
celebrō, -āre, -āvī, -ātum to visit often, make well-known
celer, celeris, celere quick, fast
cēlō, -āre, -āvī, -ātum to hide
cēna, -ae *f.* dinner
centum *indeclinable number* hundred
cernō, -ere, crēvī, crētum to separate, distinguish, pick out
certāmen, certāminis *n.* race, contest, struggle
certō, -āre, -āvī, -ātum to struggle, decide by contest
certus, -a, -um certain, sure, reliable
cervus, -ī *m.* deer
cēterus, -a, -um the rest, the other
cibus, -ī *m.* food
Cicerō, Cicerōnis *m.* Cicero (*Roman orator, statesman, and author*)
cingō, -ere, cinxī, cinctum to surround, wrap
cinis, cineris *m.* ash
circā *adv. and prep.* + *acc.* around, near
circumeō, circumīre, circumiī, circumitum to go around
citō *adv.* quickly
citus, -a, -um quick, fast
cīvis, cīvis *c.* citizen
cīvitās, cīvitātis *f.* state, city; citizenship
clāmō, -āre, -āvī, -ātum to shout
clāmor, clāmōris *m.* shouting, ruckus
clārus, -a, -um clear, bright; famous; obvious
classis, classis *f.* fleet
claudō, -ere, clausī, clausum to close, conclude
coepī, coepisse, coeptum *defective* to have begun
cōgitō, -āre, -āvī, -ātum to think, ponder
cognōscō, -ere, cognōvī, cognitum to learn; (*in the perfect*) to know, be acquainted with

cōgō, -ere, coēgī, coactum to compel, force, drive, gather
cohors, cohortis *f.* a company, retinue
colligō, -ere, collēgī, collectum to gather, collect
colloquor, -ī, collocūtus sum to talk together, converse
collum, -ī *n.* neck
colō, -ere, coluī, cultum to pay attention to, nurture, cultivate
color, colōris *m.* color
combūrō, -ere, combussī, combustum to burn up
comes, comitis *c.* buddy, companion
commissātiō, commissātiōnis *f.* (drinking) party
committō, -ere, commīsī, commissum to connect, combine; entrust
commūnis, -e common, approachable
comparō, -āre, -āvī, -ātum to prepare, buy, furnish
complector, -ī, complexus sum to hug, embrace
complūrēs, complūra several, very many
compōnō, -ere, composuī, compositum to put, put together, arrange
concēdō, -ere, concessī, concessum to go away, withdraw, yield
condō, -ere, condidī, conditum to found, build; put in safe keeping, hide
conferō, conferre, contulī, collātum to bring together, compare, engage
conficiō, -ere, confēcī, confectum to finish
confīdō, -ere, confīsus sum + *dat.* to trust
confiteor, -ērī, confessus sum to confess, admit
congredior, -ī, congressus sum to gather
coniunx, coniugis *c.* spouse
cōnor, -ārī, -ātus sum to try, attempt
consentiō, -īre, consensī, consensum to agree
consequor, -ī, consecūtus sum to follow closely, pursue, catch up to
consilium, -ī *n.* plan, advice, consultation; assembly
constituō, -ere, constituī, constitūtum to stand or set (something) up; decide
constō, -āre, constitī to stand together, stand still, stop
construō, -ere, construxī, constructum to build, set up
consul, consulis *m.* consul (*chief magistrate*)
consulō, -ere, consuluī, consultum to consult
contemnō, -ere, contempsī, contemptum to despise

Latin-English Glossary

contineō, -ēre, continuī, contentum to hold (in), contain

continuō *adv.* immediately, without missing a beat

contrā *adv. and prep. + acc.* against, facing, opposite

conveniō, -īre, convēnī, conventum to come together, meet; be fitting, agree

convertō, -ere, convertī, conversum to turn around

convīvium, -ī *n.* party

convocō, -āre, -āvī, -ātum to call together

cōpia, -ae *f.* abundance
  cōpiae, -ārum *f.pl.* supplies; troops

cōpiōsus, -a, -um abundant

cor, cordis *n.* heart

cōram *adv.* in person, openly

Corinthus, -ī *f.* Corinth

cornū, -ūs *n.* horn, wing (*of a battle line*)

corpus, corporis *n.* body

cōtīdiē *adv.* every day, daily

crāpula, -ae *f.* hangover

crās *adv.* tomorrow

creātiō, creātiōnis *f.* begetting; election

crēdō, -ere, crēdidī, crēditum *+ dat.* to trust, rely on, believe

creō, -āre, -āvī, -ātum to create; elect

crescō, -ere, crēvī, crētum to grow

crēta, -ae *f.* clay, chalk

crīmen, crīminis *n.* accusation, guilt, alleged crime

crūdēliter *adv.* cruelly

crustulum, -ī *n.* cookie

culpa, -ae *f.* guilt, blame, fault

cum *conj.* when; since, because; although

cum *prep. + abl.* with

cunctus, -a, -um all (*as a group*)

cupidus, -a, -um *+ gen.* desirous (of), eager (for)

cupiō, -ere, cupīvī, cupītum to desire, long for, want

cūr *adv.* why

cūra, -ae *f.* care, attention, concern, anxiety

cūrō, -āre, -āvī, -ātum to take care of

currō, -ere, cucurrī, cursum to run

cursus, -ūs *m.* course, route, direction

custōdia, -ae *f.* guardianship, care, custody

custōdiō, -īre, custōdīvī, custōdītum to take care of

custōs, custōdis *m.* guard, guardian

dē *prep. + abl.* down from, from; concerning, about

dea, -ae *f.* goddess

dēbeō, -ēre, -uī, -itum to owe; ought, be bound

decet, -ēre, decuit *impersonal* it is right/suitable; should

decus, decoris *n.* honor, distinction

dēfendō, -ere, dēfendī, dēfensum to defend, drive off

dēferō, dēferre, dētulī, dēlātum to bring down, report

dēfessus, -a, -um tired

dēficiō, -ere, dēfēcī, dēfectum to fall short, fail; desert, rebel

deinde *adv.* from that place; then, next

dēleō, -ēre, dēlēvī, dēlētum to destroy

Delphī, -ōrum *m.pl.* Delphi

dēmonstrō, -āre, -āvī, -ātum to show

dēnique *adv.* finally, at last

densus, -a, -um thick, dense

descendō, -ere, descendī, descensum to climb down

dēsīderō, -āre, -āvī, -ātum to desire, want, long for

dēsum, dēesse, dēfuī, dēfutūrus to be down, fail, fall short

deus, -ī *m.* god

dexter, dextra, dextrum right

dextra, -ae *f.* right hand

dīcō, -ere, dixī, dictum to tell, say

diēs, -ēī *m.* day

difficile *adv.* with difficulty

difficilis, -e difficult

digitus, -ī *m.* finger, toe

dignitās, dignitātis *f.* reputation, dignity, honor, worth

dignus, -a, -um worthy, fitting

dīligens, dīligentis careful, attentive

dīligō, -ere, dīlexī, dīlectum to love, esteem, pick out

dīmittō, -ere, dīmīsī, dīmissum to send away, abandon

discēdō, -ere, discessī, discessum to leave, go away

discō, -ere, didicī to learn

diū *adv.* for a long time

dīversus, -a, -um different, turned in different directions

dīves, dīvitis wealthy

dīvidō, -ere, dīvīsī, dīvīsum to divide
dīvīnus, -a, -um divine
dīvitiae, -ārum *f.pl.* riches
dīvus, -a, -um divine, deified
dō, dare, dedī, datum to give
doceō, -ēre, docuī, doctum to teach
doleō, -ēre, -uī, -itum to feel pain; (*impersonally*) cause pain
dolor, dolōris *m.* pain, grief
dolus, -ī *m.* trick
dominus, -ī *m.* master
domus, -ūs *f.* house, home
dōnec *conj.* until; while
dōnō, -āre, -āvī, -ātum to give (*as a gift*)
dōnum, -ī *n.* gift
dormiō, -īre, dormīvī, dormītum to sleep
dubitō, -āre, -āvī, -ātum to doubt, hesitate
dubium, -ī *n.* doubt
dubius, -a, -um doubtful
dūcō, -ere, duxī, ductum to take (someone/ something somewhere), lead
dulcis, -e sweet, pleasant
dum *conj.* while
duō, -ae, -ō two
dūrus, -a, -um hard, tough
dux, ducis *m.* leader

ē (ex) *prep. + abl.* out (of), from
ecce *interj.* look!
edō, ēsse/edere, ēdī, ēsum to eat
efficiō, -ere, effēcī, effectum to do, effect, bring it about that
effugiō, -ere, effūgī to escape
ego *pron.* I
ēgredior, -ī, ēgressus sum to go out, leave
ēheu *interj.* alas!
ēliciō, -ere, ēlicuī, ēlicitum to lure
ēligō, -ere, ēlēgī, ēlectum to pick out, choose
emō, -ere, ēmī, emptum to buy
enim *conj.* because, since, you see (*introduces an explanation or clarification of the preceding statement*)
ensis, ensis *m.* sword
eō, īre, iī (īvī), itum to go
epistula, -ae *f.* letter (*correspondence*)
eques, equitis *m.* horseman, knight (*a member of the Roman social class between patricians and plebeians*)
equus, -ī *m.* horse

ergō *adv.* so, thus, therefore
ēripiō, -ere, ēripuī, ēreptum to grab, to take out violently
errō, -āre, -āvī, -ātum to wander; be wrong
et *conj.* and, also, too, even
etiam *adv.* still, yet, even, also
etsī *adv.* even if
ēveniō, -īre, ēvēnī, ēventum to come out; result
ēventus, -ūs *m.* outcome
excipiō, -ere, excēpī, exceptum to take out, take up, catch, receive
excitō, -āre, -āvī, -ātum to rouse, awaken
exemplar, exemplāris *n.* model, example
exemplum, -ī *n.* example, precedent
exeō, exīre, exiī, exitum to go out; end
exerceō, -ēre, -uī, -itum to make strong, train; harass
exercitus, -ūs *m.* army
existimō, -āre, -āvī, -ātum to think, judge, evaluate
exitus, -ūs *m.* act of going out; outcome
expellō, -ere, expulī, expulsum to drive out, throw out
experior, -īrī, expertus sum to try, test, prove
explicō, -āre, -āvī, -ātum to explain
exspectō, -āre, -āvī, -ātum to wait for
extrā *prep. + acc.* outside (of)
extrēmus, -a, -um outermost

fābula, -ae *f.* story
facile *adv.* easily
facilis, -e easy
facinus, facinoris *n.* crime, deed
faciō, -ere, fēcī, factum to make, do
factum, -ī *n.* deed, action
fallō, -ere, fefellī, falsum to deceive
falx, falcis *f.* scythe, sickle
fāma, -ae *f.* rumor; reputation
fātum, -ī *n.* fate, destiny; misfortune
fax, facis *f.* torch
fēles, fēlis *f.* cat
fēlix, fēlīcis lucky; happy
fēmina, -ae *f.* woman, a female
fenestra, -ae *f.* window
ferē *adv.* nearly, almost
feriō, -īre to strike
ferō, ferre, tulī, lātum to carry, bring, bear; endure
ferrum, -ī *n.* iron; sword
ferus, -a, -um wild

fessus, -a, -um tired
festīnō, -āre, -āvī, -ātum to hurry
festus, -a, -um pertaining to a holiday
fidēlis, -e trustworthy, loyal
fidēs, -eī *f.* trust
fīdō, -ere, fīsus sum to trust
fīgō, -ere, fixī, fixum to fasten, affix
figura, -ae *f.* form, shape
fīlia, -ae *f.* daughter
fīlius, -ī *m.* son
fingō, -ere, finxī, fictum to shape, form
fīniō, -īre, fīnīvī, fīnītum to finish, end
fīnis, fīnis *m.* end, boundary
    fīnēs, fīnium *m.pl.* territory
fīō, fierī, factus sum to be made, be done; be;
    become; happen (*used as the passive of* **faciō**)
flamma, -ae *f.* flame, fire
flectō, -ere, flexī, flexum to bend
fleō, -ēre, flēvī, flētum to weep
flōs, flōris *m.* flower
flūmen, flūminis *n.* river
fluō, -ere, fluxī, fluxum to flow
foedus, -a, -um foul, horrible
fons, fontis *m.* a spring, fountain
forīs *adv.* outside, outdoors
forma, -ae *f.* shape, image
forsitan *adv.* perhaps, maybe
fortis, -e strong; brave
fortiter *adv.* bravely
fortūna, -ae *f.* luck, chance, fortune
Forum, -ī *n.* the Forum
fossa, -ae *f.* ditch, furrow
frangō, -ere, frēgī, fractum to break
frāter, frātris *m.* brother
frīgidus, -a, -um cold
frons, frontis *f.* forehead; front
frustrā *adv.* to no avail, in vain
fuga, -ae *f.* flight, escape
fugiō, -ere, fūgī to run away, flee, escape
fulgur, fulguris *n.* flash of lightning
fūmus, -ī *m.* smoke
fundō, -ere, fūdī, fūsum to pour
fundus, -ī *m.* bottom
fūnus, fūneris *n.* funeral
fūr, fūris *c.* thief
furtim *adv.* secretly, stealthily

Gallia, -ae *f.* Gaul (*region*)
Gallus, -ī *m.* Gaul (*person*)

Gallus, -a, -um Gallic
gaudeō, -ēre, gāvīsus sum to rejoice, be happy,
    party
gaudium, -ī *n.* joy, happiness
geminus, -a, -um twin
gens, gentis *f.* family, clan; nation, race
genū, -ūs *n.* knee
genus, generis *n.* birth, origin; type, kind
Germānia, -ae *f.* Germany
Germānus, -ī *m.* German
gerō, -ere, gessī, gestum to carry; wage (*war*);
    accomplish; wear (*clothes*)
gladius, -ī *m.* sword
glōria, -ae *f.* glory, fame
gracilis, -e slender
gradior, -ī, gressus sum to step, go
Graecia, -ae *f.* Greece
Graecus, -a, -um Greek
grātia, -ae *f.* charm; thanks
    grātiā + *gen.* for the sake of
grātus, -a, -um pleasing
gravis, -e heavy; serious
graviter *adv.* seriously, sorely
grex, gregis *m.* flock, herd; group

habeō, -ēre, -uī, -itum to have, hold; consider,
    regard
habitō, -āre, -āvī, -ātum to live (*in a place*), dwell,
    inhabit
haereō, -ēre, haesī, haesum to stick
haud *adv.* not
herba, -ae *f.* grass, a plant
heri *adv.* yesterday
heu *interj.* yikes!
hīc *adv.* here
hic, haec, hoc this, the latter
hiems, hiemis *f.* winter
hinc *adv.* from here
hircus, -ī *m.* goat
hodiē *adv.* today
homō, hominis *m.* person, human being
honōs, honōris *m.* honor; political office
hōra, -ae *f.* hour, time
hortor, -ārī, -ātus sum to urge, encourage
hortus, -ī *m.* garden
hospes, hospitis *c.* host; guest; stranger
hostis, hostis *c.* enemy
    hostēs, hostium *c.pl.* the enemy
hūc *adv.* to this place

hūmānus, -a, -um human; kind
humus, -ī *f.* ground, soil

iaceō, -ēre, -uī, -itum to recline, lie
iaciō, -ere, iēcī, iactum to throw
iactō, -āre, -āvī, -ātum to buffet
iam *adv.* now, already, at this point in time
iānua, -ae *f.* door
ibi *adv.* there, in that place
ibidem *adv.* in the same place
īciō, -ere, īcī, ictum to strike
īdem, eadem, idem the same
ideō *adv.* for that reason
igitur *adv.* therefore
ignis, ignis *m.* fire
ignōrō, -āre, -āvī, -ātum not to know
ignoscō, -ere, ignōvī, ignōtum to forgive
ignōtus, -a, -um unknown
ille, illa, illud that, the former
illīc *adv.* there
imāgō, imāginis *f.* portrait, image
imitor, -ārī, -ātus sum to copy
immō *adv.* actually, on the contrary, rather
impedīmenta, -ōrum *n.pl.* baggage
imperātor, imperātōris *m.* general; emperor
imperium, -ī *n.* power, command
imperō, -āre, -āvī, -ātum + *dat.* to give an order
impleō, -ēre, implēvī, implētum to fill up
impōnō, -ere, imposuī, impositum to put on
improbus, -a, -um substandard; naughty
in *prep.* + *acc.* in, into, onto, to, at, against; + *abl.* in, on
inānis, -e empty
incendium, -ī *n.* fire
incipiō, -ere, incēpī, inceptum to begin
inde *adv.* from that place; then
induō, -ere, induī, indūtum to put on, dress
inferō, inferre, intulī, illātum to bring in, introduce
inferus, -a, -um lower
ingenium, -ī *n.* talent; disposition, nature, character
ingens, ingentis huge
ingredior, -ī, ingressus sum to step in, enter; begin
inimīcus, -a, -um unfriendly
inquam, inquis, inquit, *etc. defective verb introducing a direct quotation* to say
insidiae, -ārum *f.pl.* trap, trick, ambush

insignis, -e outstanding, distinguished
instituō, -ere, instituī, institūtum to set up; instruct; decide
instruō, -ere, instruxī, instructum to build, equip
insula, -ae *f.* island; apartment building
integer, integra, integrum whole, intact, pure
intellegō, -ere, intellexī, intellectum to understand, be aware of, appreciate
inter *prep.* + *acc.* between, among
intereā *adv.* meanwhile
interficiō, -ere, interfēcī, interfectum to kill
interrogō, -āre, -āvī, -ātum to ask
intrā *prep.* + *acc.* inside, within
intrō, -āre, -āvī, -ātum to enter
inūtilis, -e useless
inveniō, -īre, invēnī, inventum to come upon, find
invideō, -ēre, invīdī, invīsum to cast the evil eye; envy
invidia, -ae *f.* envy
ipse, ipsa, ipsum *intensive pron.* -self
īra, -ae *f.* anger
is, ea, id *demonstrative pron./adj.* he, she, it, they; this, that (*referring to something recently mentioned*)
iste, ista, istud *demonstrative pron.* that (*often with contempt*)
ita *adv.* like this, in this way, thus
Italia, -ae *f.* Italy
itaque *adv.* and so, therefore
item *adv.* likewise
iter, itineris *n.* route, way; journey, trip
iterum *adv.* again
iubeō, -ēre, iussī, iussum to order
iūcundus, -a, -um content, happy
iūdex, iūdicis *m.* judge
iugum, -ī *n.* yoke; mountain ridge (*anything that joins*)
iungō, -ere, iunxī, iunctum to join, connect
Iuppiter, Iovis *m.* Jupiter
iūrō, -āre, -āvī, -ātum to swear
iūs, iūris *n.* a right; law
iussus, -ūs *m.* order, command
iustitia, -ae *f.* justice
iustus, -a, -um just, fair, lawful; suitable
iuvenis, -is *c.* young person
iuvenis, -e young
iuvō, -āre, iūvī, iūtum to help, please
iuxtā *prep.* + *acc.* very near

kalendae, -ārum *f.pl.* calends (*the first day of the Roman month*)

labor, labōris *m.* work, effort; suffering
lābor, -ī, lapsus sum to slip
labōrō, -āre, -āvī, -ātum to work, suffer
lacrima, -ae *f.* tear
laetus, -a, -um happy; fat
lapis, lapidis *m.* stone
lateō, -ēre, -uī to lie hidden
Latīnus, -a, -um Latin
lātrō, -āre, -āvī, -ātum to bark
lātus, -a, -um wide
laudō, -āre, -āvī, -ātum to praise
laus, laudis *f.* praise
lavō, -āre, -āvī, -ātum to wash
lectus, -ī *m.* bed
legiō, legiōnis *f.* legion
legō, -ere, lēgī, lectum to choose, pick, gather; read
lentus, -a, -um slow
leō, leōnis *m.* lion
levis, -e light, gentle
lex, lēgis *f.* law
libens, libentis glad, happy, willing
libenter *adv.* gladly
liber, librī *m.* book
līber, lībera, līberum free
līberō, -āre, -āvī, -ātum to set free
lībertās, lībertātis *f.* freedom
licet, -ēre, licuit/licitum est *impersonal* it is allowed/okay; may
lignum, -ī *n.* wood
līmen, līminis *n.* threshold
lingua, -ae *f.* tongue; language
littera, -ae *f.* letter (*of the alphabet*)
　litterae, -ārum *f.pl.* letter (*correspondence*), literature
lītus, lītoris *n.* beach, shore
locus, -ī *m.* place
　locī, -ōrum *m.pl.* specific places; literary passages
　loca, -ōrum *n.pl.* places (*somehow connected*)
longē *adv.* far
longus, -a, -um long, tall
loquor, -ī, locūtus sum to talk, speak
lūdō, -ere, lūsī, lūsum to play, deceive
lūdus, -ī *m.* game, play; school

lūmen, lūminis *n.* light, lamp; eye
lūna, -ae *f.* moon
lupus, -ī *m.* wolf
lux, lūcis *f.* light, daylight; eye

madidus, -a, -um drunk
maestus, -a, -um sad, gloomy
magis *adv.* more
magister, magistrī *m.* master, director, teacher, captain
magnitūdō, magnitūdinis *f.* greatness, size
magnopere *adv.* greatly
magnus, -a, -um big, large, great; loud
magus, -a, -um magical
male *adv.* badly
mālō, malle, māluī to want more, prefer
malus, -a, -um bad, evil
mandō, -āre, -āvī, -ātum to entrust, order
māne *indeclinable noun* morning
maneō, -ēre, mansī, mansum to stay
manus, -ūs *f.* hand; band of men, posse
mare, maris *n.* sea
Mars, Martis *m.* Mars
māter, mātris *f.* mother
māteria, -ae *f.* raw material, lumber
mēcum with me
medeor, -ērī + *dat.* to heal
Mediolānum, -ī *n.* Milan
medius, -a, -um (the) middle (of)
membrum, -ī *n.* limb, body part
meminī, meminisse *defective,* + *gen.* to be mindful, remember
memor, memoris mindful
memoria, -ae *f.* memory
memorō, -āre, -āvī, -ātum to remind, mention
mens, mentis *f.* mind
mensa, -ae *f.* table
mensis, mensis *m.* month
mereō, -ēre, -uī, -itum to deserve, earn
merīdiēs, -ēī *m.* noon, midday
metuō, -ere, metuī, metūtum to fear
metus, -ūs *m.* fear
meus, -a, -um my
mīles, mīlitis *c.* soldier
mille *indeclinable adj.* thousand
　mīlia, mīlium *n.pl. noun* thousands
minimē *adv.* in the least
minister, ministrī *m.* helper, subordinate
minus *adv.* less

mīror, -ārī, -ātus sum to wonder at, marvel, be amazed

mīrus, -a, -um amazing, wonderful

misceō, -ēre, miscuī, mixtum to mix

miser, misera, miserum unfortunate, unhappy, pitiful, miserable, poor

mītis, -e soft, mild

mittō, -ere, mīsī, missum to send, release, throw (*to make something go away under its own power*)

modo *adv.* just, only

modus, -ī *m.* way, method; measure

moenia, moenium *n.pl.* fortifications

molestus, -a, -um annoying

mollis, -e soft, smooth, flexible

moneō, -ēre, -uī, -itum to warn, advise

monita, -ōrum *n.pl.* warnings

mons, montis *m.* mountain

monstrō, -āre, -āvī, -ātum to show

mora, -ae *f.* delay, pause

morbus, -ī *m.* disease, illness

mordeō, -ēre, momordī to bite

morior, -ī, mortuus sum (*fut. part.* **moritūrus**) to die

moror, -ārī, -ātus sum to delay, wait, stay, kill time

mors, mortis *f.* death

morsus, -ūs *m.* bite

mortālis, -e mortal, destined to die

mortuus, -a, -um dead

mōs, mōris *m.* characteristic, custom
mōrēs, mōrum *m.pl.* character, morals

moveō, -ēre, mōvī, mōtum to move

mox *adv.* soon

mulier, mulieris *f.* woman

multitūdō, multitūdinis *f.* large number

multum *adv.* much, a lot

multus, -a, -um much, many

mundus, -ī *m.* the world

mūnus, mūneris *n.* gift; duty, an office

mūrus, -ī *m.* (outer) wall

mūtō, -āre, -āvī, -ātum to change; move

nam *conj.* because, since, for

narrō, -āre, -āvī, -ātum to tell (*in story form*)

nascor, -ī, nātus sum to be born

natō, -āre, -āvī, -ātum to swim

nātūra, -ae *f.* nature

nātus, -ī *m.* son, child

nāvigō, -āre, -āvī, -ātum to sail

nāvis, nāvis *f.* ship

-ne *enclitic attached to the end of the first word of a clause to convert it to a yes/no question*

nē *conj.* not, lest

nec *see* **neque**

necessārius, -ī *m.* a close relative/friend

necessārius, -a, -um unavoidable

necesse necessary

necessitās, necessitātis *f.* necessity

necō, -āre, -āvī, -ātum to kill

nectar, nectaris *n.* nectar

neglegō, -ere, neglexī, neglectum to neglect

negō, -āre, -āvī, -ātum to deny, say no

negōtiōsus, -a, -um busy

negōtium, -ī *n.* business

nēmō, nēminis *c.* no one, nobody

nemus, nemoris *n.* grove

neque (nec) *conj.* and … not, nor
neque … neque neither … nor

nesciō, -īre, nescīvī, nescītum not to know

neuter, neutra, neutrum neither

niger, nigra, nigrum black

nihil (nīl) *indeclinable noun* nothing

nimis *adv.* too much, very much, excessively

nisi *conj.* if not, unless, except

nix, nivis *f.* snow

nōbilis, -e well-known, famous; of high birth

noceō, -ēre, -uī, -itum + *dat.* to harm, be harmful, hurt

noctū *adv.* at night

nōlō, nolle, nōluī to be unwilling, not want

nōmen, nōminis *n.* name

nōminō, -āre, -āvī, -ātum to name, mention

nōn *adv.* not

nōndum *adv.* not yet

nōnne *introduces a question expecting a* yes *answer*

nōs *pron.* we

noscō, -ere, nōvī, nōtum to learn; (*in the perfect*) to know, recognize

noster, nostra, nostrum our

notō, -āre, -āvī, -ātum to mark, note

nōtus, -a, -um known

novus, -a, -um new, young; strange

nox, noctis *f.* night

nūbēs, nūbis *f.* cloud

nūdus, -a, -um naked

nullus, -a, -um no, none, not any

num *introduces a question expecting a no answer*

nūmen, nūminis *n.* divine will, nod; deity

numerus, -ī *m.* number

nummus, -ī *m.* coin

numquam *adv.* never

nunc *adv.* now

nuntiō, -āre, -āvī, -ātum to announce

nuntius, -ī *m.* messenger; message

ob *prep. + acc.* on account of; in front of; in exchange for

obstō, -āre, obstitī, obstātum to block

obvius, -a, -um in the way, on hand

occāsiō, occāsiōnis *f.* opportunity

occīdo, -ere, occīdī, occīsum to kill

occurrō, -ere, occurrī, occursum to meet

oculus, -ī *m.* eye

ōdī, ōdisse, ōsum to hate

offerō, offerre, obtulī, oblātum to offer

officium, -ī *n.* duty, respect

oleō, -ēre, -uī to smell, stink

ōlim *adv.* once upon a time, at that time

omnis, -e all, every, whole

opera, -ae *f.* work

   operam dare to pay attention

oportet, -ēre, oportuit *impersonal* it is proper; should, ought

oppidum, -ī *n.* town

oppugnō, -āre, -āvī, -ātum to attack

ops, opis *f.* abundance

   opēs, opum *f.pl.* wealth, resources

optō, -āre, -āvī, -ātum to want, desire, choose

opus, operis *n.* a work

   opus est there is need

ōra, -ae *f.* shore

ōrātiō, ōrātiōnis *f.* speech, eloquence

ōrātor, ōrātōris *m.* spokesman, orator

orbis, orbis *m.* circle

ordō, ordinis *m.* row; rank, (social) class

orior, -īrī, ortus sum to rise

ornō, -āre, -āvī, -ātum to decorate

ōrō, -āre, -āvī, -ātum to beg, ask, plead; speak, pray

ōs, ōris *n.* mouth, face

os, ossis *n.* bone

ostendō, -ere, ostendī, ostentum to show

ōtium, -ī *n.* free time, leisure

paene *adv.* almost

paenitet, -ēre, paenituit it causes regret, makes one feel sorry

pandō, -ere, —, pansum to open up, stretch

pānis, pānis *m.* bread

pār, paris equal

parcō, -ere, pepercī, parsum + *dat.* to spare, forgive, be lenient

parens, parentis *c.* parent

pāreō, -ēre, -uī, -itum + *dat.* to obey, be obedient

pariēs, parietis *m.* (interior) wall

pariō, -ere, peperī, partum to give birth, produce

parō, -āre, -āvī, -ātum to prepare, get ready; obtain

pars, partis *f.* part; direction

parum *adv.* little, not much; not enough, too little

parvus, -a, -um little, small

passus, -ūs *m.* (foot)step

pateō, -ēre, -uī to lie open/exposed

pater, patris *m.* father

patior, -ī, passus sum to suffer, experience

patria, -ae *f.* fatherland, native country

paucī, -ae, -a few

paulus, -a, -um little

pauper, pauperis poor

pax, pācis *f.* peace

pectus, pectoris *n.* chest, heart

pecūnia, -ae *f.* money, property

pellō, -ere, pepulī, pulsum to drive

pendō, -ere, pependī, pensum to hang, weigh; pay

per *prep. + acc.* through, along; over; throughout; because of

percutiō, -ere, percussī, percussum to hit, strike

perdō, -ere, perdidī, perditum to lose, destroy, waste

pereō, perīre, periī, peritum to die; go through, be lost

perficiō, -ere, perfēcī, perfectum to complete

pergō, -ere, perrexī, perrectum to continue

perīculōsus, -a, -um dangerous

perīculum, -ī *n.* danger

permittō, -ere, permīsī, permissum to allow, send through; throw

pernoctō, -āre, -āvī, -ātum to spend the night

perpetuus, -a, -um continuous

persequor, -ī, persecūtus sum to pursue, overtake

persuādeō, -ēre, persuāsī, persuāsum
+ *dat.* to persuade, make convincing
perveniō, -īre, pervēnī, perventum to arrive
pēs, pedis *m.* foot
petō, -ere, petīvī, petītum to look for, ask;
head for a place; attack
philosophia, -ae *f.* philosophy
pictor, pictōris *m.* painter
pietās, pietātis *f.* duty, devotion (*especially to gods or country*)
piget, -ēre, piguit it annoys, irritates, disgusts
pila, -ae *f.* ball
pingō, -ere, pinxī, pinctum to paint
pirum, -ī *n.* pear
piscis, piscis *m.* fish
pius, -a, -um dutiful
placeō, -ēre, -uī, -itum + *dat.* to please, be pleasing
placidus, -a, -um peaceful, quiet
plānē *adv.* obviously, clearly
plaudō, -āre, -āvī, -ātum to applaud
plēnus, -a, -um full
plūrimus, -a, -um very much; (*pl.*) very many
plūs, plūris *indeclinable sg. noun* more
plūrēs, plūra *adj. in pl.* many
pōculum, -ī *n.* cup
poena, -ae *f.* penalty, punishment
poēta, -ae *m.* poet
pompa, -ae *f.* parade
pōnō, -ere, posuī, positum to put, lay
pontus, -ī *m.* sea
populus, -ī *m.* a people
porta, -ae *f.* gate
portō, -āre, -āvī, -ātum to carry, bring
possum, posse, potuī to be able, can
post *prep.* + *acc.* after, behind
posteā *adv.* afterwards
postquam *conj.* after
postulō, -āre, -āvī, -ātum to ask, demand
potens, potentis powerful, capable
potestās, potestātis *f.* power, ability
potior, -īrī, potītus sum to obtain
prae *prep.* + *abl.* in front of, before
praebeō, -ēre, -uī, -itum to offer
praecipiō, -ere, praecēpī, praeceptum to teach; take in advance
praecipuē *adv.* especially
praecipuus, -a, -um special

praedīcō, -ere, praedixī, praedictum to predict, warn
praedō, praedōnis *m.* robber, mugger
praeficiō, -ere, praefēcī, praefectum to put in charge (of)
praemium, -ī *n.* reward
praepōnō, -ere, praeposuī, praepositum to put in charge (of)
praestō, -āre, praestitī, praestitum to surpass
praesum, praeesse, praefuī to be in charge (of)
praeter *prep.* + *acc.* except, beyond
praetereō, praeterīre, praeteriī, praeteritum to go past
precor, -ārī, -ātus sum to pray, beg
premō, -ere, pressī, pressum to press, push
pretium, -ī *n.* price; worth
prex, precis *f.* prayer, request
prīmus, -a, -um first
princeps, principis *c.* leader, chief
principium, -ī *n.* beginning
prior, prius former
prius *adv.* earlier, first
prīvō, -āre, -āvī, -ātum to deprive
prō *prep.* + *abl.* on behalf of, for; in exchange for, instead of; in front of
prōcēdō, -ere, prōcessī, prōcessum to go ahead
procul *adv.* at a distance, far
prōdō, -ere, prōdidī, prōditum to betray, hand over
proelium, -ī *n.* battle
prōgredior, -ī, prōgressus sum to go forward, advance
prōiciō, -ere, prōiēcī, prōiectum to throw forward
prōmittō, -ere, prōmīsī, prōmissum to promise; send ahead
prope *prep.* + *acc.* near
properō, -āre, -āvī, -ātum to hurry
prōpōnō, -ere, prōposuī, prōpositum to put forward, tell
proprius, -a, -um one's own, peculiar
propter *prep.* + *acc.* on account of; near
prōsum, prōdesse, prōfuī, prōfutūrus to benefit, be useful
proximus, -a, -um next, closest
pūblicus, -a, -um public
pudet, -ēre, puduit it causes shame
pudor, pudōris *m.* shame, modesty
puella, -ae *f.* girl
puer, puerī *m.* boy, child

pugna, -ae *f.* a fight
pugnō, -āre, -āvī, -ātum to fight
pulcher, pulchra, pulchrum beautiful, handsome
pulsō, -āre, -āvī, -ātum to hit, knock
pūniō, -īre, pūnīvī, pūnītum to punish
pūrus, -a, -um pure, clean, simple
putō, -āre, -āvī, -ātum to think; value

quaerō, -ere, quaesīvī, quaesītum to look for, ask
quālis, -e what kind of
quam *adv.* how; as, than
quamquam *conj.* although, even though
quandō *conj.* when
quantus, -a, -um how great, how much
quārē *adv.* how, why, for what reason
quasi *adv.* as if
-que *enclitic conj.* and
    -que ... -que both ... and
queror, -ī, questus sum to complain
quī, quae, quod *pron./adj.* who, which; that
quia *conj.* since, because
quīdam, quaedam, quoddam *pron./adj.* a certain (person/thing)
quidem *adv.* of course, indeed
    nē ... quidem not even ...
quiēs, quiētis *f.* rest, sleep
quīn *conj.* why not, but
quis, quis, quid *pron.* who, what
quisquam, quisquam, quidquam *pron.* anyone, anything
quisque, quaeque, quodque *pron./adj.* each, every
quisquis, quisquis, quidquid *pron.* whoever, whatever
quō *adv.* to what place
quod *conj.* because; that
quōmodo *adv.* how
quondam *adv.* formerly, at some point (in time)
quoniam *conj.* since, because
quoque *adv.* also, too
quot *indeclinable adj.* how many

rāmus, -ī *m.* branch
rapiō, -ere, rapuī, raptum to seize, grab, take (*forcefully*)
rārus, -a, -um scattered, rare
ratiō, ratiōnis *f.* reason, account, business
recēdō, -ere, recessī, recessum to go back

recipiō, -ere, recēpī, receptum to accept, take back
rectus, -a, -um straight, correct
recurrō, -ere, recurrī, recursum to run back
reddō, -ere, reddidī, redditum to give back, surrender; repeat
redeō, redīre, rediī, reditum to go back
referō, referre, rettulī, relātum to bring back; report; reply
rēgīna, -ae *f.* queen
regiō, regiōnis *f.* region, line, direction
rēgius, -a, -um royal
regnō, -āre, -āvī, -ātum to rule
regnum, -ī *n.* royal power, kingdom, kingship
regō, -ere, rexī, rectum to rule, guide
regredior, -ī, regressus sum to go back, return
relinquō, -ere, relīquī, relictum to abandon, leave (behind)
reliquus, -a, -um left behind, remaining
repellō, -ere, reppulī, repulsum to drive off/back
repente *adv.* unexpectedly, suddenly
reperiō, -īre, repperī, repertum to find
requīrō, -ere, requīsīvī, requīsītum to demand, ask; miss
rēs, reī *f.* thing; matter, affair, situation, problem
respiciō, -ere, respexī, respectum to look back
respondeō, -ēre, respondī, responsum to answer, correspond
retineō, -ēre, retinuī, retentum to hold back, keep
reveniō, -īre, revēnī, reventum to come back
revertō, -ere, revertī, reversum to turn back
revocō, -āre, -āvī, -ātum to call back
rex, rēgis *m.* king
rīdeō, -ēre, rīsī, rīsum to laugh, smile
rīpa, -ae *f.* river bank
rogō, -āre, -āvī, -ātum to ask, beg
Rōma, -ae *f.* Rome
Rōmānus, -a, -um Roman
ruber, rubra, rubrum red
rumpō, -ere, rūpī, ruptum to break, burst
ruō, -ere, ruī to rush
rūpes, rūpis *f.* cliff
rursus *adv.* back, backward
rūs, rūris *n.* the country, countryside
rusticus, -a, -um rural

sacer, sacra, sacrum sacred, holy
sacerdōs, sacerdōtis *c.* priest/priestess
saeculum, -ī *n.* a generation, lifetime, an age
saepe *adv.* often
saevus, -a, -um fierce, savage
sagitta, -ae *f.* arrow
saltem *adv.* at least
salūs, salūtis *f.* health
salūtō, -āre, -āvī, -ātum to greet
sanctus, -a, -um holy, sacred, inviolable
sanguis, sanguinis *m.* blood
sapiēns, sapientis wise
sapientia, -ae *f.* wisdom
sapiō, -ere, sapīvī to know, be wise; have taste
satis *adv.* enough
saxum, -ī *n.* rock
scelestus, -a, -um wicked, evil
scelus, sceleris *n.* crime, evil deed
scientia, -ae *f.* knowledge, skill
scīlicet *adv.* of course, apparently
sciō, -īre, scīvī, scītum to know
scrībō, -ere, scripsī, scriptum to write, scratch, carve
secundus, -a, -um second, following; favorable
sēcūrus, -a, -um carefree, safe
sed *conj.* but, rather
sedeō, -ēre, sēdī, sessum to sit, stay put
semper *adv.* always
senātus, -ūs *m.* senate
senescō, -ere, senescuī to grow old, age
senex, senis old
sensus, -ūs *m.* feeling, sense
sententia, -ae *f.* opinion, thought, meaning
sentiō, -īre, sensī, sensum to feel, perceive, experience, realize
sepeliō, -īre, sepelīvī, sepultum to bury
sepulcrum, -ī *n.* grave, tomb
sequor, -ī, secūtus sum to follow
sermō, sermōnis *m.* conversation, talk
serviō, -īre, servīvī, servītum + *dat.* to be a slave, serve
servō, -āre, -āvī, -ātum to save, keep, guard, protect
servus, -ī *m.* slave
seu *conj. see* **sīve**
sī *conj.* if
sīc *adv.* like this, in this way, thus
sīcut *conj.* as, like
sīdus, sīderis *n.* star, constellation

signum, -ī *n.* sign, signal, seal
silentium, -ī *n.* silence
silva, -ae *f.* forest
similis, -e similar, like
simul *adv.* at the same time
sine *prep.* + *abl.* without
singulus, -a, -um single, individual
sinō, -ere, sīvī, situm to allow, endure
sinus, -ūs *m.* curve, fold; bay
situs, -ūs *m.* location
sīve (seu) *conj.* or if
    sīve ... sīve whether ... or
socius, -ī *m.* ally
sōl, sōlis *m.* sun
soleō, -ēre, solitus sum to often/usually (do something), be accustomed to / in the habit of (doing something)
sollicitus, -a, -um upset, anxious, worried
sōlus, -a, -um alone, only
solvō, -ere, solvī, solūtum to loosen, untie; pay
somnus, -ī *m.* sleep
sonō, -āre, sonuī, sonitum to make a sound
soror, sorōris *f.* sister
spargō, -ere, sparsī, sparsum to scatter, sprinkle
spatium, -ī *n.* space, period; pause
speciēs, -ēī *f.* sight, appearance
spectō, -āre, -āvī, -ātum to watch, look at
speculum, -ī *n.* mirror
spērō, -āre, -āvī, -ātum to hope, expect
spēs, speī *f.* expectation, hope
spīritus, -ūs *m.* breath, life, spirit
statim *adv.* immediately
statua, -ae *f.* statue
stella, -ae *f.* star
sternō, -ere, strāvī, strātum to spread, stretch
stō, stāre, stetī, statum to stand, stay
strepitus, -ūs *m.* noise, ruckus
strepō, -ere, strepuī, strepitum to make a terrible racket
studeō, -ēre, -uī + *dat.* to be eager, be busy with
studium, -ī *n.* eagerness, fondness
stultus, -a, -um stupid, foolish
sub *prep.* under, beneath, at the foot of (+ *acc. for motion toward*; + *abl. for place where*)
subeō, subīre, subiī, subitum to go under, approach
subiciō, -ere, subiēcī, subiectum to toss under
subitō *adv.* suddenly
sublīmis, -e high

sum, esse, fuī, futūrus to be, exist
summus, -a, -um highest
sūmō, -ere, sumpsī, sumptum to take, assume
super *prep.* over, above (+ *acc. for motion toward*; + *abl. for place where*)
superbus, -a, -um proud, arrogant
superō, -āre, -āvī, -ātum to overcome, conquer, win, overtake
supersum, superesse, superfuī, superfutūrus to survive, remain
suprā *adv. and prep.* + *acc.* over, above
surgō, -ere, surrexī, surrectum to rise
suscipiō, -ere, suscēpī, susceptum to undertake; accept
sustineō, -ēre, -uī to support, uphold
suus, sua, suum *reflexive possessive pron.* his own, her own, *etc.*

taberna, -ae *f.* inn, bar
tabula, -ae *f.* board, tablet; painting
taceō, -ēre, -uī, -itum to be quiet
taedet, -ēre, taesum est it bores, makes tired
tālis, -e such, of such a kind
tam *adv.* so, to such a degree
tamen *adv.* nevertheless, anyway, yet
tamquam *conj.* like, just as
tandem *adv.* finally, at last
tangō, -ere, tetigī, tactum to touch
tantum *adv.* only
tantus, -a, -um so great, so big
tardus, -a, -um slow, late
tectum, -ī *n.* roof; house
tegō, -ere, texī, tectum to cover
templum, -ī *n.* sacred area, temple
temptō, -āre, -āvī, -ātum to try, test
tempus, temporis *n.* time
tendō, -ere, tetendī, tentum/tensum to stretch; try
tenebrae, -ārum *f.pl.* dark, darkness, gloom
teneō, -ēre, tenuī, tentum to hold, have
tener, tenera, tenerum tender, soft
tergum, -ī *n.* back
terra, -ae *f.* land, soil
terreō, -ēre, -uī, -itum to frighten
tertius, -a, -um third
texō, -ere, texuī, textum to weave
theātrum, -ī *n.* theater
timeō, -ēre, -uī to fear, be afraid of
timor, timōris *m.* fear

tollō, -ere, sustulī, sublātum to raise; carry away; destroy
torus, -ī *m.* bed, couch; knot, lump
tot *indeclinable adj.* so many
tōtus, -a, -um whole, entire
trādō, -ere, trādidī, trāditum to hand over, surrender
trahō, -ere, traxī, tractum to pull, drag
trans *prep.* + *acc.* across, over
transeō, transīre, transiī, transitum to cross
trēs, tria three
tristis, -e sad, gloomy
triumphus, -ī *m.* triumphal parade, victory
Trōia, -ae *f.* Troy
Trōiānus, -a, -um Trojan
tū *pron.* you (*sg.*)
tum *adv.* at that time, then
tunc *adv.* at that time, then
turba, -ae *f.* crowd, mob
turpis, -e ugly, shameful
turris, turris *f.* tower
tūtus, -a, -um safe
tuus, tua, tuum your (*sg.*)

ubi *conj.* where; when
ullus, -a, -um any
ultimus, -a, -um last, farthest
ultrā *adv. and prep.* + *acc.* on the far side (of)
umbra, -ae *f.* shadow, shade
umquam *adv.* ever
ūnā *adv.* together
unda, -ae *f.* water, wave
unde *adv.* from what place
undique *adv.* from all sides
ūniversus, -a, -um all together
ūnus, -a, -um one
urbs, urbis *f.* city
usque *adv.* all the way, completely
ūsus, -ūs *m.* use; practice, skill
ut (utī) *conj.* when; in order that; with the result that; as, because (*with the subjunctive, introduces clauses of purpose/result, indirect command, or a negative clause after a verb of fearing*)
uterque, utraque, utrumque each (*of two*)
ūtilis, -e useful
ūtilitās, ūtilitātis *f.* usefulness
utinam *particle* Oh, would that …, If only …, I wish that …

ūtor, -ī, ūsus sum + *abl.* to use; benefit oneself (by means of)

ūva, -ae *f.* grape

uxor, uxōris *f.* wife

vacuus, -a, -um empty, hollow

vādō, -ere to go

valdē *adv.* very, very much, really, strongly

valeō, -ēre, -uī, -itum to be well/strong

vallum, -ī *n.* rampart

varius, -a, -um diverse, different

vātēs, vātis *c.* priest, prophet; poet

-ve *enclitic conj.* or

vehō, -ere, vexī, vectum to carry; (*in the middle voice* + *abl.*) to ride

vel *conj.* or (*nonlimiting choice between things*)

vēlōcitās, vēlōcitātis *f.* speed

velut *adv.* like, as

vendō, -ere, vendidī, venditum to sell

veniō, -īre, vēnī, ventum to come

vēnor, -ārī, -ātus sum to hunt

ventus, -ī *m.* wind

Venus, Veneris *f.* Venus; charm, beauty

vēr, vēris *n.* spring (*season*)

verberō, -āre, -āvī, -ātum to beat

verbum, -ī *n.* word

vereor, -ērī, -itus sum to fear, be afraid

vērō *adv.* indeed, yes, really

versus, -ūs *m.* a turn; row, line (*especially of poetry*)

vertō, -ere, vertī, versum to turn

vērus, -a, -um true, real

vesper, vesperis *m.* evening

vester, vestra, vestrum your (*pl.*)

vestis, vestis *f.* clothing

vetō, -āre, vetuī, vetitum to forbid

vetus, veteris old

via, -ae *f.* road, way

vīcīnus, -a, -um neighboring

—, vicis *f.* change

victor, victōris *m.* winner

victōria, -ae *f.* victory

vīcus, -ī *m.* village

videō, -ēre, vīdī, vīsum to see; (*in passive voice*) to seem, appear, be seen

vigilia, -ae *f.* (night) watch, vigil

vigilō, -āre, -āvī, -ātum to be awake, watch

vincō, -ere, vīcī, victum to conquer

vīnum, -ī *n.* wine

vir, virī *m.* man

virga, -ae *f.* a switch, green twig

virgō, virginis *f.* young woman

virtūs, virtūtis *f.* manliness, courage

vīs, vīs *f.* **vīrēs, vīrium** *f.pl.* force, strength

vīsitō, -āre, -āvī, -ātum to visit

vīta, -ae *f.* life

vitium, -ī *n.* crime, vice, flaw

vīvō, -ere, vixī, victum to live

vīvus, -a, -um alive, living

vix *adv.* barely, with difficulty

vocō, -āre, -āvī, -ātum to call, summon

volō, -āre, -āvī, -ātum to fly

volō, velle, voluī to be willing, want

voluptās, voluptātis *f.* pleasure

vōs *pron.* you (*pl.*)

vōtum, -ī *n.* vow

vox, vōcis *f.* voice

vulnus, vulneris *n.* wound

vultus, -ūs *m.* expression (*facial*)

zōna, -ae *f.* girdle, band, sash

INDEX

An italic page number identifies a page that
contains a declension chart for the noun, pronoun,
or adjective, or a conjugation chart for the verb.

Index